The
Mormon Cult

Jack B. Worthy

See Sharp Press • Tucson, Arizona

See Sharp Press
P.O. Box 1731
Tucson, AZ 85702-1731

Web site: www.seesharppress.com

Worthy, Jack B.
    The Mormon cult : a former missionary reveals the secrets
of Mormon mind control / Jack B. Worthy (pseud.) – Tucson,
Ariz. : See Sharp Press, 2008

ISBN 1-884365-44-2
ISBN 9781884365447

Includes bilbiographical references and index.

Summary: This book describes the author's work as a missionary in
Hong Kong and his experience working in the cinema in Hong Kong
after being excommunicated. The author presents an exposé of
Mormonism's inherent racism and sexism as revealed in official church
documents, including the Book of Mormon and proclamations by
the church's "prophets."

1. Mormon Church – China – Hong Kong. 2. Mormons – Biography.
3. Mormon Church – Controversial literature. 4. Motion pictures –
China – Hong Kong. 1. Title.

289.3

Cover design by Kay Sather. Interior design by Chaz Bufe.

Printed in Canada

Contents

Introduction (by Richard Packham) 1

Preface 5

A Note on Terminology 7

1. A Thumbnail History of Mormonism 9

2. The Indoctrination Process 15

3. Life Before My Mission 53

4. My Mission in Hong Kong 65

5. Excommunication and Life After Mormonism 161

Glossary of Mormon Terms 191

Recommended Reading & Viewing 209

Index 213

For Angie

Cult, n. 1. A system of religious worship and ritual. 2. A religion or sect considered extremist or false.

—*The American Heritage Dictionary* (Third Edition)

"I suspect that there are few who know better the reality of Satan and his henchmen than does the full-time missionary, for the missionary is exposed to the fiery darts of the adversary, which come whistling overhead as he or she labors in the front lines in our war against sin."

—Elder Carlos E. Asay of the Presidency of the First Quorum of the Seventy, "Opposition to the Work of God," *Ensign*, Nov. 1981, p. 67.

Acknowledgments

I want to thank Richard Packham for writing such a fitting introduction. I also want to thank Richard for the excellent comments he gave after reading an earlier draft of this book, and for allowing me to use an adaptation of the glossary of Mormon terms from his web site (home.teleport.com/~packham/).[1] I wish to thank Emily Strauss, who was gracious enough to read two drafts of this book and give very insightful suggestions regarding content and style. She also encouraged me to keep working on the book at times when I needed such encouragement.

I am tremendously grateful to my family for never making me feel like an outsider in a culture that often ostracizes those who leave or are kicked out. I especially thank my wife and daughter. I never could have finished this book without their love and support. They have proved beyond a shadow of a doubt that life outside of Mormonism can be full of blessings that can be named and counted one by one. They have proved themselves very capable of replacing God in that popular Mormon hymn that I sang so often as a child:

> Count your blessings
> Name them one by one
> Count your blessings
> See what [They] hath done . . .

---

1. His well written and very interesting website is an invaluable resource for learning about Mormonism—so invaluable, in fact, that it is occasionally down because of heavy traffic, or because it is hacked by people (in all likelihood Mormons) who don't like it. You can go to a mirror site when that happens: http://geocities.com/packham33.

Introduction

Almost everyone who lives in any of the civilized or semi-civilized countries of the modern world has encountered Mormon missionaries at one time or another. Always in pairs, young men about twenty years old, dressed in dark trousers, white shirt and tie, wearing a plastic name badge reading "Elder So and so—Church of Jesus Christ of Latter-day Saints." Or, less often, the missionaries are young women, in their early twenties. Always together, always pleasant and smiling, always wanting to give you a message about religion.

These missionaries seem to be everywhere, which is hardly surprising, since the LDS Church has over 50,000 of them working full time around the globe. This Mormon army is probably the largest modern religious proselytizing force in the world. It's all the more amazing, then, that these young people are not paid by their church, but are financing their two-year missions with their own savings, or with money from their families back home.

Jack B. Worthy was one of these missionaries. In many ways, Jack's story is typical, and in other ways quite atypical.

Good autobiographical writing allows the reader to experience someone else's life, to live for a while in another's skin. And Jack quickly allows the reader to "become" that devout Mormon boy who voluntarily gave up two years of his young adulthood to serve God and to save souls.

What is typical about Jack's experience is the idealism and faith with which he embarked on his intensive mission in the service of God. Like all missionaries, he submitted himself to rigorous weeks of preliminary training at the LDS Missionary Training Center in Provo, Utah, where the regimen is as restrictive and severe as in almost any monastery. Since Jack had been called to a foreign mission, his training also included a crash course in a foreign language.

But what is not quite so typical about Jack's mission experience is the effect it had on his life and on his relationship to his church.

Almost all former missionaries (generally called "returned missionaries" or "RMs") agree that their two-year missions were fundamentally life changing. Many return with a firm "testimony" of Mormonism, even though they may have had unspoken doubts before. Many insist that their missions were "the best two years of my life!" The mission experience, aside from its religious effects (both on the missionary and upon the converts), almost always enables the missionary to acquire skills that will later prove invaluable in post-mission life: self-confidence, speaking skills, sales techniques, self-discipline, planning, record keeping, and—for those who serve in foreign countries—the ability to speak another language. Mormon missionaries frequently become successful in business or government at least in part because of the skills and training acquired on their missions.

For Jack B. Worthy, however, his mission did not strengthen his testimony. One of the surprising facts about the missionary experience is that it can just as easily destroy a missionary's testimony as build it up. The church is aware of this, although its leaders do not admit it officially. In private, however, they acknowledge that two out of every five missionaries will eventually leave the church, largely because of their mission experience. Some missionaries even abandon their mission before completing it, in spite of tremendous pressure to finish it "honorably," and despite the shame they must endure when they return home. Regardless of the real reason for not completing a mission, the folks back home generally assume that the missionary was sent home early because of some terrible sin (usually assumed to be sexual) committed while on the mission.

In this book, Jack takes us on his journey of awakening to the problems with his mission and his church. Facing up to reality, removing the rose-tinted spectacles, seeing the ugly facts, is rarely a pleasant experience for anyone. It is a necessary step to becoming an adult, however, and we see this process occurring in this honest young man.

Another fundamental change in Jack's life, which was a direct result of his mission, was that he ultimately chose to return to the site of his mission (Hong Kong) and settle there permanently. Whereas missionaries are under strict rules not to adapt to native customs or to participate in native culture (or even read local newspapers or watch local television), Jack, no longer a missionary, was no longer bound by those rules, and now had the task of integrating himself into the local culture.

As someone of a completely different ethnicity and background, he faced a severe challenge, in spite of his mission-learned mastery of the language. But he succeeded.

One of the frequent effects of leaving the religion of one's youth—especially if it is an all-embracing, all-controlling religion, such as Mormonism (as much a culture as a faith)—is the burning desire to write about one's life-changing experience. In a way, that's a form of self-therapy. Jack's story is by no means the only account in print of a former Mormon missionary's apostasy. But it is certainly one of the most interesting and most readable.

And that is partly because it is rather unusual. Jack's life after his mission has by no means been ordinary. I have never had the opportunity to meet Jack personally, but we have been acquainted for a number of years through the Internet, mostly in connection with various ex-Mormon e-mail discussion groups. I have been able to share in the progress of this book over several years, and have enjoyed the many stories of his experiences as a student in Texas, as a resident of San Francisco's Chinatown, and his later careers in Hong Kong, ranging from movie actor to equipment salesman.

Jack is presently a teacher at a Hong Kong school, and is working toward an advanced degree in Chinese Studies. He is completely integrated into Chinese life, married to a Chinese woman, and involved in raising a family. His observations about the similarities of Chinese culture and Mormon culture are especially insightful.

You are about to share a glimpse into a very interesting life.

—Richard Packham, Founder, Ex-Mormon Foundation

Preface

The most common question people ask me is how I went from being a Mormon missionary to being irreligious. Until now, I never had a short answer to this question, because my transition was long and complex. But finally I have a brief response that even my publisher likes: read this book.

People often ask me what Mormons believe, and that usually leads to an interesting follow-up question: How could anyone believe *that?* My answer to these questions is the same: read this book.

On several occasions I have woken from nightmares, relieved to find out that my nightmare was just that—only a bad dream. In these dreams, I had committed a terrible act that would adversely affect the rest of my life. Each time after waking, I suddenly realized that I wouldn't suffer the terrible consequences of that act, because I had not actually committed it.

Only once in my life have I woken from a dream and thought, "Oh no! It really happened!" Rather than waking from a nightmare, I had woken from a pleasant dream into a nightmare. What I had forgotten while sleeping came flooding back when I awoke. I had committed an act that is, according to Mormon doctrine, second only to murder, and that entails a fate worse than death.

This book tells the story of my privileged birth, indoctrination, and missionary service. It tells of my sin and my excommunication from the Mormon Church for committing this sin—a sin for which I will pay, I am told, for all eternity. And if I understand that correctly, that is a long time.

There is a missionary story that clearly illustrates just how seriously Mormon culture judges my crime. In 1998 Elder Bradley Borden, a Mormon missionary, was stabbed by drunken Russians while serving his mission in Russia. Dale Borden, Bradley's father, was contacted by Church leaders after the incident. Brother Borden said that when he realized Church leaders were contacting him about his missionary son, he was "worried that [Bradley] had done something unworthy." In other words, Brother Borden was worried that his son Bradley had done what I did on my mission. Bradley hadn't, however, and Brother Borden was therefore relieved to hear that his son had instead been stabbed in the stomach, suffering wounds to his upper intestines, liver and pancreas. Brother Borden quoted a Mormon cliché: "You see, we'd rather have [our son] come home in a pine box than do something unworthy."[1]

Bradley's companion, Elder José Manuel Mackintosh, was stabbed to death.

I was less fortunate; I returned home unharmed and unworthy.

---

1. *The Arizona Republic,* October 19, 1998.

A Note on Terminology

Some of the terms that follow are either unique to Mormonism or are used by Mormons in unique ways. The first time such terms appear, they are in **bold type**. The glossary at the back of the book provides definitions for all of them.

A Thumbnail History
of Mormonism

There are many fascinating books on Mormon history for those who want to read about it in depth. For readers who are so inclined, I have included a bibliography. To set the scene for this book, however, only a quick sketch of the religion's history is necessary.

The official name of the organization commonly known as "The Mormon Church" is **The Church of Jesus Christ of Latter-day Saints**, or the LDS Church for short. The LDS Church claims that, in the spring of 1820, a fourteen-year-old farm boy named **Joseph Smith, Jr.** wanted to know which of all the churches on earth was true. So one day he went to the woods near his home in Palmyra, New York to ask God for an answer. To Joseph's astonishment, Jesus Christ and God the Father appeared floating in a pillar of light directly above him. Jesus told Joseph that he "must join none of [the churches that existed at that time], for they were all wrong."[1]

Three-and-a-half years later, on September 21, 1823, Joseph was praying in his room when another pillar of light appeared. This time it was an angel that Joseph saw floating in the air above him. The angel kindly introduced himself as **Moroni**, a **prophet** who, according to

---

1. The only thing that God the Father said was, "This is My Beloved Son. Hear Him!" It makes one wonder why God even bothered to go along for the ride. The only point of His being there was probably to show that God and Jesus are two separate beings, with bodies of flesh and bone. This is a doctrine that Joseph Smith evolved over time, and there are some small changes in the *Book of Mormon* that show this change of doctrine. There are seven versions of this **First Vision**, which is the official title of this vision that Joseph had of God the Father and Jesus Christ. The only version of the First Vision that is actually in Joseph Smith's handwriting does not mention God the Father, so it appears that this change in doctrine inspired changes to both the *Book of Mormon* and to the details of the First Vision. It is also interesting to note that after the time that the First Vision is supposed to have taken place, Joseph Smith joined the Methodist Church. That must have taken some real guts. These facts are not part of the official story, so we can rest assured that they are insignificant and ignore them.

Mormon doctrine, used to live in ancient America. Moroni told Joseph about a book whose pages were made of gold.[2]

This book of gold, later to become known as the **gold plates** (or golden plates), contained a record of the people who lived in ancient America. Moroni said that the gold plates were buried on the Hill **Cumorah**, located miraculously close to the farm where Joseph lived. Joseph was allowed to see the gold plates the next day, and once a year for four years thereafter. Finally, four years and one day after first meeting Moroni, Joseph was allowed to heft those beautiful plates home.

The now-twenty-one-year-old Joseph translated the gold plates into a book of scripture called the ***Book of Mormon***. The official story of this so called translation emphasizes Joseph's use of something called the **Urim and Thummim**, a tool used by ancient prophets to translate texts from one language to another. It consisted of two seer stones in silver bows attached to a breastplate. The angel Moroni had been thoughtful enough to include the Urim and Thummim with the gold plates. However, according to written witness accounts, Joseph apparently didn't use the Urim and Thummim much. Perhaps he felt a bit silly wearing a breastplate.

The translation technique Joseph seemed to prefer, instead, involved the use of a seer stone that was placed into the bottom of a top hat. Joseph would then stick his face into the hat containing the seer stone.[3] Buried inside the pitch blackness of the hat, Joseph would then wait. "[I]n the darkness [of the hat,] the spiritual light would shine. A piece of something resembling parchment would appear, and on that appeared the writing. One character [from the gold plates] at a time would appear, and under it was the interpretation in English."[4] Picture a man leaning down with his face buried deep into a top hat, transcribing one "Reformed Egyptian" character at a time to his assistant. Another method of "translation" involved Joseph sitting hidden, along with the golden plate, behind a hanging sheet. In each case the transcriber never saw the golden plates. Even when Joseph was in view,

---

2. Now that caught the attention of this poor farm boy. Even the officially sanctioned version of this story says that Joseph was tempted to use the golden plates for financial gain.

3. This seer stone is still in the Mormon Church's possession today.

4. *David Whitmer, An Address to All Believers in Christ,* Richmond, Mo.: n.p., 1887, p. 12 (quoted in "A Treasured Testament," by Russell M. Nelson, *Ensign,* July 1993, p. 61).

using the Urim and Thummim or the stone in the hat, the plates were kept hidden from the transcribers.[5]

To assure the transcribers that the plates were real, Joseph allowed them to hold the plates while they were wrapped in a cloth. The only witnesses actually allowed to set their eyes upon the plates were two of Joseph's brothers, his father, and five other men who all belonged to a family named Whitmer, and who were all close friends of the Smith family. In his book, *Roughing It*, Mark Twain pans the *Book of Mormon*, saying that its translation truly was a miracle if Joseph Smith stayed awake throughout, because the book is "chloroform in print." Referring to the eight witnesses, Twain noted that he "could not feel more satisfied and at rest if the entire Whitmer family had testified" to the authenticity of the plates. Obviously Mark Twain was not convinced, and since the angel Moroni took the plates back after the *Book of Mormon* was published, nobody other than the original witnesses will ever see them. What Joseph did is referred to as a translation, but, if one takes the witness accounts at face value, then the *Book of Mormon* is actually the product of a breathtaking ability to dictate an entire book piecemeal.[6] Mormons claim that was a humanly impossible feat, and therefore the *Book of Mormon* could not be a product of Joseph Smith's imagination. However, memorizing entire books *is* possible. Chinese scholars used to memorize Confucian texts in their entirety, and many people have managed to memorize the Koran. Which is harder to believe, that Joseph Smith dictated a 531-page story, or that it came from out-of-sight golden plates handed to him by an angel?

On May 15, 1829, during the time when Joseph and his assistant Oliver Cowdery were writing—excuse me, translating—the *Book of Mormon*, they were visited by John the Baptist, who conferred the

---

5. Joseph had three assistants: His wife, Emma Smith; Martin Harris; and Oliver Cowdery.

6. In spite of the *Book of Mormon*'s numerous flaws, it's amazing that any kind of book at all could be written this way. As far as its being a "translation," however, the whole process seems very suspect. Why did Joseph Smith get the gold plates if he never viewed them throughout the entire "translation" process? They remained covered, out of sight of both the scribe and the translator. Also, anyone who has ever gone beyond a few weeks of learning a second language can tell you that translating from one language to another is not a process of literal translation of one word (or character) at a time. You may come across occasional simple sentences that you can translate word for word, from one language to another, but you won't get very far, let alone through an entire book, doing word-for-word translation without creating gibberish.

Aaronic Priesthood on them. Later that same month, Peter, James, and John visited Joseph and Oliver conferring the **Melchizedek Priesthood** on them. These priesthood powers were thus restored back to the Earth, having previously vanished with the death of Christ's disciples.

The first edition of the *Book of Mormon* was printed on March 26, 1830. Less than two weeks later, on May 6, the LDS Church[7] was officially organized. *The Book of Mormon* is considered by the Latter-day Saints to be divine scripture.[8] So is the Holy Bible. So is a book called the ***Doctrine and Covenants***, which is a collection of revelations that Jesus Christ gave personally to Joseph Smith. And so is a book called the ***Pearl of Great Price***, part of which Joseph Smith "translated" from some ancient Egyptian papyri that the LDS Church had purchased, along with a couple of Egyptian mummies that that their owner had been lugging around and showing for a fee. (So, in addition to Prophet, Seer, and Revelator, Joseph also had the title of Translator.)

Unfortunately, The Papyri have subsequently been translated by Egyptologists, showing that Joseph Smith had no clue whatsoever as to what was actually written on them. His so-called translation was entirely fabricated.[9]

The *Book of Mormon* has been referred to by Mormon leaders as the keystone of the LDS Church, because the Church either stands or falls based on whether this book is true or false. The *Book of Mormon* begins with a story about a family of Israelites who were commanded by God to go to America in 600 BC. We learn from the book that the American Indians, those people who were unfortunate enough to be discovered in 1492, are the cursed, black-skinned descendents of one of those Israelites named Laman. He was bad. And because he was bad, God made his descendents black. "[W]herefore, as they were white, and

---

7. It was first called The Church of Jesus Christ. That later became The Church of the Latter-day Saints. Then those two names were combined and became The Church of Jesus Christ of Latter-day Saints. We are told that the name of the Church was revealed to Joseph Smith by God. Apparently God is not only a jealous God, but a fickle God.

8. There is unequivocal evidence showing that the *Book of Mormon* is not what it claims. It contains many anachronisms and mistranslations copied straight from the Bible. For a detailed treatment of this, see "A Linguist Looks at Mormonism," by Richard Packham at: http://home.teleport.com/~packham/linguist.htm.

9. Joseph "translated" them as if they were written by the biblical patriarch Abraham, but they were actually common funeral papyri that were written around the time of Christ, which dates them roughly 1,700 years after the time of Abraham.

exceeding fair and delightsome, that they might not be enticing unto my people, the Lord God did cause a skin of blackness to come upon them. And thus saith the Lord God, I will cause that they shall be loathsome unto thy people . . ."[10]

Laman's descendents, known as the **Lamanites**, were of course lazy and wicked, and they killed all the white people. The white people that they killed were descendents of Laman's brother Nephi, who remained white because he was good. All of this explains why Columbus found no white people when he landed on the shores of America, only black-skinned, "loathsome" people.

God later commanded Joseph Smith to marry lots of women, and he reluctantly obeyed. As the story goes, he didn't want to comply but was forced to do so by an angel with a flaming sword. (The early Mormons were severely persecuted for a variety of reasons—polygamy was just one of them.)

Eventually, Joseph Smith was murdered by a mob, and Brigham Young took his place as prophet. Soon after that, there was an incredible, very deadly, cross country exodus of Mormon pioneers, some of whom were my ancestors. The exodus ended with the majority of Mormons settling in Utah. Since that time, the LDS church has grown into an organization with millions of members spanning the globe. It is now extremely wealthy and a significant number of members hold high positions in government.[11]

The rest of this book is a description of the culture that has resulted from the establishment, survival, and growth of this very American religion called Mormonism. First, I will describe how Mormon children are indoctrinated. Second, I will explain what Mormon children are indoctrinated to believe. Third, I'll explain what they are commanded to do. And then I will tell my story.

---

10. *Book of Mormon*, 2 Nephi: 5:21–22.

11. At the following web site, there is a list of past and present LDS members who hold, or have held, positions in government: http://famousmormons.net/pol.html.

The Indoctrination Process

"With very few exceptions, the religion which a man accepts is that
of the community in which he lives, which makes it obvious
that the influence of environment is what has led
him to accept the religion in question."

—Bertrand Russell, *Why I am Not a Christian*

The Mormon Show

The Truman Show was a movie about a television reality show of the
same name: "The Truman Show." The TV show was filmed inside a
giant domed studio the size of a small town. The town inside the dome
was an artificial world in which everything, including the ocean and the
sky, was human made. Truman, the first person lucky enough to be
legally owned by a corporation, was born inside the town, and was
raised to believe that the human-made, corporate-owned studio he
lived in was a real and natural world. Everyone in Truman's life, his parents, his friends, and his associates, were all actors, each doing their
part to create his false reality. Everyone except Truman knew that his
life was a manufactured reality.

In an interview within the movie, the actor who played the part of
Truman's best friend in the television show said, "It's all true. It's all
real. Nothing here is fake. Nothing you see on this show is fake. It's
merely controlled." In a sense, that was true. Truman's reality was
entirely designed and controlled by humans, but because he believed
in it, it was his reality and was therefore every bit as real to him as everyone else's reality is to them.[1]

In another interview within the movie, the woman who played the
part of Truman's wife said that "The Truman Show" "is a lifestyle. It's a

---

1. An obvious question of ethics arises: should anyone be granted the right to knowingly
fabricate another's reality? If so, who should have that right, and why? If not, who
should stop them, and how? Obviously there are no easy answers to these questions
when they refer to people's own children.

noble life. It is . . . a truly blessed life." She believed that doing her part, day in and day out, to perpetuate Truman's belief in a fabricated reality was a noble, blessed calling.

Mormon indoctrination attempts to duplicate what was done in "The Truman Show." Rather than using a physical dome to separate Mormons from the outside world, The Mormon Show uses a psychological dome, locking Mormons safely inside a feeling-based reality. This feeling-based reality has to coexist alongside a contradictory fact-based reality, so keeping the dome impermeable is no easy task. **Apostle**[2] James E. Faust told **members** they must work harder at it, saying, "Somehow, some way, we must try harder to make our homes stronger so that they will stand as sanctuaries against the unwholesome, pervasive moral dry rot around us."[3]

Just like Truman's friends and family, the actors in The Mormon Show are trained to consciously create a false reality for children, both their own and the children of others, members and nonmembers alike. They are made to believe that doing so is "a noble [and] blessed life."

All cultures inculcate subjective views of the world in children. All cultures are therefore guilty of raising children to have inaccurate views of reality. However, this usually occurs unintentionally on a subconscious level.

Because all cultures see things differently, it should be obvious that no single culture has an entirely accurate view of reality. Unfortunately, however, people have a propensity to believe that one culture sees things much more clearly than the rest. They also believe that they were lucky enough to be born into the one and only superior culture. The anthropological term for this is ethnocentricity.

Mormon culture makes a very conscious effort to teach children to believe in a specific version of reality, and it warns them about the dangers of contrary beliefs and ideas. All cultures with beliefs and practices that differ greatly from Mormon culture are said to be wrong and misguided at best, and inspired by Satan at worst. Rather than trying to reduce children's natural tendency toward ethnocentricity, Mormonism strongly encourages it.

---

2. The lexicon of Mormonism includes terms that are unfamiliar to outsiders, and it defines some familiar words differently (for example, Jews are "Gentiles"). All these terms (or phrases) are defined in the glossary at the back of the book.

3. James E. Faust, "The Greatest Challenge in the World—Good Parenting," *Ensign*, November 1990, p. 32.

The Mormon Show uses a very effective three-step program of child indoctrination: first, indoctrinated parents are commanded to indoctrinate their children; second, parents and others who are responsible for teaching children are given detailed instructions on how to indoctrinate them; and third, they carry out the indoctrination. Mormonism then adds one key ingredient that makes the whole process of indoctrination work very well: Mormons teach children that the truth of Mormonism is proved through feelings. This means that no evidence is required, and that no amount of conflicting empirical evidence could ever prove **the Church** to be false.

The Lord Commands You to Indoctrinate Children

A key book of LDS scripture is called the *Doctrine and Covenants* (*D&C*), which, if you recall, is a collection of revelations given to Joseph Smith and other church leaders during Smith's time. To Mormons, the *D&C* is no less the word of God than is the Bible. In fact, the commandments from the Lord that are recorded in the *D&C* are more powerful and immediate than commandments recorded in the Bible because they are comparatively contemporary and are directed specifically at Mormons. In the *D&C*, God commands parents to indoctrinate their children to be Mormons: "But I [God] have commanded you to bring up your children in light and truth" (*D&C* 93:40). And all Mormons clearly understand that there is only one source of "light and truth."

There is another verse in the *D&C* that is more explicit, and church leaders frequently quote it when they want to remind parents about God's commandment to indoctrinate their children. The verse says, "And again, inasmuch as parents . . . teach [their children] not to understand [church] doctrine . . . the sin be upon the heads of the parents" (*D&C* 68:25). In the April 1902 **General Conference**, Apostle Matthias F. Cowley quoted this verse, and in case anyone missed the point, he then explained that God meant it is "a sin to thus neglect the sons and daughters that have been committed to our care. . . . [I]t is the duty of every father and mother to . . . indoctrinate them in the principles of the **gospel**."[4]

---

4. Matthias F. Cowley, *Conference Report*, April 1902, p. 72.

President Spencer W. Kimball was the prophet when I was growing up. Regarding parents' duties to indoctrinate their children, he said, "We must be energetic and devoted in supporting the efforts of parents to build **testimonies** and faith in their children."[5] In a **fireside** talk given in San Salvador, El Salvador in January 1997, President Gordon B. Hinckley told members to "[r]ear [children] in the nurture and admonition of the Lord. God will hold those accountable who do not do so." Being told to do something by a prophet of God is not the same as getting advice from a friend. It is the equivalent of being commanded directly by God.

Dwan J. Young used to be the Primary General President, heading the top tier of the organization called **Primary**. This organization is in charge of indoctrinating the Church's young children. Sister Young extended the commandment to teach children when she said, "we are all teachers of children—parents, aunts, uncles, grandparents, priesthood leaders, **ward** members, neighbors."[6] The obvious conclusion from this is that all Mormon adults are commanded by God to indoctrinate all children.

How to Indoctrinate Children

Mormon parents who are indoctrinated themselves will naturally want to indoctrinate their children, while those who are not indoctrinated will do whatever they think is best, regardless of what Church leaders say. In other words, the commandment to indoctrinate one's children is most effective with the parents who are most likely to do it anyway. Therefore, church leaders focus heavily on keeping adults indoctrinated, and then supplement this with explicit instructions for indoctrinating children.

Child indoctrination is a frequent theme in the *Ensign*, one of the Church's official monthly magazines. The *Ensign* contains a regular feature called "Family Resource Guide," which advertises reading and audio materials designed to help members indoctrinate their children. A Bible verse, Proverbs 22:6, heads this regular feature: "Train up a child in the way he should go: and when he is old, he will not depart

---

5. Spencer W. Kimball, "Train Up a Child," *Ensign*, April 1978, p. 2.

6. Dwan J. Young, "Teach Children the Gospel," *Ensign*, May 1988, p. 78.

from it." That sums up the ultimate goal of the indoctrination: to ensure that children believe in Mormonism so strongly and so deeply that their belief can't be erased or replaced by other belief systems. The instructions for indoctrination include three parts:

1. Start when children are very young.
2. Frequently tell them you know the Church is true.
3. Get them to frequently say they know the Church is true.

Start When Children Are Very Young

Brother and **Sister** Hasler wrote an article for the *Ensign*, using a title inspired by Proverbs 22:6, "Train up a Child." They said that their sixteen-year-old son told them he was now at an age where he had to learn things for himself. The Haslers reluctantly agreed, but they were content in the fact that years of indoctrination had permanently affected their son. They said:

> Years of **family home evening**, family prayer, and scripture study [in short, years of indoctrination] had laid a foundation that he could reject, perhaps, but not ignore. Once truth is etched in the heart by the Spirit of the Holy Ghost, it becomes an integral part of a person and must be dealt with. A child so taught will never be the same![7]

An important part of this lesson from the Haslers is that parents must indoctrinate their children starting when they are very young. Waiting until a child is sixteen is much too late. In fact, age is often cited as a critical factor. Thomas S. Monson,[8] former **First Counselor** in the Church's **First Presidency**, and current prophet, said, "The formative years of a child should be used for building a life firmly set in a foundation of the gospel."[9] **Elder** Monson also warned parents against exposing children under eight to information that contradicts Mormon beliefs:

---

7. John W. and Marjorie E. Hasler, "Train Up a Child," *Ensign*, April 1999, p. 50.

8. In January 2008, Monson succeeded President Gordon B. Hinckley as the LDS prophet.

9. Thomas S. Monson, "An Invitation to Exaltation," *Tambuli*, August–September 1986, p. 2.

Dr. Glenn Doman, a prominent author and renowned scientist, reported a lifetime of research in the statement: "The newborn child is almost an exact duplicate of an empty computer, although superior to such a computer in almost every way . . . What is placed in the child's brain during the first eight years of his life is probably there to stay. If you put misinformation into his brain during this period, it is extremely difficult to erase it." This evidence should provoke a renewal of commitment in every parent: "I must be about my Father's [God's] business."[10]

In my case, I'm sure that my indoctrination into the Church began as soon as I was old enough to talk. I can't remember that far back, of course, but that is what happens to all children of active members. It's an integral part of growing up Mormon. An important part of the process consisted of adults in the church repeatedly telling me a standard list of specific "truths." My parents taught me to fully trust those adults and assured me that the things those adults told me were true. Parental indoctrination is firmly reinforced by indoctrination from other adults.

Sister Anne G. Wirthlin, First Counselor in the Primary General Presidency, referring to a group of two and three year olds, said, "In their pure, childlike faith, their spirits were receptive to the truths they were being taught."[11] She then went on to explain the method by which those LDS children's indoctrination would be ensured: "That experience will be repeated for them in their nursery class Sunday after Sunday." Adding some scientific backup, she quoted from an article entitled "Fertile Minds" from *Time* magazine: "From birth, a baby's brain cells proliferate wildly, making connections that may shape a lifetime of experience. The first three years are critical."[12]

Church leaders obviously understand that human cognitive development is a natural biological process that can be manipulated by controlling the environment in which children grow and develop. Predictably, however, the fact that children are such easy targets of indoctrination is interpreted as being part of Heavenly Father's plan.

---

10. Thomas S. Monson, "Teach the Children," *Ensign*, November 1997, p. 17.

11. Anne G. Wirthlin, "Teaching our Children to Love the Scriptures," *Ensign*, May 1998, p. 9.

12. J. Madeleine Nash, "Fertile Minds," *Time*, February 3, 1997, p. 49.

Sister Wirthlin rhetorically asked, "Is it surprising that our Father in Heaven fashioned the minds of very young children to be so capable of learning at a time when they need to be taught who they are and what they must do?" But Heavenly Father obviously didn't think it through, since it works equally well for all belief systems, and church leaders admit this every time they warn parents against exposing their children to any belief system other than Mormonism.[13]

---

13. On March 17, 1997, *Mother Jones* contributing writer Michael Krasny interviewed biologist Richard Dawkins, author of *The Selfish Gene.* The following excerpt from that interview gives an explanation quite different from Anne Wirthlin's as to why children are so gullible:

MK: You're known for your atheism and your comment that "religion is a virus." Are you more tolerant toward religion these days?

RD: No. I am often asked to explain as a biologist why religion has such a hold. The theory is this: When a child is young, for good Darwinian reasons, it would be valuable if the child believed everything it's told. A child needs to learn a language, it needs to learn the social customs of its people, it needs to learn all sorts of rules—like don't put your finger in the fire, and don't pick up snakes, and don't eat red berries. There are lots of things that for good survival reasons a child needs to learn.

So it's understandable that Darwinian natural selection would have built into the child's brain the rule of thumb, "Be fantastically gullible; believe everything you're told by your elders and betters."

That's a good rule, and it works. But any rule that says "Believe everything you're told" is automatically going to be vulnerable to parasitization. Computers, for example, are vulnerable to parasitization because they believe all they're told. If you tell them in the right programming language, they'll do it. Computer viruses work by somebody writing a program that says, "Duplicate me and, while you're at it, erase this entire disk."

My point is that the survival mechanism that makes children's brains believe what they're told—for good reason—is automatically vulnerable to parasitic codes such as "You must believe in the great juju in the sky," or "You must kneel down and face east and pray five times a day." These codes are then passed down through generations. And there's no obvious reason why it should stop.

There's an additional factor in the virus theory, which is that those viruses that are good at surviving will be the ones that are more likely to survive. So, if the virus says, "If you don't believe in this you will go to hell when you die," that's a pretty potent threat, especially to a child. Or, if it says, "When you become a little bit older you will meet people who will tell you the opposite of this, and they will have remarkably plausible arguments and they'll have lots of what they'll call evidence on their side and you'll be really tempted to believe it, but the more tempted you are, the more that's just Satan getting at you." This is exactly what many creationists in this country have been primed with.

Frequently Tell Them the Church Is True

Being successfully indoctrinated is referred to as "having a **testimony**," which is a church member's knowledge that the Church, and everything that goes along with it, is true. Adults are taught how to help their children gain their own personal testimonies. Apostle Loren C. Dunn told parents they should:

> . . . bear their testimonies to their children in the home—actually express to your children exactly what it is about the Church you know to be true. If we think our children know these things just because they live in the same house with us, we are mistaken. We need to say the words so our families can feel the same spirit of testimony that we have felt.[14]

The December 1989 *Ensign* included an article titled, "How to Help Our Children Gain a Testimony." It said parents need to tell their children that they know the Church is true. It said, "No matter what their ages, our children need to hear our testimonies and faith-promoting stories." It suggested that after Church **meetings** parents "can testify of the truthfulness of what [they] have heard and felt." Children should then be taught to say these things themselves at home. Once they "begin to feel comfortable expressing themselves at home, they can be encouraged to bear testimony in **fast and testimony meeting**."

Get Them to Frequently Say That the Church Is True

The core steps for building testimonies in children are quite simple: parents bear their testimonies to their children and then instruct their children to do the same, first privately, then publicly. Elder Carl B. Cook of the Quorum of the **Seventy** quoted Apostle Henry B. Eyring, who said, "First we can teach some sacred truth. Then, we can testify that we know what we have taught is true."[15] Elder Cook explained that the home is the best place to teach children how to "express heartfelt feelings" as "a prelude to testimony bearing." He said that an "integral

---

14. Loren C. Dunn, "How to Gain a Testimony," *Ensign*, Jan. 1973, p. 84.

15. Henry B. Eyring, quoted in "When Children Want to Bear Testimony," *Ensign*, December 2002, p. 29.

part of family communication" should be the discussion of gospel principles and the sharing of spiritual feelings. He provided examples of scripts that parents can use. One script went like this: "Today in **sacrament meeting** I felt the **Spirit** confirming the truth of the counsel given by our **bishop**." The next step is to then get children to say such things themselves, and Elder Cook suggested some questions parents could ask to get their children started: "Would you like to tell me what you are feeling now? What did you feel in your heart as we discussed this principle?"

Bearing these testimonies at home is only the beginning. Elder Cook said, "Parents are responsible to teach their young children how to bear their testimonies in public settings, [which is] a natural extension of the testimony bearing experiences family members have at home."[16] Similar instructions have also come straight from the top in the form of a letter from the First Presidency dated May 2, 2002:

> Parents and teachers should help children learn what a testimony is and when it is appropriate for them to express it. It may be best to have younger children learn to share their testimonies at such times as family home evening or when giving talks in Primary until they are old enough to do so in a fast and testimony meeting.

To return to my own upbringing, I was made to speak specific "truths" to an audience, which is a very powerful reality-molding technique. Mom, or a Sunday school teacher, stood at my side and carefully whispered the words into my ear for me to repeat. In this manner, I told large groups of people that I "knew" Joseph Smith was a prophet, that this was God's one and only true Church, and that the *Book of Mormon* is the word of God. I was thus initiated into a culture in which such proclamations of knowledge are publicly made again and again and again by every active member. And only by active members who are respected members of the Mormon community—which is something even young children understand. Performing this type of guided and coaxed public witnessing is an integral and constant part of growing up a Latter-day Saint.

Children are trained to stand in front of hundreds of people and say that they know the Church, and everything else that goes along with

---

16. Carl B. Cook, "When Children Want to Bear Testimony," *Ensign*, December 2002, p. 29.

it, is true. They are not expected to merely profess belief or faith; they are expected to profess knowledge. Elder Emerson R. West said, "We should have the courage to say 'I know', [sic] [which is] a powerful and moving phrase when spoken with sincere conviction."[17] It is powerful and moving because when we repeatedly say to other people that we "know" something is true, our belief in it increases. Apostle Boyd K. Packer said, "A testimony is to be *found* in the *bearing* of it!" [his emphasis]. He said this after admitting that "[i]t is not unusual to have a [Mormon] missionary say, 'How can I bear testimony until I get one? How can I testify that God lives, that Jesus is the Christ, and that the gospel is true?'" Then, as if it should be obvious, he rhetorically asked, "Can you not see that it will be supplied as you share it?"[18]

And indeed it will, which is why the Mormon method of social indoctrination is so successful. It is a culture of ubiquitous public witnessing, and every respected member absolutely must participate. Elder West admitted that "children are limited in knowledge and experience," but added that "they have positive feelings about the gospel which they can learn to recognize and share." In other words, they should be taught to accept "positive feelings" as evidence of truth, and "should be taught early in life to bear their testimonies."[19] According to Apostle Packer, the result will be that Mormon children go from "saying" the Church is true to "knowing" that it's true. In the same way, they will also "know" that Joseph Smith was a prophet and that the *Book of Mormon* is the word of God.

The magic ingredient that makes it all work so well is that everything is based on feelings. There are *Ensign* articles that teach parents and Primary teachers to build up children's trust in them, and then to use this trust to convince the children that any feelings they have while learning about the Church are from the Holy Ghost. Adult members are instructed to tell children that they, the children, have felt the Spirit, which is telling them that the things they have just been taught are true.

As a result of this methodical psychological programming, children's testimonies become linked to the natural, tingly feelings that everyone experiences in life. These types of feelings can come from lis-

---

17. Emerson R. West, "This I Know," *Ensign*, December 1993, p. 26.

18. Boyd K. Packer, "The Candle of the Lord," *Ensign*, January 1983, p. 51.

19. Emerson R. West, "This I Know," *Ensign*, December 1993, p. 26.

tening to music, or from feeling nervous before and during public speaking, which is a frequent activity for Mormons that begins in childhood. Mormon children are raised to believe that these natural human feelings and emotions are the promptings of the Spirit, which is telling them that the Church is true. They are taught that no amount of information can trump these feelings, no matter how high its quality, how logical, or how plentiful. Anyone who tries to persuade Mormons that Mormonism is untrue has been influenced by Satan and his followers to say such things. And Mormons who are tempted to consider any evidence that disproves the Church are *themselves* influenced by Satan.[20]

This powerful and effective method of mind control links the truth of Mormonism to both pleasant and unpleasant emotions. Believers have been conditioned to feel anything from calmness to ecstasy when exposed to anything even remotely linkable to the Church's truthfulness. It is referred to as a **burning in the bosom**. Such pleasant feelings may be triggered by hearing a talk at church, by singing a hymn, by being in the presence of other Mormons (especially Mormon leaders), or simply by thinking about something church related while sitting at home on the sofa.

At the same time, believers are conditioned to feel anything from slight anxiety to outright panic when exposed to whatever church leaders have defined as bad; of course it is impossible to provide an exhaustive list, so members often must decide for themselves what is or isn't "bad." Uncomfortable feelings come from committing (or even contemplating) a Mormon-defined sin, by reading what is, or might be, considered to be "anti-Mormon" literature (this book you're now reading, for example), by hearing someone criticize the Church or its leaders, or, most interestingly, by being in any cultural environment that is too foreign to allow Mormons to feel the Spirit, which is equated with the pleasant feelings described above. There seems to be a direct correlation, therefore, between the strength of a person's testimony on the one hand, and the degree to which he or she is ethnocentric on the other; each strengthens and reinforces the other.

All of an indoctrinated member's feelings, both pleasant and unpleasant, are interpreted as a form of evidence that proves Mormonism to be true. Those who end up losing their belief in Mormonism are amazed to eventually discover that their feelings prove

---

20. See footnote 13.

only one thing: humans have emotions that are triggered by any number of things for any number of reasons. They discover this when those feelings interpreted as being from the Spirit continue to manifest themselves even after they leave the Church. These feelings are not Mormon; they are human. The only thing unique about Mormon feelings is the frequency and intensity with which they are focused on and developed, as well as, of course, the interpretation they are given.

One person who lost his belief in the Church is Simon Southerton, a former bishop from Australia, who recalls:

> Australia beat America in the America's Cup yacht race. To most Americans this was a non-event but for many Australians it was a huge thrill. Australia came from behind in the series to snatch victory in the face of almost certain defeat. I felt intensely warm feelings in my heart, as though it was going to burst. I had felt similar feelings when I was teaching discussions as a missionary. I could not understand why the strong emotional feelings I felt with such an event were essentially indistinguishable from what I had learned to interpret as the feelings of the Spirit. They were similar to the feelings I felt as I watched *The Sound of Music*, or *Fiddler on the Roof* or *Les Miserables*.[21]

After shaking free of Mormon indoctrination, former believers realize, somewhat embarrassedly, that the same emotions that proved to them that the Church was true are just as effective at proving the divinity of football, first dates, and their favorite singer.

Edward T. Hall is an anthropologist who is considered by many to be the founder of intercultural communication studies. When trying to understand another culture, he said:

---

21. Simon is a genetics scientist who wrote *Losing a Lost Tribe: Native Americans, DNA, and the Mormon Church* (Signature Books, 2004). It provides scientific evidence that challenges the Church's claim that American Indians are descendants of Jews.

In Simon's story explaining his departure from Mormonism, he refers to "a statement published by the Smithsonian Institute in Washington D.C. concerning the *Book of Mormon*. In very strong language this statement spoke of a complete lack of evidence for any connection between the Old World and the New World." He explains that "[t]his is significant because the *Book of Mormon* teaches that America was populated by a very small group of Jews that traveled from Jerusalem around 600 B.C. [and] I had been told in seminary [the Mormon version of catechism] that the Smithsonian had been known to use the *Book of Mormon* in their research [to study ancient America]. The statement utterly refuted this claim. In fact the Smithsonian have grown tired of responding to Mormons who regularly contact them to see how the *Book of Mormon* is helping them out."

It is so important to pay attention to your feelings. . . . The main thing that marks my methodology is that I really do use myself as a control. I pay very close attention to myself, my feelings because then I have a base. And it is not intellectual.[22]

His methodology is similar to Mormon indoctrination. However, whereas Dr. Hall focuses on his feelings in order to understand and appreciate certain aspects of other cultures, as well as his own, Mormons use their feelings to judge the traits of other cultures as either good or bad, depending on how closely they resemble Mormon culture. Dr. Hall's goal is to *reduce* ethnocentricity, while the goal of Mormonism is to *increase* ethnocentricity and to use it as a tool to strengthen the psychological dome that houses the reality of The Mormon Show.

The Doctrine in Indoctrination

Now you know how testimonies are born, nurtured, and cemented into place. Once a member has a testimony, he or she believes whatever **the brethren** say. In fact, believing everything the brethren say is the very definition of "having a testimony." With that in mind, let's take a look at what the brethren have said over the years.

Where Did We Come From?

Mormon doctrine is best told as a story, which all started once upon a time on a planet that revolves around a very big star at the center of the universe.[23] A single day on that planet is equal to a thousand of our

---

22. "Gifts of Wisdom: An interview with Dr. Edward T. Hall," *The Edge: The E-Journal of Intercultural Relations*, Summer 1998, Vol. 1 (3).

23. ". . . and I saw the Stars that they were very great, and that one of them was nearest unto the throne of God; ...and the name of the great one is Kolob, because it is near unto me, for I am the Lord thy God. ... And the Lord said unto me ... that Kolob was after the manner of the Lord, according to its times and seasons in the revolutions thereof, that one revolution was a day unto the Lord, after his manner of reckoning, it being one thousand years according to the time appointed unto that whereon thou standest. This is the reckoning of the Lord's time, according to the reckoning of Kolob."
—*The Pearl of Great Price*, First Edition, The Book of Abraham, p. 23 (Published By F. D. Richards, 1851)

earth years. The name of the big star is **Kolob**, and an important man lies under Kolob's radiance on the planet that revolves around it. The piece of work this man is best known for is the planet we presently occupy. He has created uncountable others, but this is the only one that is so incredibly wicked that, in the end, the whole thing will need to be firebombed.

Before we were all born—in fact, before anyone who has ever lived on Earth was born—we all lived together with this man, whom we now call **Heavenly Father**. We technically have no beginning because we have all existed eternally as intelligences. Our spirits have a beginning, however, and they were created by Heavenly Father, which is why we call him Heavenly Father. You don't hear about his companions much, but you know the old cliché: behind every successful man lies a successful woman. In this case there are several, because, according to Brigham Young, Heavenly Father was a polygamist.

In the same way that our lives begin and end here on Earth, just like our parents' lives did, we also have the same type of beginning and ending as our heavenly parents. They, like us, started out as people, and we, like them, can become gods. Because we have "been born of Him in the Spirit," we have "inherited the very attributes which He possesses" and are therefore "God's embryo."[24] In other words, if you're good and do what you're told, you'll grow up to be exactly like God.

Our two eldest siblings were really smart boys. You have probably heard of them. The name of the first born was Jesus and the second was Lucifer.[25] They separately drew up plans to create Earth and then have us all be born there so that we could get physical bodies, die, be judged according to our behavior, and then finally be resurrected with perfect

---

24. "We are His children in very deed, having been born of Him in the spirit, and we have inherited the very attributes which He possesses. They are in us, and they make us God's embryo, We believe that as we are now God once was, and . . . He has become what He is, and as He is, man may become, on the same principle."
—Elder George F. Richards, *Conference Report*, April 1913, p. 82.

(The ultimate goal of each of us, therefore, is to someday become a God [or one of the behind-the-scenes wives of a God] and create our own planets so that we can inhabit them with the bodies of our own spirit children, and, if we choose, think of our own special ways to destroy the ones that don't listen.)

25. "He [Jesus] was the Firstborn of the great family to which we belong, so we call him not only our Redeemer, but our Elder Brother."
—President Charles W. Penrose, *Conference Report*, April 1920 (morning session), p.32.

bodies that are forever in their prime—something even Estée Lauder doesn't promise.

Lucifer presented his proposal first, which is always a disadvantage. He suggested to Heavenly Father that everyone should get perfect scores on their tests. He said this could be done simply by giving everyone no choice but to follow all the test's rules. A lot of people—spirits, that is—thought this was a great idea. There must have been a lot of mumbling and head nodding, just as there would be if a teacher proposed giving every student an A+ on the French Literature final.

(Speaking of head nodding, this is a good time to point out that when we were spirits in the **pre-existence**, we had "the same shape and form as the physical body. The spirit body then has arms, legs, a head, and a mind."[26] When we are in our prime in this life, we look like our spirits do, and after we die, we'll get our same bodies back, blemish and handicap free, and forever in their prime. Not a bad deal, really.)

Jesus' proposal was much more complicated than Lucifer's. His idea was to give everyone the choice to either follow or break the rules, a concept called **free agency**. We would all be graded according to how closely we followed the rules, with the breaking of some rules being judged more severely than others.

The thing that may have clinched the deal for Jesus was the fact that, in his proposal, he said all the glory would go to Heavenly Father in the end. By contrast, Lucifer, who was going to do all the work making everyone obey the rules, didn't offer to hand all the glory over to Heavenly Father. What did I tell you about going first? Lucifer probably would have changed a couple of details in his proposal if he'd known what Jesus was going to say.

It was understood that everyone would sin if they had free agency, but people could repent of most sins and be forgiven. For that to work, according Jesus' plan, Jesus would be born on Earth, get tortured, and be crucified. The fact that this made absolutely no sense was explained away as being incomprehensibly profound.

We know that Heavenly Father chose Jesus' plan and that we are now living it out. Therefore, to see the details of the plan, all we have to do is examine the history of our world. As is often the case, Brigham Young provides us with the most intriguing version. According to him,

---

26. Elder Eldred G. Smith, Patriarch to the Church, *Conference Report*, October 1964, p.10.

Heavenly Father, Michael the archangel, and the Adam who lived in the Garden of Eden are all the same person. That means Heavenly Father is not only the father of our spirits but is the human ancestor of all of us as well.

Heavenly Father (Adam) moved into the Garden of Eden, which was located in Jackson County, Missouri, with one of his wives named Eve. Roughly 4000 years later, when it was Jesus' turn to appear on the scene, Heavenly Father physically begat Jesus in the flesh with the woman we all know as the Virgin Mary. In other words, He "knew" Mary in the biblical sense but respected her enough in the morning to allow her to keep the title of Virgin. You may be tempted to smile, but don't; Brigham Young threatened damnation upon anyone who makes light of this doctrine.[27]

This deal with Mary was perhaps another detail of Jesus' plan that appealed to Heavenly Father. But whatever the reason, Heavenly Father was not the only one who chose Jesus' plan; most spirits did as well. Of those who did, they either really liked the plan, or they realized there was going to be a serious conflict and decided it was safer to choose the stronger side, the one with Heavenly Father on it. "We should also keep in mind that the greatest of all military men was the Son of God himself [Jesus]. In the war in heaven [that ensued from this argument], he led the forces of righteousness against the rebellion of Lucifer."[28] It must have been pretty obvious which side would win, so two-thirds of the spirits stood safely behind it. The remaining one third of the spir-

---

27. "When our father Adam came into the garden of Eden, he came into it with a *celestial body*, and brought Eve, *one of his wives*, with him. He helped to make and organize this world. He is MICHAEL, *the Archangel*, the ANCIENT OF DAYS! about whom holy men have written and spoken—HE *is our* FATHER *and our* GOD, *and the only God with whom* WE *have to do* . . . When the Virgen [sic] Mary conceived the child Jesus, the Father had begotten him in his own likeness. He was *not* begotten by the Holy Ghost. And who is the Father? He is the first of the human family; and when he took a tabernacle, it was begotten by *his Father* in heaven, after the same manner as the tabernacles of Cain, Abel, and the rest of the sons and daughters of Adam and Eve . . . Jesus, our elder brother, was begotten in the flesh by the same character that was in the garden of Eden, and who is our Father in Heaven. Now, let all who may hear these doctrines, pause before they make light of them, or treat them with indifference, for they will prove their salvation or damnation."
—Brigham Young, *Journal of Discourses*, 1:50–51 (April 9, 1852) [emphasis in original]
28. Sterling W. Sill, Assistant to the Council of the Twelve, *Conference Report*, October 1970, p.79.

its, all of whom wanted to fight for a guarantee of good grades, joined Lucifer's rebellion.

"[T]here was war in heaven, actual combat,"[29] and it was a fight to the finish. Jesus and "the loyal spirit hosts . . . vanquished Lucifer and his rebellious legions, winning the right to take bodies upon this planet."[30] Lucifer and his warriors were cast from heaven, sentenced to an eternity without bodies, and they now dwell on earth, still in spirit form, tempting us all to do dastardly things to ourselves and each other, all because they're sore losers and therefore want us all to fail our tests.

Not everyone on the side of righteousness fought so valiantly. Some played it safe and said they were for Jesus' plan, but when there was a call for volunteers to go to the front lines, they probably looked around at nothing in particular and whistled nonchalantly. Suffice it to say they didn't raise their hands, and they are now paying a price for it.

Apostle George F. Richards said, "The Negro is an unfortunate man. He has been given a black skin." Even worse, according to Elder Richards, is that black[31] men are "not permitted to receive the Priesthood and the ordinances of the **temple**, necessary to prepare men and women to enter into and enjoy a fullness of glory in the **celestial kingdom**." The reason for this is "that as spirit children of our Eternal Father they were not valiant in the fight. . . . [They were not] valiant in the **spirit world** in that war in heaven. Somewhere along the line were these spirits, indifferent perhaps, and possibly neutral in the war." Elder Richards then warned that "it does not pay in religious matters, matters that pertain to our eternal salvation, to be indifferent, neutral, or lukewarm."[32] Just look at what having such attributes did to black people: it made them black people.

The Church's second prophet, Brigham Young, explained that we "see some classes of the human family that are black, uncouth, uncomely, disagreeable and low in their habits, wild and seemingly deprived of nearly all the blessings of the intelligence that is generally bestowed

---

29. Melvin J. Ballard, *Conference Report*, October 1918, p.149.
(There is no explanation anywhere in official Mormon literature as to how spirits could engage in "actual combat.")

30. Orson F. Whitney, of the Council of the Twelve, *Conference Report*, October 1925, p.101.

31. I do not use the term African-American because Mormon doctrine regarding black people refers to all blacks of African origin, wherever they might live today.

32. George F. Richards, *Conference Report*, April 1939, pp. 58–59.

upon mankind." The prophet Brigham then kindly explained how this class of humans originated. They are the result of a curse that was put on Cain because "Cain slew his brother." The consequence of this act of murder was that "the Lord put a mark upon him, which is the flat nose and black skin"—the unfortunate state that Apostle Richards was referring to. But it gets worse, Brigham Young tells us that after the flood "another curse is pronounced upon the same race—that they should be the 'servants of servants;' [sic] and they will be, until that curse is removed; and the Abolitionists cannot help it, nor in the least alter that decree."[33]

Some readers are surely wondering why Cain's descendents weren't all drowned in the flood. It turns out, according to President John Taylor, that after the flood "the curse that had been pronounced upon Cain was continued through Ham's wife, as he had married a wife of that seed. And why did it pass through the flood? Because it was necessary that the devil should have a representation upon the earth . . ."[34]

The curse to be servants did not end with the Civil War or the Civil Rights Movement, nor will it ever end; it will last forever. In a talk given at Brigham Young University (BYU) on August 27, 1954, Apostle Mark E. Petersen explained how this works, interpreting it as something "merciful":

> Isn't the mercy of God marvelous? Think of the Negro, cursed as to the priesthood . . . This Negro, who, in the pre-existence lived the type of life which justified the Lord in sending him to earth in the lineage of Cain with a black skin, and possibly being born in darkest Africa . . . In spite of all he did in the pre-existent life, the Lord is willing, if the Negro accepts the gospel with real, sincere faith, and is really converted, to give him the blessings of baptism and the gift of the Holy Ghost. If that Negro is faithful all his days, he can and will enter the celestial kingdom. He will go there as a servant, but he will get celestial glory.[35]

---

33. Brigham Young, *Journal of Discourses*, Vol. 7, 1859, p. 290.

34. John Taylor, President of the Church of Jesus Christ of Latter-day Saints, *Journal of Discourses*, Vol. 22, August 28, 1881, p. 304.

35. This concept of blacks being blessed by being in the presence of greatness, even as servants, is not unlike what Hegel believed. He wrote that "The polygamy of the Negroes has frequently for its object the having many children, to be sold, every one of them, into slavery." He thought they looked upon slavery as "the occasion of the increase of human feeling among the Negroes," and that it enabled them to participate "in a higher morality and the culture connected with it."

Blacks aren't the only race of people that started out as whites but ended up cursed. As mentioned earlier, the *Book of Mormon* tells us why Native Americans aren't white people like they used to be: "wherefore, as they were white, and exceeding fair and delightsome, that they might not be enticing unto my people, the Lord God did cause a skin of blackness to come upon them. And thus saith the Lord God, I will cause that they shall be loathsome unto thy people."[36] These loathsome people look an awful lot like Asians, so it's only natural that Mormons might wonder about all the other dark skinned races around the world.

In the same speech quoted above, Elder Petersen cleared this up for them:

> Is there reason then why the type of birth we receive in this life is not a reflection of our worthiness or lack of it in the pre-existent life?. . . [C]an we account in any other way for the birth of some of the children of God in darkest Africa, or in flood-ridden China, or among the starving hordes of India, while some of the rest of us are born here in the United States? We cannot escape the conclusion that because of performance in our pre-existence some of us are born as Chinese, some as Japanese, some as Latter-day Saints. . . . A Chinese, born in China with a dark skin, and with all the handicaps of that race seems to have little opportunity. But think of the mercy of God to Chinese people who are willing to accept the gospel. In spite of whatever they might have done in the pre-existence to justify being born over there as Chinamen, if they now, in this life accept the gospel and live it the rest of their lives they can have the Priesthood, go to the temple and receive endowments and sealings, and that means they can have exaltation.

This means that all people of color were less valiant than whites in the War in Heaven, and their dark skin is the smoking-gun proof. Since we know that all people of color were not truly in favor of Jesus' plan, then that means only a minority of all the spirits in heaven were. Of the two-thirds of heaven's spirits who were allowed to be born on Earth, only the white ones were decidedly in favor of Jesus' plan, and even a lot of those seem to have changed their minds.

Reading the Bible, one can only wonder if perhaps the war is still being fought. At one point, for example, Heavenly Father wiped out nearly everyone on our planet, saying he wished none of his kids had

---

36. *Book of Mormon*, 2 Nephi: 5:21–22

ever been born.[37] The linguist Noam Chomsky, who as a child read the Bible in Hebrew with his Hebrew scholar father, observed that:

> [T]he Bible . . . is basically polytheistic, with the warrior God demanding of his chosen people that they not worship the other Gods and destroy those who do—in an extremely brutal way, in fact. It would be hard to find a more genocidal text in the literary canon, or a more violent and destructive character than the God who was to be worshipped.[38]

Bertrand Russell said, "We read in the Old Testament that it was a religious duty to exterminate conquered races completely, and that to spare even their cattle and sheep was an impiety."[39] Russell was criticizing what Mormon Apostle Robert D. Hales referred to as "a marvelous story about Samuel and Saul . . . Before one battle, Samuel told Saul to utterly destroy the Amalekites and all of their animals, as Samuel had been told by the Lord." Unfortunately, however, "[a]fter their victory, Saul and his army brought back the best of the animals." This was a sad state of affairs. "Saul had practiced selective obedience because he had [not] destroyed all the animals."[40] Elder Hales thinks it is one's duty to murder anything that moves if that is what God's spokesman tells one to do.

It seems logical to conclude that the genocidal extermination of the Amalekites, the Canaanites, and nearly all the people of Noah's time was an extension of the War in Heaven. And the fight appears to have continued into present times in the form of the Cold War and the "War on Terror." Apostle Ezra Taft Benson said that "communism is turning out to be the earthly image of the plan which Satan presented in the pre-existence. The whole program of socialistic-communism is essentially a war against God and the plan of salvation—the very plan which we fought to uphold during 'the war in heaven.'" Benson said, "The fight against godless communism is a very real part of every man's duty

---

37. "And it repented the LORD that he had made man on the earth, and it grieved him at his heart. And the LORD said, I will destroy man whom I have created from the face of the earth; both man, and beast, and the creeping thing, and the fowls of the air; for it repenteth me that I have made them."
—Genesis 6:6–7

38. Noam Chomsky, Internet *ChomskyChat* forum, May 1998.

39. Bertrand Russell, *Unpopular Essays*, p. 163 (Unwin Paperbacks, 1950).

40. Robert D. Hales, "Return with Honor," *Ensign*, June 1999, p. 7.

who holds the priesthood . . . a struggle against the evil, satanical priest-craft of Lucifer. Truly it can be called, 'a continuation of the war in heaven.'"[41]

This means we can praise the biblical tactics carried out by the United States against Cambodian peasant farmers when President Nixon said, "I want them to hit everything," and Kissinger passed on this genocidal order to carry out a "massive bombing campaign in Cambodia [using] [a]nything that flies on anything that moves."[42]

We can also be assured of the righteous nature of the "War on Terror." Just when the U.S. started bombing Afghanistan, President Hinckley said that "[t]he conflict we see today is but another expression of the conflict that began with the War in Heaven."[43] And two years later, just before quoting verses about the War in Heaven from the book of Revelation, President Hinckley concluded that "[t]he present war [in Iraq] is really an outgrowth and continuation of that conflict [in Afghanistan]."[44]

This theological "war" also extends to domestic politics. Many African-Americans weren't just fence sitters during the Cold War; they were decidedly on the wrong side of the war. Apostle Benson warned us that "the so-called civil rights movement as it exists today is a Communist program for revolution in America."[45]

Apostle Benson was very devoted to preventing the advancement of African-Americans' political power. He even allowed one of his talks to be used as the foreword to an overtly racist book titled *The Black Hammer: A Study of Black Power, Red Influence and White Alternatives,* by Wes Andrews and Clyde Dalton (Desco Press, 1967). On page 83 the book mentions "the Negro's need for complete subservience to the Great White Fathers in Washington." The most appalling feature of the book is its cover, featuring the decapitated, profusely bleeding head of a black man. Ezra Taft Benson later went on to become the Church's prophet, seer and revelator from 1985 to 1994. He was the top spokes-

41. Ezra Taft Benson, *Conference Report,* October 1961, pp. 70–71.

42. Elizabeth Becker, *New York Times,* 27 May 2004.

43. Gordon B. Hinckley, "The Times in Which We Live," *Liahona,* January 2002, p. 83.

44. Gordon B. Hinckley, "War and Peace," *Liahona,* May 2003, p. 79.

45. Ezra Taft Benson, September 1967. Quoted in *The Mormon Hierarchy: Extensions of Power,* by D. Michael Quinn, 1997, p. 98.

man for Heavenly Father, meaning he was responsible for telling us all how to live our lives.[46]

While growing up, I was fully aware of, and accepted, the Church's racist doctrines as they were taught to me at the time. By the time I came along, it was no longer official doctrine that blacks were cursed descendents of Cain who stood on the sidelines during the War in Heaven. The Church did still have official racist teachings, however, and these had long been public knowledge; so had the fact that black men were not allowed to hold the priesthood. As a result, BYU was being boycotted, and some universities were refusing to compete with BYU's sports teams. Even more seriously, the IRS was considering denying the Church its tax-free status as a religion.

Inevitably, the prophet soon received a revelation from God, and in 1978 men with "flat nose[s] and black skin" were suddenly allowed to hold priesthood power. Roughly coinciding with this revelation, members were told that the story about the origin of blacks—that they were fence sitters in the War in Heaven and descendents of Cain—was nothing but a speculative theory with unknown authorship. Most members, including myself, were ignorant of the fact that the Church's former apostles and prophets were the actual authors of this "theory," and that it had previously been taught openly as gospel truth.

I had accepted this ludicrous story about the origin of black people as fact, and then pushed it aside as a speculative theory when I was told to do so. Like all members, I did not consider these beliefs to be racist, nor did I comprehend in the least how utterly cruel and disgusting it is to indoctrinate dark skinned children to believe that their appearance is a curse from God. The Church has never apologized for, nor officially retracted, any of its racist doctrines. The teaching that Native Americans were cursed by God with "a skin of blackness . . . [and that God] cause[d] that they shall be loathsome" is still official, canonized doctrine. And, I'm sorry to say, there are plenty of dark skinned children born and raised inside the dome of The Mormon Show.

Now you know the story of where we all came from, and you know the how-the-elephant-got-its-trunk type story that explains why we all look the way we do. But why are we here? What sort of test did Jesus prepare for us?

---

46. See D. Michael Quinn's *The Mormon Hierarchy: Extensions of Power*, 1997, Chapter 3, for a detailed treatment of Ezra Taft Benson. Quinn reviews Benson's dedication to radical anti-communism and his avid support of the John Birch Society.

Why Are We Here?

We were sent here to get bodies and be tested. Our lives must therefore be entirely devoted to scoring high on the test, which has two parts:

1. Believe
2. Obey

What must we believe? We must believe the story of our origin, which you now know. We must believe in Heavenly Father, the same God written about in the Bible, and in His son, Jesus Christ, and in the Holy Ghost. We must believe that they are three separate beings, two of which now have bodies of flesh and bone. We must believe everything in the Bible, as far as it is translated correctly. We must believe in the *Book of Mormon*, which has no mistranslations because Joseph Smith did such a marvelous job. We must believe that God has one, and only one, true church, which is The Church of Jesus Christ of Latter-day Saints. We must believe that the men at the head of this Church are prophets and apostles of God, and that their job is to tell us what God requires us to do.

We must believe all these things. We must believe them so strongly that we can publicly say we "know" they are true. And if we don't believe they are true, then we must publicly say "we know these things are true" until we believe what we say.

To make the test hard, our memories of our pre-existence were entirely wiped out so that we would have to believe in Heavenly Father on faith alone. We have to believe He is real, despite the fact that He gave us reasoning capabilities, and despite the fact that "[n]one of us has ever seen this being; none of us has ever heard him, except in the silence of our own heads; none of us can produce a piece of evidence as large as a mustard seed that what we think of as God is anything more than a thought. . . . [W]e have no trace [of God], except for the testimony of scribes writing of events neither they nor those around them ever witnessed."[47] And we must believe in Him despite there being

---

47. Stephen Chapman, a columnist and editorial writer for the *Chicago Tribune*, during a debate in late 1999 with former *New Republic* editor Andrew Sullivan on the question, "Is there a God?"

plenty of evidence contradicting the stories we've been told by His prophets, for example the tale about the world being approximately six thousand years old.

In order to make the test extra difficult, the prophet Joseph Smith spoke of the inhabitants of the moon, whom he described as tall people that dress like Quakers and live to approximately one thousand years of age. As if that wasn't hard enough, the prophet Brigham Young tested us even further when he told us about "the inhabitants of the sun. Do you think it is inhabited? I rather think it is. Do you think there is any life there? No question of it; it was not made in vain. It was made to give light to those who dwell upon it, and to other planets; . . ." In the same sermon, he warned us "who the real fanatics are: they are they who adopt false principles and ideas as facts, and try to establish a superstructure upon a false foundation. They are the fanatics; and however ardent and zealous they may be, they may reason or argue on false premises till doomsday, and the result will be false."[48]

There is a simple formula to the belief portion of the test. I was taught on several occasions that all one really needs to believe is that Joseph Smith was a prophet of God. If you believe that, then you will believe that he saw Heavenly Father and Jesus Christ in a vision. You will believe that he translated the *Book of Mormon* with the help of God, and that it is therefore the word of God. You will also believe that the Church Smith founded is God's only true church. In short, if you believe that Joseph Smith was a prophet, you will believe every single thing about Mormonism.

It's that simple. All you have to do is believe that this man who had at least thirty-three wives, and who "propos[ed] to females as young as twelve, [had] sexual relationships with polygamous wives as young as fourteen, . . . [and] marriage and sexual cohabitation with foster daughters, . . ."[49] was a prophet of God, who was chosen by Him to tell all of us exactly how to live our lives in order to pass Jesus' test. If we believe that about Joseph Smith, then by logical extension we will believe it about his successor Brigham Young and every other prophet up to the present day. All that is required of Mormons is that they believe and obey what these men say. Brigham Young, who had more

48. Brigham Young, *Journal of Discourses*, Vol. 13, July 24, 1870, p. 271.
49. D. Michael Quinn, *The Mormon Hierarchy: Origins of Power*, p. 89.

than fifty wives, said, "I have never yet preached a sermon and sent it out to the children of men, that they may not call Scripture."[50]

The second part of the test is to obey the Church's leaders, referred to as **General Authorities**. Everything Mormons are required to do is referred to as a "commandment" from God (meaning a commandment from the Church's General Authorities), and a constant preoccupation in Mormon culture is working out the details of these commandments. Members frequently talk about what, exactly, they are required to do or not do; they analyze and discuss what the prophets, apostles, and other General Authorities meant when they said this or that. This is necessary because many of God's commandments are far from clear.

Take the commandment from Exodus 20:13, for example: "Thou shalt not kill." Like all commandments, it is an imperative in the second person. That means that God, the speaker of the command, is excluded. This commandment was not broken, therefore, when He drowned all His children except for a select few in Noah's day. It is we humans who must never kill.

This would be clear and simple if God didn't give us conflicting commandments, such as the one from Exodus 22:18: "Thou shalt not suffer a witch to live." Suddenly we're confused. Who decides who the witches are? Who is to kill them? How?

The Mormon doctrine of **blood atonement** is a more recent example of a commandment that conflicts with "Thou shalt not kill." According to this doctrine, some sins are not covered by Christ's atonement, and therefore require the sinner to personally atone for his or her own sin. This personal atonement requires the sinner's life to be taken and his or her blood to be literally shed onto the ground. Addressing the members of the Church, Brigham Young said:

> Will you love your brothers and sisters . . . when they have committed a sin that cannot be atoned for without the shedding of their blood? Will you love that man or woman well enough to shed their blood? . . . I could refer you to plenty of instances where men have been righteously slain, in order to atone for their sins . . . This is loving our neighbor as ourselves; if he needs help, help him; and if he wants salvation and it is necessary to spill his blood on the earth in order that he may be saved, spill it . . . That is the way to love mankind.[51]

---

50. Brigham Young, *Journal of Discourses*, Vol. 13, January 2, 1870, p. 95.

51. Brigham Young, *Journal of Discourses*, Vol. 4, 1857, pp. 219–220.

More confusion. Who decides which people are guilty of a blood atonement sin? Who is supposed to show their love for these people by killing them? How should the killing be done so as to properly fulfill its purpose?

The General Authorities deliver sermons semi-annually in Salt Lake City at General Conferences. Devout members greatly look forward to these sermons.[52] Sermons at modern day General Conferences don't include anything as controversial as the doctrine of blood atonement. In fact, most Mormons would be very surprised to read the above quote from Brigham Young. Instead, today's members learn the latest official policy regarding which books and movies are appropriate to read and watch, or how a woman can best fulfill her roles as wife, mother, and homemaker. Regarding the role of women, Sister Julie Beck, the **Relief Society** General President, said in a General Conference in 2007 that Mormon mothers with testimonies "desire to have children"; that "young couples should not postpone having children"; that mothers are in charge of "cooking, washing clothes and dishes, and keeping an orderly home"; and that they should consider "their homes as a pre-missionary training center" for their sons. How can a woman ever know for sure if she is adequately fulfilling these "commandments"?

Mormons frequently discuss what types of thoughts, behaviors and lifestyles are acceptable for **worthy** Mormons. Is it okay to drink coke? How many children are enough? Under what circumstances is it all right for a woman to work outside the home? Can tithing be calculated after taxes rather than before?

The **law of tithing** requires members to give ten per cent of their income to the Church. A predecessor to the law of tithing was God's command to establish the **United Order of Enoch** (also called the **law of consecration**). Speaking to church members—through Joseph Smith of course—God said, "consecrate all thy properties, that which thou hast unto me, with a covenant and a deed which can not be broken; and they shall be laid before the bishop of my church . . ."[53] This Order of Enoch was a communalistic order that attempted to follow the Marxist ideal, "from each according to his ability, to each according to his need."

---

52. I loved listening to General Conferences when I was a teenager. You can see and hear the most recent session online at www.lds.org.

53. *A Book of Commandments*, 1833, Chapter XLIV, verse 26.

Church members had a hard time with this commandment. God soon "saw [that they] could not live it, and [therefore] revealed the law of tithing to take its place temporarily."[54] The Church will some day reinstate the law of consecration when its members are ready to abide by this higher law, but "[b]efore we [try again to] enter upon the law of consecration, which is the celestial law of God in finance, it is necessary that we should take the training that we are now having under the law of tithing."[55] For the time being, then, members are only required to obey the law of tithing, a much easier law that merely requires members to pay ten percent of their total income to the Church.

Growing up in the Church, I frequently heard people discuss whether tithes should be calculated before taxes or after. Church leaders have never officially said anything about this, but many members, even those struggling to make ends meet, pay ten percent of their gross income to be sure they are fully complying with the law of tithing.

It is difficult to exaggerate the importance that the Church places on the commandment to pay one's tithes. To help members out, the *Ensign* occasionally includes articles that teach fiscal responsibility and budgeting. Why budget? Because, as an April 1998 *Ensign* article explains, it "ensures we can pay our tithing and other offerings." Not only is the ability to pay tithing a benefit of budgeting, it is an essential step in the budgeting process. This is because the Lord provides financial blessings to those who pay their tithes. It is only logical, therefore, that tithe payers will have an easier time making ends meet than non-tithe payers. And if we carry this logic one step further, we will see that people can actually come out of poverty by tithing to the Church. Finally, a solution to world poverty.

A former prophet actually suggested this for all the miserably poor people living in the Philippines. President Hinckley, Heavenly Father's mouthpiece, gave a talk to the Cebu Mission missionaries in 1997. He told them that if poor Filipinos, "even living in poverty and misery . . . will accept the gospel and live it, pay their tithes and offerings, even though those be meager, . . . they will have rice in their bowls and clothing on their backs and shelter over their heads. I do not see any other solution." Hinckley's piece was—yes—titled "Solution For Poverty."[56]

---

54. Elder Reed Smoot, *Conference Report*, October 1901, p. 6.

55. Apostle Francis M. Lyman, *Conference Report*, October 1899, p. 34.

56. *Ensign*, August 1997, p. 7.

Some commandments are related to marriage. Early on, polygamy was a requirement. Brigham Young said, "The only men who become Gods, even the Sons of God, are those who enter into polygamy."[57] To help the men obey this commandment in peace, Brigham warned all the members—I'm sure he was talking especially to the women here—not to "deny the plurality of wives," or, he said, "I promise that you will be damned." He said they weren't even allowed to "deny it in [their] feelings."[58]

Surprisingly, some women complained. Not surprisingly, Brigham Young couldn't stand their whining and warned them to pipe down or leave. He made an announcement to "all the women of this community," saying, "I am going to give you [two weeks to] . . . determine whether you wish to stay with your husbands or not, and then I am going to set every woman at liberty and say to them, . . . [they] have got to do one of two things; either round up their shoulders to endure the afflictions of this world, and live their religion, or they may leave . . ."

Giving his own wives the benefit of the doubt, the prophet said, "I know what my women will say; they will say, 'You can have as many women as you please, Brigham.'" But he was displeased with other women in the community, saying he wanted to "go somewhere and do something to get rid of the whiners." He wanted "the wives and the children [to] say amen to what [the man] says, and be subject to his dictates, instead of their dictating the man, instead of their trying to govern him."

He instructed the men to "say to [their] wives, '. . . [I]f you stay with me you shall comply with the law of God, and that too without any murmuring and whining. You must fulfil the law of God in every respect, and round up your shoulders to walk up to the mark without any grunting.'" "Sisters, I am not joking," Brigham insisted, "there is no cessation to the everlasting whining of many of the women in this Territory." He was so frustrated by it, he resorted to prophetic threats, saying, "[I]f the women will . . . continue to despise the order of heaven, I will pray that the curse of the Almighty may be close to their heels, and that it may be following them all the day long." Needless to say, this threat was extremely frightening to those who believed it.

---

57. Brigham Young, *Journal of Discourses*, Vol. 11, August 9, 1866, p. 269.
58. Brigham Young, *Journal of Discourses*, Vol. 3, July 14, 1855, p. 266.

Being sympathetic to the women's plight, Brigham acknowledged that he understood Heavenly Father had put "a curse upon the woman that is not upon the man, namely, that 'her whole affections shall be towards her husband,' and what is the next? 'He shall rule over you.'" This is God's doing, though. Brigham was merely an obedient servant who was passing on the message. He warned these women, who surely had nowhere else to go: "[Y]ou must bow down to it, and submit yourselves to the celestial law [of polygamy]. You may go where you please, after two weeks from to-morrow; but, remember, that I will not hear any more of this whining."[59]

Later, when the Church wanted Utah to become a state, the then-prophet received a revelation. Polygamy on Earth is no longer a commandment, though it is still possible in the afterlife for those who do well on their tests. On Earth, Mormon women no longer have to share their husbands, and the curse of their husbands ruling over them has been gradually diluted. In the pre-1990 temple ritual, sister members had to raise their right hands, as in a court of law, and were told to "solemnly covenant and promise before God, angels, and these witnesses at this altar that you will each observe and keep the law of your husbands, and abide by his [sic] counsel in righteousness. Each of you bow your head and say 'Yes.'" Changes were made to the ritual in 1990, and an LDS woman is now only required to "obey the Law of the Lord, and to hearken unto the counsel of her husband, as her husband hearkens unto the counsel of the Father."

President Hinckley said that "in attaining the highest degree of glory in the celestial kingdom, the man cannot enter without the woman, neither can the woman enter without the man."[60] And members must go through certain rituals to make it to the highest degree of glory. In addition to being baptized and becoming a member of the LDS Church, they must also go through a marriage ceremony inside a temple, which **seals** them to their spouses in **celestial marriage**. If not, then "when they are out of the world they neither marry nor are given in marriage; but are appointed angels in heaven, which angels are ministering servants, to minister for those who are **worthy** of a far more, and an exceeding, and an eternal weight of glory."[61]

---

59. Brigham Young, *Journal of Discourses*, Vol. 4, September 21, 1856, pp. 55–57.

60. Gordon B. Hinckley, "Daughters of God," *Ensign*, November 1991, p. 97.

61. *Doctrine and Covenants* 132:16.

The fate of people who never marry, or who have spouses that aren't worthy, is to end up serving, for all eternity, those people who succeeded at the very thing they failed at. Talk about twisting the knife. This encourages people to put pressure on their spouses to remain faithful and obedient Mormons. Married Mormons who stop believing that the Church is true find themselves in a very awkward situation. They must either live a lie or risk breaking up their families. It's a very effective way to retain (tithe paying) members who would otherwise opt out without hesitation.

The chances of making it to the highest degree of glory in the Celestial Kingdom are better for men than for women, because a man can be sealed to more than one woman. Men have it better in another way as well: women who are sealed to husbands in the temple must first go through the temple's endowment ceremony, which is the ceremony where they are made to promise that they will "hearken unto the counsel of [their] husband[s]." (The intention of this book isn't to convert people to Mormonism, but some men just might consider ten percent of their income to be worth the benefit of having wives that are commanded to "hearken unto the[ir] counsel.")

Unworthy members and nonmembers are not allowed inside the temple, and they are therefore forced to wait outside while the wedding of a loved one takes place. Imagine not being allowed to attend your child's wedding—how cruel! If your child joins the Church and you are a nonmember, or an unworthy member, that is exactly what will happen. Unworthy members with testimonies already feel a tremendous sense of shame and guilt for being unworthy. This is compounded by the public display of unworthiness when they are refused admission to the weddings of relatives or friends.

There is a series of commandments called the **law of chastity**. This law includes a list of specific taboos related to sex and modesty. Girls and women must dress modestly. Everyone must "[a]bstain from premarital sex, petting, necking, sex perversion, masturbation, and preoccupation with sex in thought, speech, and action," according to a Church pamphlet titled "For the Strength of Youth." Beginning at the age of twelve, girls and boys are interviewed one on one by their bishops and specifically asked about such things as "Do you masturbate?" "Have you ever participated in heavy petting?" or "Do you have immoral thoughts?" are also common queries, although the explicitness of the questions is up to the bishop. Some will just ask, "Do you obey the law of chastity?" or "Are you morally clean?" Mormon youth understand what those questions mean, and know that they are supposed to confess any form of sexual behavior or "unclean" thoughts.

There is a commandment called the **Word of Wisdom** that strictly forbids members from drinking any alcohol, coffee, or tea. Members are advised to refrain from drinking caffeinated soft drinks as well. They absolutely must not use tobacco or any type of drugs whatsoever, other than medicinal drugs. In fact, Utah leads the nation in per capita use of antidepressants, which many speculate is related to the high demands the Church puts on mothers with testimonies.[62]

Members are commanded to attend church regularly. They must keep the **Sabbath**, which means, in addition to attending church, they must never shop, eat in restaurants, see movies, or patronize any business on Sundays.

Members must never speak ill of, or disagree with, Church leaders. Apostle N. Eldon Tanner said, "When the prophet speaks the debate is over."[63] The brethren have said that members must never criticize the brethren [General Authorities], even if the criticism is true. You would think they would try to say this with a straight face, but I saw Apostle Dallin H. Oaks say it on the PBS special called "The Mormons," and, amazingly, he said it with a grin.[64] Perhaps they can't help themselves. To appreciate their difficulty, try saying the following to someone without smiling: "You must never criticize me, even if the criticism is true."

The last commandment I'll mention is the command to do missionary work. Joining the Church and keeping the commandments are the only way anyone can return to live with Heavenly Father. Therefore, members have been commissioned to do their very best to get anyone and everyone to join the Church.

Elder Bruce R. McConkie said, "[W]e have an affirmative, positive, definite obligation resting upon us to do missionary work. This matter

---

62. Dr. Kent Ponder, a Mormon psychologist who did doctoral reasearch on the psychology of cognitive-dissonance conflict, wrote an open letter to LDS therapists that describes in some detail the problems caused by the Mormon one-size-fits-all culture. He titled it "Mormon Women, Prozac® and Therapy." It is available on two web sites: http://packham.n4m.org/prozac.htm
and http://www.exmormon.org/mormon/mormon197.htm.

63. N. Eldon Tanner, "The Debate Is Over," *Ensign*, August 1979, p. 2.

64. "The Mormons" can be viewed online at: http://www.pbs.org/mormons/view/.

of carrying the gospel message to the world is not something that we can choose to do or not, if and when we may find it to be convenient. We are under covenant to do it 'at all times . . . and in all places . . . even until death.'"[65] It is supposed to be constantly on members' minds when associating with nonmembers, and for especially devout Mormons it always is. Mormons are like Amway representatives: all their acquaintances are potential converts.

This commandment to do missionary work had a major impact on me because all Mormon boys are commanded to serve fulltime **missions** when they turn nineteen. Not long before I began my mission, Elder Robert L. Blackman of the Quorum of the Seventy addressed "the young men of the Church." He told us that President Kimball had "stated that every young man should serve a mission." He then rhetorically asked, "Do you sustain him as a prophet? If you do, your only response should be, 'When? I'll be prepared.'"[66]

Despite such statements, Mormons go out of their way to tell nonmembers that all missionaries serve voluntarily. In actuality, though, the only voluntary missionaries are girls and retired couples. All the boys are commanded to go, and they clearly understand this because they hear it constantly while growing up inside the reality bubble of The Mormon Show. Elder Christian Hans, who served as a missionary in the Arkansas Little Rock Mission, was quoted in *New Era* saying that "[e]ligible boys are commanded to serve missions."[67] Saying that missionaries all go voluntarily, however, sounds less cultish, so that is what members say to nonmembers. But all Mormon boys know the truth.

Ezra Taft Benson said, "The Lord needs every young man between the ages of 19 and 26, worthy, prepared, and excited about serving in the mission field."[68] Elder H. Bryan Richards of the Quorum of the Seventy told parents to teach their sons that God "wants every able and worthy young man to serve a mission."[69] A **Gospel Doctrine** manual

---

65. Bruce R. McConkie, of the First Council of the Seventy, *Conference Report*, October 1960. His quote was from Mosiah 18:9 in the *Book of Mormon*.

66. Robert L. Backman, "To the Young Men of the Church," *Ensign*, November 1980, p. 40.

67. "Q&A: Questions and Answers," *New Era*, December 1992, p. 17.

68. *The Teachings of Ezra Taft Benson*, 1988, p. 178.

69. H. Bryan Richards, "As for Me and My House, We Will Serve the Lord," *Ensign*, November 1998, p. 43.

says, "Through his prophets, the Lord has repeatedly commanded every worthy, able young man to serve a full-time mission."[70] President Thomas S. Monson, the current prophet, said, "The command to go has not been rescinded. Rather, it has been reemphasized. Today thousands of missionaries are serving in response to the call."[71] In case anyone still didn't get it, Elder William R. Bradford of the Seventy spoke to Mormon boys and their parents, specifically addressing any of them who "would justify [them]selves in not doing [their] duty to God [by serving a mission]":

> If I could speak separately to each of you young men and your parents who so justify, I would say with all the power of speech I could generate, Just who do you think you are? What right do you have to match your wisdom with that of God, who through His prophets has issued a firm decree, a solemn mandate, that the restored gospel must be declared to all the world by the voice of His disciples? This means you! [72]

Now you know where we came from, and that we are here to believe and obey. Now let's look at what we can expect after we die, depending on how well we do on our test.

Where Will We Go After We Die?

A three-tier grading system was sketched out in Jesus' plan. People will go to one of three kingdoms according to how well they do on the test. The Celestial Kingdom will be the highest, the brightest, and the best. Father in Heaven will live there and will never visit any of the lower kingdoms because he refuses to be in the presence of anyone who is anything less than perfect. The second kingdom will be called the Terrestrial Kingdom, and it will be like the moon is to the sun in comparison to the Celestial Kingdom. Jesus, and anyone living in the Celestial Kingdom who wants to, can visit relatives and friends down in

---

70. *Old Testament Gospel Doctrine*, 33: Sharing the Gospel with the World, p. 162.
(Gospel Doctrine is the name of the Sunday school class that adults attend. It is where adults discuss what God's commandments are, and all discussions are based on Gospel Doctrine lesson manuals that are written at the Church's headquarters.)

71. Thomas S. Monson, "The Army of the Lord," *Tambuli*, April 1990, p. 28.

72. William R. Bradford, "Sanctification through Missionary Service," *Ensign*, November 1981, p. 49.

the Terrestrial Kingdom. The lowest kingdom is the Telestial Kingdom. It will be like the stars are to the moon in comparison to the Terrestrial Kingdom. This is where all the really serious sinners will end up, but even this place will be so much better than Earth, according to Joseph Smith, who saw all the kingdoms in a vision, that if any of us saw it we would want to commit suicide on the spot so we could go there immediately.

It is ironic that a religion that threatens its members with the loss of salvation to keep them in line teaches that even the worst sinners will end up in a place that is paradise compared to Earth. The eternal misery and despair that sinners will suffer is going to come from knowing that, as good as the Telestial Kingdom is, things still could have been much, much better. For all eternity, sinners will angrily mumble, "Damn it! I should have believed in that story about Joseph Smith and the gold plates!"

The Purpose of the Indoctrination

The reasons for creating The Mormon Show are not too hard to see and understand if you live outside the dome. The system allows a relatively small group of people to control a lot of other people. Church leaders are respected and revered to a very high degree. I have heard many stories of people crying because they were in the presence of an apostle or a prophet, which is reminiscent of the young Red Guards, who, during the Cultural Revolution in China, wept uncontrollably with joy at the sight of Chairman Mao in Tiananmen Square. Having that kind of power over people is, without doubt, intoxicating.

The Mormon reality dome allows leaders to direct people's lives under the pretext that they are merely passing on messages from Heavenly Father, the great director in the sky. In the early days of the Church, there was little concern for what outsiders thought. Church leaders were therefore able to design a social structure upon a belief system that pandered to their primal instincts, forcing women to fully and subserviently take on the roles that the leaders wanted them to play. Charles Darwin pondered the lifestyles of primeval man, and his conclusion brings to mind the lives of Joseph Smith and Brigham Young:

Judging from the social habits of man as he now exists, and from most savages being polygamists, the most probable view is that primeval man aboriginally lived in small communities, each with as many wives as he could support and obtain, whom he would have jealously guarded against all other men. Or he may have lived with several wives by himself, like the Gorilla.[73]

More and more, church leaders have been forced to concern themselves with what the rest of the world thinks. As a result, the brethren's rhetoric and the Church's doctrines have gradually changed over the years to become more palatable to gentiles; polygamy was rejected and people of all colors are now allowed membership on equal terms— racist doctrines aside. The result is that most Church members today would be surprised to read at least some of the preceding quotes from Church leaders.

I believe the greatest motivation for Church leaders today is the reward of being highly revered. After becoming indoctrinated, members stay because they fear losing their eternal salvation, or they fear losing their family, or they fear that leaving the Church would result in unhappiness and misery because they are indoctrinated to believe that that is what would happen, or they fear all of these things at once. Since indoctrinated members will choose to stay anyway, it seems logical that they would have a strong incentive to climb the ladder of Mormon political power. Despite a popular misconception, financial incentives are certainly not the driving force, because for any man to get anywhere near the top of the central hierarchy that runs the Church, he must prove himself through years of devotion, in the form of donated time and money at the local level, where there is no paid ministry.

What is life like for the average member? Life in the Mormon dome cannot be simplistically described as the endurance of psychological and financial exploitation combined with a very rewarding camaraderie with a community of like-minded people who derive a sense of purpose in obeying the commandments. The Mormon community is a social network that welcomes every member with open-armed enthusiasm to every single planned activity—and there is a never-ending supply of planned activities. To people who would normally be left out of, or per-

---

73. Charles Darwin, *The Descent of Man*, 1871. This view of primeval life has been disproven by modern anthropological research, which finds serial monogamy to be the most common type of marriage practiced in band and tribal societies.

haps ignored at, social gatherings in other types of communities, Mormonism offers a pleasant lifestyle. Teenagers who might be bullied or insulted at school would appreciate feeling fully accepted at all of the well-planned and highly structured Church activities. And if they'd ever miss an activity, Church members would likely go out of their way to tell such teenagers that they were missed.

At the same time, however, the Mormon community can be a source of serious misery for those with traits or personalities that clash with its clearly defined norms of acceptable behavior and its endless list of expectations. Some people are inherently more curious, and therefore develop an unquenchable desire to reconcile modern-day Church statements with previous Church statements, such as those from Brigham Young. Their investigations and questions will be sincere, and will stem from knowing that the brethren, from Joseph Smith to the present-day prophet, are divinely inspired. Therefore they assume that today's Church leaders could only consider their reading the sermons of early Church leaders and reading about early Church doctrine as a good thing. When curious members who follow this path are told to "be careful," many of them realize something isn't quite the way it should be.

Gay people are also misfits in Mormon culture. If a person is gay, this fact absolutely must be kept secret. Gay Mormons learn to hate themselves. Few are ever accepted by their families for who they are.

Another type of person who doesn't feel entirely comfortable as a Mormon is one who has a strong need to express himself or herself in unique and artistic ways. The repetitive lifestyle of Mormonism that demands conformity of dress and behavior, and major time commitments to Church activities, feels boring and bland to artists and nonconformists.

Leaving the Mormon reality dome usually damages family relationships in painful ways, so people with traits and personalities that clash with the culture suffer whether they stay or go. Sadly, members are taught to believe that Mormonism is right for every single human on the planet—that the Church is perfectly compatible with every person who has all the good traits of human nature. If a person has trouble fitting in, therefore, there is something seriously wrong with that person. If a member is unhappy, unmotivated, or if their life seems meaningless or unfulfilling, then the solution is always the same: they need to be more diligent in obeying the commandments and carrying out their Church duties. This is the only path to happiness, they are told. The irony, however, is that it is the same path that led to their unhappiness.

For better or worse, I am a product of The Mormon Show. It molded me throughout my formative years, and my heritage goes back to its beginning on both sides of my family. What follows is a description of the part I played, a part that strays strikingly far from the script.

Life Before My Mission

An Elite Birth

My childhood was as "apple pie" as they come. I grew up in Nebraska with its steamy summers, brittle winters, and those few days of absolute paradise that separate the two. I came into the world five years to the day after Madonna was born, and fourteen years to the day before Elvis died. I'm not sure if that's auspicious or ominous, but I do know that according to official Mormon doctrine I was one of the privileged elite. I was born white, American, Mormon, and male. My **patriarchal blessing** even tells me I was born "into a Royal Family . . . being a descendent of Abraham."

My mother lost a lot of blood when I was born. It almost killed her, and that made me extra special: if something comes at a high price, people tend to believe that it's especially valuable. Because of my supposed greatness, my mother held high expectations for me. Active members with strong testimonies measure success according to a person's achievements within the Church, and my mother thought I was going straight to the top. "There's the future president of the Church," she said, looking down at the precious newborn creature in her arms—a prophecy I was reminded of whenever my behavior warranted it.

It was no trivial claim. The President of the Church is a prophet of God, no different from Abraham, Moses, or Isaiah. It's the highest position a mortal can hold.

Not long after my return from the hospital, I was given a **baby's blessing** during a fast and testimony meeting. This blessing officially gave me my name, which was then recorded in the Church's records. I was blessed by my father, who was assisted by other Melchizedek Priesthood holders.

Baby's blessings look rather like a group huddle at a basketball game, but the men involved are all wearing suits and ties rather than jerseys and trunks, and their palms are facing upward instead of downward. The baby lies atop their collected palms and is rocked up and down to keep it calm and quiet. When this doesn't work, and it often doesn't, the baby's cries flood the **chapel** through a microphone that is held up to the blesser's mouth by one of his assistants.

I was now officially a member on record. I had to strive to be "perfect" and "Christ-like" and was supposed to feel guilty each time I inevitably fell short. A lot was expected of me, but I had good and loving parents, so this didn't translate into parental pressure—it merely set up my parents for great disappointment.

We went to church every Sunday without fail. Before each meal we folded our arms across our chests, closed our eyes, and bowed our heads while one of us said the **blessing**. We frequently had family prayers, which were almost always given down on our knees, either facing each other in a circle, or with each of us leaning with our elbows resting on a chair. On Mondays, we had family home evening, which included prayers and a church-related lesson.

When I turned eight, I was baptized in our church's baptismal font, a large, rectangular, box-shaped tub that descended below floor level. There was a small room in front of the font with enough space for about twenty people to view the baptism. The room and font were positioned between the men's and women's bathrooms, and stairs led from each bathroom down into the font from either side. When it was almost time, my father and I went into the bathroom and changed into white trousers and white shirts.

Barefoot and looking like angels, my father and I descended the steps into the font, which was like walking down the steps of a swimming pool. There was a bathtub-type faucet near the top of one of the font's walls that, if I recall correctly, had to run for about an hour before each baptism. The water was a nice, warm temperature. It went almost up to my chest. My father put his left arm around my shoulders and raised his right arm, as one does when being sworn into political office, or at a court of law. Then he said, "Having been commissioned of Jesus Christ, I baptize you in the name of the Father, and of the Son, and of the Holy Ghost. Amen." Holding me with both his hands, he gently pushed me backward and submerged me entirely.

From the first breath I took upon emerging from the waters of baptism, I was held accountable for everything I said and did. At least that's what I was taught, and in a very serious manner, but at that age kids will be kids. My behavior didn't change, and I went on doing typical boy things, such as liberating frogs from creek banks and introducing them to the luxury of a cardboard box. I later progressed from doing typical boy things to doing typical teenager things. But Mormons don't want their kids to be typical; they want them to be peculiar, which means that they want them to be unusually religious and righteous.[1]

Had I grown up in one of the largely (or entirely) LDS communities in Utah or Idaho, I would have had a real "Truman Show" upbringing, and perhaps I never would have strayed from being "peculiar." But my indoctrination did not take place in isolation. I was exposed to the real world with all its wonderful temptations, and from the ages of twelve to sixteen, my behavior and desires conformed more to the wilder sides of the 1970s American youth culture than to the Church's ideals of strong faith and strict obedience.

That doesn't mean my indoctrination failed. My upbringing "had laid a foundation that [I] could reject, perhaps, but not ignore." The Church had become "an integral part of [me, which was something that had to] be dealt with. A child so taught will never be the same!"[2] Even though I had submitted to peer pressure that caused me to wander away, my indoctrination ensured my eventual, prodigal-son return. After a few years of wandering off the straight and narrow path that leads to God's kingdom, I made a sudden, dramatic change. I began to wholeheartedly play the role of a believer in The Mormon Show—something all faithful members with rebellious children dream about.

In the Wake of the Sixties

The '60s was a time when future presidents and legislators—and it would be unfair to the respected field of journalism if I didn't mention Sam Donaldson and his colleagues—smoked marijuana. Bill Clinton

---

1. "The Latter-day Saints are expected to be a peculiar people, because of their lives and examples; and they are expected to preach the Gospel by example, if they are not always called upon to preach by precept."
—Apostle Francis M. Lyman, *Journal of Discourses*, Vol. 3, October 9, 1892, p. 162.

". . . that we might become . . . a peculiar people—peculiar only in that we keep the commandments of God and work righteousness upon the earth."
—President Joseph F. Smith, *Journal of Discourses*, Vol. 3, July 16, 1893, pp. 310–311.

2. "Train Up a Child," by John W. and Marjorie E. Hasler, *Ensign*, April 1999, p. 50.

said he never inhaled, and when Sam heard what Bill said, he made sure everyone knew that he himself did inhale.

As a young teenager, I had thick, flowing red hair that reached to my shoulders, and I regularly broke the Word of Wisdom. With nothing much to do growing up amid the fields of wheat, corn, and sorghum in Nebraska, it should come as no surprise that in the wake of the '60s I began smoking pot in the sixth grade. My friends and I hoped that the tetra-hydro-cannabinol it contained would affect our minds, and to our delight it worked every time.

We were young boys who called each other "man" and got "fried" smoking weed imported from Mexico. Adopting the working class image designed by the marketers at the Miller Brewing Company, we also had our "Miller Times." Rather then immediately following tough work shifts, however, our Miller Times came whenever we could get someone's older brother to buy us some beer.

An eight-year-old Jewish boy lived in our neighborhood. When I was in junior high, he would come running over to my friend's house after school with a tiny handful of Thai stick that he'd gotten from his kitchen fridge, which was where his father kept his stash. The boy then smoked it with us, but, like Clinton, he never inhaled. He didn't seem to care for it, and was probably only in it for the pats on his back and the high fives he got each time he ran over with a tightly clenched fist-ful of the good stuff. This was part of a rebellious, peer-conforming phase of mine that lasted until I saw the light at the age of sixteen, when Heavenly Father, through the Holy Ghost, told me to stop.

My consumption of marijuana and alcohol was taken much more seriously by my parents and myself than it was by my **nonmember** friends. I therefore guarded the secret of my smoking and drinking with religious vigor, and whenever I was among members I dutifully behaved as I was expected to. There's a joke that says it's all right to go fishing with two Mormons but not one, because one Mormon will drink all your beer. Mormons who don't live the **gospel** (often referred to as **Jack Mormons**) are careful to keep their sins out of view of other Mormons who may spread the news back to fellow Church members. I hid my sins and partook of the sacrament unworthily, which is typical of young Mormon kids who participate in worldly sins.

Short of running away from home, there is little if anything that a sinful child of active Mormon parents can do to avoid going through the motions of being a believing Mormon. So throughout my child-hood I was an active participant in the organization; I went to church every single Sunday and attended other church activities during the week. I dutifully attended all my bishop **interviews**; and I lied. When I turned twelve, I was **ordained** a **deacon** in the Aaronic Priesthood and started blessing and passing the sacrament. At fourteen, I was ordained a **teacher**.

None of my church participation was by choice, but there were attempts to make me believe it was. One Sunday, for instance, I asked my mother if I had to go to Primary. "You're old enough to decide that for yourself," she said. That got my attention. I wasn't sure how to respond. I was ten years old at the time, and I did feel old enough to decide this for myself. As her words sunk in, I felt pleasantly surprised about the control I seemed to have suddenly been granted over my own church attendance.

"I decide not to go," I said.

She smiled kindly and said, "You made the wrong decision. Now get dressed."

Like all good parents, my mother did her very best to persuade me to want the things she believed were good for me. She was no different from those parents who try patiently and creatively to get their children to enjoy doing homework and eating vegetables. But I, like most nor-mal children, wasn't easily convinced. And my mother, like most par-ents, resorted to making me understand the inevitable: you'll be hap-pier if you like it, but like it or not, you're going to do it.

Freedom and happiness in Mormonism are connected to obedi-ence and belief; it is a concept that compels Mormon youth to become true believers. Church leaders don't merely want people to obey—they want them to desire to be obedient. A time tested technique for accom-plishing this is to make members feel uncomfortable, and therefore unhappy, if they break any of the Church's commandments.

During a talk,[3] Elder Jack H. Goaslind of the Presidency of the Seventy quoted a scripture from the *Book of Mormon* that all Mormons know by heart: "Behold, I say unto you, wickedness never was happi-ness" (Alma 41:10). Of course "wickedness" is defined as breaking any of Heavenly Father's commandments, so Elder Goaslind was just stating

---

3. "Happiness," by Jack H Goaslind, *Ensign*, May 1986, p. 52.

the obvious when he went on to say, "The commandments are guides to happiness." Mormon indoctrination makes members believe that people who don't follow the Church's commandments are neither truly free nor truly happy.

This concept is nothing new. Religious leaders throughout history have said that when people learn to desire doing whatever God commands, they will be happy and free. Confucius said, "At [the age of] seventy, I could follow the dictates of my own heart; for what I desired no longer overstepped the boundaries of right." Rulon Jeffs, the former leader of the notorious **Fundamentalist** Church of Jesus Christ of Latter Day Saints, said, "I want to tell you that the greatest freedom you can enjoy is in obedience."[4] And even mainstream Mormons can tell you exactly who Rulon wanted his community of believers to obey: Rulon Jeffs.

My mom was patient with me, knowing in her heart that my rebel phase would end someday, and that I would eventually mend my ways, cut my Samson-length hair, and serve a mission for the Church. She was right about everything; I abandoned my wicked ways to walk the less contentious road of belief. Deep down I "knew," like all Mormons do, that it was the only path to freedom and happiness, something that was strongly reinforced on the 26th of June 1979, the day I received my **patriarchal blessing.**

The stake patriarch laid his hands on my head and, "by the authority of the Holy Melchizedek Priesthood," told me that before I came to this earth I had covenanted to fulfill certain responsibilities. I had made these covenants with both Heavenly Father and my "earthly parents." The patriarch said, "you must make the choice from this point forth as to what your course will be." If I did what the brethren said I was supposed to do, I would "preside over branches of the Church" and would "be able to handle [weighty matters] as the Lord would handle them were He here to take care of them Himself." The patriarch also said, "the windows of Heaven will be opened and pour out upon you."

Those blessings would only come to me if I were obedient, however. The patriarch warned that disobedience "would destroy you and deny you that blessing which would otherwise be yours. For with that same degree of illumination that can come to you by the Spirit of the

---

4. Quoted in *Under the Banner of Heaven,* by Jon Krakauer, p. 12.

Lord, in the opposite direction darkness and confusion would be yours if you do not follow the path of righteousness." My patriarchal blessing made it very clear that there was no middle road for me. I was either going to have the windows of heaven opened to me, or I was going suffer darkness and confusion to that "same degree."

The patriarch recorded the blessing and a hard copy was later typed up for me to keep and refer to. My own personal promises and threats from God had thus been canonized, and I was encouraged to read and ponder it often.

My Conversion and Testimony

Sooner or later, like all indoctrinated children of active LDS parents, I had to decide which direction to take regarding the Church. It was "an integral part of [me that] must be dealt with." I doubt any child of active member parents has escaped being converted to one degree or another. The only real questions about conversion are, How strongly? At what age? and, Will it stick? For me it came very strongly at the age of sixteen, and it stuck hard—for about five years, with effects that lingered for at least a decade beyond that.[5]

It's not surprising that I had a strong conversion at a relatively early age. I had better-than-average experiences growing up in the Church. Even throughout my rebellious, long-haired phase I was well accepted and liked by members of all ages. I had a personality that the Mormon culture rewards. I was outgoing, humorous, confident, and a relatively good speaker compared to many of my church-going peers. I was the son of well-liked, respected parents, both of whom almost always held at least one calling or another. My dad even served as our ward bishop for a time.

I had the right type of personality, so it was not difficult for me to fit comfortably into the Church's culture; as well, outright rejection of

---

5. I'm talking about religious belief only; culturally, I will always be a Mormon and will always feel most at home and in tune with other Americans raised as Mormons. Ironically, the religious beliefs of Mormons prevent many of them from having a close and meaningful relationship with someone like myself, which is why there is a community of ex-Mormons. We associate with each other to replace the relationships we've lost.

it would have made my home life very unpleasant. On top of that, my deep rooted indoctrination made me feel guilty and scared about my sins at the subconscious level. All things considered, it seems only natural that my intense Mormon indoctrination would cause me to ultimately reject mainstream American youth culture. Conforming to the expectations of my parents and the Church made life easier because it eliminated the guilt, fear, and contention I experienced as a sinner. The family contentions were minor in my case because I had exceptional parents, but I implicitly understood there would be problems if I never converted.

My conversion took place soon after I was ordained a **priest**. That sounds like an impressive title, but it's just the natural progression of all sixteen-year-old male Mormons who pass the **interview** with their bishop—whether honestly or not. My conversion was a watershed event that changed my life profoundly. I grew up surrounded by people literally testifying to me over and over that they knew the Church was true. Nevertheless, I still had to find out for myself. I needed a testimony of my own. I had to know for myself that all of it was true.

A person could go about this by studying empirical historical evidence from reasonably objective sources. He or she could also look at obviously subjective sources with varying and conflicting opinions in an attempt to understand all the differing views and biases. That is what a rational person would do. But I was raised inside the Mormon dome, so studying it in that way never crossed my mind. I had been taught early on that the only reliable evidence about the Church—in fact the only evidence at all worth looking at—comes from the Church itself. This evidence can be undeniably confirmed, not through logical, deductive reasoning, but by the emotional feelings we were taught from early childhood to recognize as being from the Holy Ghost.

Having been born and raised in the culture, I understood these methods of acquiring knowledge very well, so I knew exactly what to do. I fasted for three days; I went seventy-two hours without a single bite of food. At the end of the fast I saw a miraculous change in my appearance: I had lost weight. That wasn't the miracle I was searching for, though, so before concluding my ritual fast—a process that purifies the body and brings one closer to God—I prayed and asked for an answer as to whether or not the Church was true. And it came. I now had a testimony. It was that quick, that simple, and that inevitable.

The natural result of gaining a testimony—one part of the giant package—was that I was going to serve a mission. It was a commandment. I understood this before I fasted, which meant I knew I would be sacrificing two years of my life for the Church. The outcome of my fast, therefore, was not trivial. Besides a two-year mission, I would also have to start living my life according to the dos and don'ts of Mormonism. Mormon kids regularly attend bishop interviews, where they are specifically asked about their compliance to the rules.

Church leaders were all boys themselves once, so they are able to give practical advice to the next generation of testosterone-filled, alpha-male candidates. They advised us to "avoid pornography like the plague," and when dirty thoughts appeared in our young minds (there was no pretending they wouldn't), they told us to replace them with wholesome thoughts by, for example, reciting a verse of scripture or humming the tune of a hymn. Pornography and lascivious thoughts were the kindling and match that lit the fire of masturbation, and that was a horrendous, guilt-inducing no-no. The advice Mormon leaders give for avoiding masturbating is impressively creative. One of the classics, tying one's hand to a copy of the *Book of Mormon*, most probably works for boys who aren't ambidextrous, but if they use a hardback copy, they risk turning an itchy nose into a bloody one when they instinctively reach to scratch it in the middle of the night.

I was required to confess to my bishop any infractions of the commandments. These confessions were, and still are, conducted face to face. The same was, and is, true for girls; and there are no female bishops. Unlike Catholic confession, in which people only confess what they choose to confess, questions about masturbating and other "sins" are specifically asked of children beginning at the age of twelve. (If not specifically asked, then questions about sexual behaviors and thoughts are asked indirectly with questions such as "Are you morally clean?" or "Do you ever have impure thoughts?" Interviews vary from bishop to bishop.) For some, this is how they first learn what the word masturbation means. The only way to forego the confession of this natural act, therefore, is to lie—taking the fifth is not an option.

When my father was bishop, he was responsible for conducting these interviews. He didn't seem to like having to ask me if I masturbated any more than I liked being asked. I clearly remember a time when he interviewed me while we were sitting in our car parked outside a McDonald's. After asking everything else that he was required to ask me, he nonchalantly said, "And you don't masturbate or anything like that, do you?" I had the feeling he wanted me to just say "no," and then we could go get our Big Macs and be done with it. Of course I complied.

There is something even worse for Mormon boys than the embarrassment of confessing a bout of masturbation to their dad or to another grown man wearing a suit and a tie: guilt, the incredible, pent-up self-loathing that makes a person's whole body weak, and his mind foggy and confused, guilt that makes it impossible to look in the mirror without despising what one sees.

My psychology professor at BYU told us that, according to studies based on private surveys, ninety-seven per cent of males have masturbated. And in his opinion the remaining three per cent were suffering from memory loss when they filled out their surveys. So if masturbation is not a question of *if*, but rather *how often*, then guilt is not a question of *if*, but *how much*.[6] Mormon culture increases the guilt by holding up the supposedly exceptional boys (who don't really exist) as ideal role models that one must try to emulate.

Bishop Vaughn J. Featherstone, Second Counselor in the Presiding Bishopric, spoke during the Priesthood session of the April 1975 general conference. In his talk, entitled "A Self-Inflicted Purging," he said:

> We shouldn't have a problem with masturbation. I know one fine father who interviewed his 11-year-old son and he said, "Son, if you never masturbate, the time will come in your life when you will be able to sit in front of your bishop at age 19, and say to him, 'I have never done that in my life,' and then you can go to the stake president when you are interviewed for your mission and tell him, 'I have never done that in my life.'" . . .
>
> The father again interviewed the young man, who is now 18 years old, and he asked the son about masturbation. The son said, "I have never done that in my life . . ."

---

6. This guilt is not only caused by proactive sins. Just believing that you don't live up to God's standards, which is practically a given in Mormonism, can depress a person. I was never comfortable looking in the mirror until I rid myself of that large baggage of guilt that very many Mormons feel, which is something that took me several years after my departure to do. This type of guilt is difficult to understand unless it is experienced first hand.

My Psychology 101 professor at BYU was a kind man, who was of course well educated in the field of psychology. Since all BYU professors are Church members, he clearly understood the culture, and therefore had well-informed, professionally based opinions about the psychological effects of growing up in the Church. Possibly, he was trying to counter some of these effects when he told us that masturbation was natural and common, and that we should feel grateful for having sexual urges and properly functioning sexual organs. He told us it meant we could live normal, happy lives. It's sad to know that there are university students who need to hear that.

Considering my lifelong indoctrination, the result of my fast was inevitable—despite the implications. If I had received no answer from the Holy Ghost, I would have remained stuck in limbo without having resolved that "integral part of [me that] must be dealt with." And if I had concluded the Church to be false, there would have been serious difficulties at home. A dependent, sixteen-year-old Mormon cannot expect his or her parents to accept such a conclusion without their applying plenty of pressure to go back and ask the Lord again and again until the right answer is reached.

Ultimately, the easiest choice for LDS children is to discover that the Church is true, and they subconsciously know it. Many Mormon boys miraculously gain strong testimonies just before they are to serve their mandatory missions. This enables them to survive the sacrifice of two years of their lives.

My conversion was not a complete sacrifice. It wasn't entirely about making commitments and avoiding unpleasantness. The pleasant aspects of Mormon culture (at least in my case) made being a believer pretty good on the whole. In fact, whenever I felt that I was in good standing with Heavenly Father, life was hard to beat. I felt totally at peace with myself. If I paid my tithes, attended all my Church meetings and activities, and abstained from clearly defined sins, then I believed I was fulfilling every one of my moral obligations as a human being.

I didn't have to fret about my hungry contemporaries at home and abroad, or the economically and politically oppressed; they resided outside of my jurisdiction. I was encouraged to feel sorry for them, but not to feel any sense of social, political or economic solidarity. And I knew that later, as a missionary, my duty would be to help people in one way and one way only: save their souls by converting them to Mormonism. I knew that ultimately that was all anyone in the world really needed.

My Mission in Hong Kong

Preparation

When I approached nineteen, the age when every worthy male member is commanded to serve a mission, I prepared myself mentally and spiritually. As required, I repented for all the sins of my past. The repentance process included confessing to the bishop, stopping all sinful behavior, and apologizing to anyone whom one's sins had adversely affected. I visited the three stores from which I had shoplifted as a youth and gave them enough money to replace what I had taken, along with an apology. An elderly cashier at Walgreen's literally applauded me when I handed her a few dollars and explained it was for the gum and candy I'd stolen four years earlier. I felt like a hero.

My mission preparation involved a series of special interviews with the bishop. The climax was an interview with the stake president. The purpose of this final interview was to make sure I had been properly cleansed of all past transgressions—to see if I was truly worthy to serve.

The stake president's interview was extremely thorough. He even asked me if I had ever had sex with an animal. I'm pretty sure it had nothing to do with the way I looked or dressed, because it's a standard question. Still, it's an odd experience to be asked this seriously and somberly by a well-groomed man, someone that your parents, friends, and Church community look up to and respect. It causes one to wonder exactly when and why this question was added to the list. For the stake president's sake, he was lucky not to have been interviewing Billy Connolly, the Scottish comedian who became famous for telling jokes like the one about sheepherders who get their sheep up against the edge of a cliff before having sex with them because it makes them push back. I'm sure Mr. Connolly would have gladly offered a long and detailed impromptu response to the stake president's question.

Unlike many prospective missionaries, I felt no pressure to serve this voluntary mission that the Lord commanded of me, because it was something I sincerely wanted to do. From the time of my fast, my testimony had never once wavered. My desire to serve the Lord was as strong as anyone's could be. I was a truly willing and faithful follower.

I had indicated on a pre-mission questionnaire that I preferred a foreign mission, but knew that I would have no choice in where I would go. Even so, I was ready to go anywhere in the world, and I was terribly disappointed when, while studying at BYU, I heard the Church announce a reduction in the length of missions from two years to eighteen months.[1] That wasn't long enough for me. In contrast, a close friend, whom I was rooming with on campus, was quite happy to hear that his mandatory service had just been reduced by half a year.[2]

The summer before my mission, I worked on our bishop's farm, feeding pigs, cleaning their pens, and castrating all the male piglets when they were a week old. One of the farmhands was a returned missionary. One day this farmhand told me about missionaries who dated girls, made out with them, and even engaged in heavy petting. He appeared to think it was important to tell me this. It didn't seem like he was warning me to be careful. It seemed as if he thought of himself as an informant who was telling me how things really were, knowing that I likely hadn't been told such things by anyone else, which was true. I felt uncomfortable hearing what he was telling me and assumed that what he had seen or heard on his mission must have been extremely unusual. I knew I needn't take any notice of it, so I brushed it aside.

To prepare myself, I spent most of my spare time reading the *Book of Mormon* and James E. Talmage's *Jesus the Christ.* I anticipated the day I would receive my mission call from the General Authorities, and was very excited when it showed up in the mail. After nervously opening it, I read that I had been "chosen to serve in the Hong Kong Mission (Cantoneese [sic] program)." I enthusiastically welcomed my fate and

---

1. Missions have since been changed back to two years.

2. It's interesting to compare my life in Mormonism to that of my friend. I was partly responsible for his becoming a bit of a beer drinker in high school. We had both quit breaking the Word of Wisdom before our senior year, however, because we had committed ourselves to living the gospel. But on prom night he chose to drink with others at a party, and it really upset me. I was very saddened by it. I couldn't understand how anyone with a testimony could do something like that.

A year later, he was happy to find out that his mission had been shortened to eighteen months, and I was upset. Ironically, I ended up hating my mission, and he ended up loving his. In fact he requested an extension and got it. He went on to become a bishop at a very young age, and is now the first counselor in his **stake presidency**.

immediately dug out a world map to see just where it was in Japan that Hong Kong was located.[3]

A few weeks after receiving my mission call, and after having found out that Hong Kong was not a city in Japan but rather a colony on the southeast coast of China that was counting down its few remaining years of British rule, I wrote a letter to all my relatives. I informed them that I would be serving in the Hong Kong mission, and that I would be learning to speak "Cantoneese."

I received two responses that surprised me. The first was from my mother, who said she wished I wasn't going so far away. I couldn't understand why she would worry about me. After all, I was going to Hong Kong to serve a mission. How could the Lord possibly allow anything bad to happen to me? The second reaction was from my sister-in-law. She said, "Be careful. Some of the most beautiful girls in the world are over there." I thought that was a very odd thing to say. I was going there to do missionary work. I wouldn't even be thinking about girls, let alone become involved with any. Why would it matter whether they were pretty or not?

A month before my mission, I received an orientation booklet in the mail along with some language materials that included two cassette tapes titled "Cantonese Sounds and Tones." I took out cassette number one, inserted it into my tape deck, and turned it up loud. Almost immediately mom and dad bolted up the stairs to see what was going on. The very clear and precisely articulated Cantonese phrases that came blaring out of the stereo speakers sounded like space aliens invading our house, or at least that was how my mom liked to retell the story.

---

3. This is indicative of the quality of the American school system: I had been an honor student in high school and had received a scholarship to BYU because of my high GPA, yet I still didn't know where Hong Kong was. I'm not the only American missionary to have failed so miserably in geography. In September 1998 we invited some Hong Kong-serving missionaries to our house for dinner, and I took the opportunity to find out if my pre-mission ignorance was unique. It turned out that one of them had thought, just as I had, that he'd been called to serve in Hong Kong, Japan. Another had studied Japanese for a year in college and therefore hoped he would be called to Japan. He knew, of course, that Hong Kong was not in Japan, but most of his friends, after hearing that he had been called to serve in Hong Kong, congratulated him on getting his wish to go to Japan. The third missionary I asked said he thought the name "Hong Kong" was a made-up name of a Chinese restaurant in his hometown in Idaho. He had no idea that the restaurant owner had named it after a city, let alone where that city was located. I forgot to ask him if, after receiving his mission call, he thought he was going to spend two years proselytizing to the cooks and waiters in that restaurant.

The Empty Sea

In October of 1982, mom, dad and I drove a thousand miles from Lincoln, Nebraska to Provo, Utah. The next day we went to the Provo temple so that I could be washed, anointed, and receive my temple **endowments**. The secret temple ceremony was very strange.[4]

I was given a white poncho called a shield, which was open down both sides. I stripped naked and put on the poncho for the washing and anointing ceremony. During the ceremony, various parts of my body were ritualistically washed with water and then anointed with **consecrated oil**. This was done symbolically by very briefly dabbing parts of my body, not actually washing them. I felt uncomfortable having my loins washed and anointed, but I accepted everything that took place in the temple as only a true believer could. I was not touched on my genitals, but sufficiently close to surprise me. There was nothing sexual about it—it was just a tad offbeat.

After my washing and anointing, I was dressed by the worker in "the garment of the Holy Priesthood," which I was to wear for physical and spiritual protection at all times from that moment onward. (Garments also act as a constant reminder of the covenants that a member has made with God in the temple.) I was then given a secret name, Elijah, which I was never ever, under any circumstances, to reveal to anyone.[5]

For the endowment ceremony we wore all white. We sat in a room with benches on either side, men on one side, women on the other. We were taught secret signs, similar to handshakes, and told their secret names. We promised that we would sooner have our throats slit from ear to ear, or be disemboweled, than to reveal these tokens and their names to outsiders. We were required to enact slicing motions across our throats and stomachs, using our thumbs to represent knives. The

---

4. I could never have remembered every detail and every word of the temple ceremony after so many years. The detailed descriptions on Richard Packham's website helped greatly in filling in the blanks: http://home.teleport.com/~packham/temples.htm.

5. I believed at the time, like almost every Mormon who's been through the temple, that my secret name was chosen especially for me. Actually, though, every person of the same sex who goes through a certain temple on a certain day gets the same name. So every other man who received his endowments in the Provo temple on the same day that I did was also given the secret name Elijah. And if I'd gone on a different day, I would have received a different name.

temple ceremonies are secret, so this was all a complete surprise to me. It didn't matter, though, because I was ready to take anything given to me by the Church and accept it as true and good by definition. I knew that if I felt uncomfortable about anything, it was my problem and was something that I needed to overcome.

The end of the endowment ceremony was as strange as anything that preceded it. It would have been even stranger were I a woman. Curtains opened, uncovering a white, translucent veil that reached to the ground. It represented the veil that separates the people on this world from the spiritual world on the other side. Each of us had to pass through this veil to get into the Celestial Room that lay just beyond the veil. The Celestial Room represented the Celestial Kingdom.

The veil was divided into sections so that many of us could "pass through the veil" at the same time. Each section had holes in it that were the same shape as the symbols on our garments. One of these symbols represented a compass, and one a square. (Joseph Smith was a Freemason and he borrowed many of the temple's symbols and rituals from the Masonic temple rituals.) A post with a mallet hanging from it was positioned next to each section of the veil. A temple worker assisted each of us to ensure that even those of us with poor memories would pass through the veil successfully.

When it was my turn I stood next to the temple worker at the veil. I was playing the part of Adam, and this temple worker was helping me to communicate with the Lord. The worker tapped the mallet on the post three times. On the other side of the veil another temple worker pretended to be the Lord. "What is wanted?" asked the Lord. I'd always had difficulty getting answers to my prayers and suddenly wanted one of those mallets.

The temple worker said, "Adam, having been true and faithful in all things, desires further light and knowledge by conversing with the Lord through the Veil."

"Present him at the Veil, and his request shall be granted," said the Lord. Then the Lord reached through a hole in the veil and gave me the first secret handshake that I had just learned in the endowment ceremony. "What is that?" he asked.

"The First Token of the Aaronic Priesthood," I said. (Whenever I forgot what to say, or when I was unsure of what to do, the temple worker standing next to me whispered it into my ear.)

"Has it a name?" asked the Lord.

Rather than just telling him the name, I said, "It has."

Perhaps rolling his eyes, the Lord said, "Will you give it to me?"

"I will," I said, "through the Veil." Then, after looking to the temple worker for guidance and approval, I whispered the secret name of the token through the veil to the Lord.

Then I did the same for all the other tokens and their names that I'd learned. Everything was going along just fine until the Lord gave me a secret handshake for which I hadn't yet been told the name.

"Has it a name?" the Lord asked.

"It has," I said again, like a child who never learns.

"Will you give it to me?"

"I cannot," I was told to say, "I have not yet received it. For this purpose I have come to converse with the Lord through the Veil."

"You shall receive it upon the Five Points of Fellowship through the Veil," said the Lord.

For the Five Points of Fellowship, the Lord and I both knelt on our left knees and slid our left arms through the holes in the veil and put our left hands on each others' backs. We put the insides of our right feet together and touched our knees together. Then we embraced breast to breast and the Lord put his mouth to my ear. I then listened very carefully, trying to remember everything he said—I really wanted to get into heaven.

The Lord said, "This is the name of the Token: Health in the navel, marrow in the bones, strength in the loins and in the sinews, power in the Priesthood be upon me, and upon my posterity through all generations of time, and throughout all eternity." Then he asked me what the name of the token was.

That was hardly fair. It was far too much to remember, especially under the circumstances. Just as I was about to give up hope of ever making it to the Celestial Kingdom, the temple worker started whispering the answer into my ear. After I repeated it, the Lord and I broke our embrace and stood up. The temple worker knocked three times again.

"What is wanted?" asked the Lord. He was very patient. He didn't sound annoyed at all.

The worker, speaking on my behalf, said, "Adam, having conversed with the Lord through the Veil, desires now to enter his presence."

The Lord said, "Let him enter," and I was in.

The Celestial Room was well lit and had fancy furniture with light colored fabrics. The chairs were a bit firmer than I prefer, but all in all it was a comfortable room. It would have made a nice reading room, and I love to read, so the Celestial Kingdom seemed like a good place to be.

It's easier to get into the Celestial Room these days. Since the rituals were significantly changed in 1990, the washing and anointing is done entirely symbolically on the forehead only, and while the person is fully clothed. There are no more references and enactments of penalties, such as disembowelment, and the Five Points of Fellowship are no longer used to pass people through the veil.

That evening, my parents drove me to a conservatively designed spread of brick buildings that lie a few blocks from BYU. After we exchanged emotional goodbyes, I stood alone at the entrance to the main building and watched my parents' olive green station wagon slowly drive away. Its tires crackled and popped over the gravelly pavement. It turned out of the parking lot and picked up speed. Growing smaller, it descended over a hill, sank into the road, and was gone.

I felt empty suddenly, and a bit lonely. Looking around I took in what was to be my home for the next eight weeks. It looked like any modern college campus might, and it offered a language program as intense as any in the world, teaching over forty languages. It was called the Missionary Training Center, or MTC for short. One person mistakenly thought I said "empty sea" when I said I would be trained for my mission at the MTC. The mistake was appropriate because learning Cantonese ten hours a day, six days a week, for eight weeks, is like filling an empty mind with a sea of information—in essence, filling up an empty sea. Recalling a specific piece of that information after those four hundred eighty grueling hours would prove to be about as easy as it was to find the Titanic.

There were eight Elders in my group, including myself.[6] On our first night there we were briefed by Elder Cornwall, a blond-haired missionary in his mid twenties. He was kind, but extremely serious. He was

---

6. Our group was composed entirely of Elders, but there are Sister missionaries as well. On average, Sisters make up just under twenty per cent of missionaries in the field. Girls don't serve missions until they are at least twenty-one and, because they are not commanded to do so, they are true volunteers. Once on a mission, however, the psychological stresses that male and female missionaries experience are probably very similar.

part of the Hong Kong-bound group of missionaries who arrived at the MTC a month before we did, and who would therefore be going to Hong Kong a month ahead of us. New groups arrived for each mission every month, and our group's size was average for the Hong Kong Mission. Elder Cornwall told us where we would sleep, how we were to be divided into pairs of companions, and where we would attend our first class the next morning.

Only Mormon Missionaries and Babies

After our early morning exercises, a shower, breakfast, and scripture study, we gathered inside our classroom. We crammed ourselves into the eight school desks that skirted the small, square room.[7] Two male teachers, both with skin as milky white as our own, walked in and started talking to each other in Cantonese. After a few minutes, one of them wrote something strange on the board, pointed to it, and shouted it out: "Yat!"

Then he pointed at us and we mimicked: "Yat!"

He wrote something else and shouted: "Yih!"

"Yih!," we yelled.

We continued doing this until we had imitated, over and again, ten different sounds. After that we played a game. Each of us, including the two teachers, were assigned a sound. We got a rhythm going—two slaps on our thighs, followed by a clap. Then a teacher started us off. At the moment when he was supposed to clap, he instead called out one Elder's assigned sound and pointed at him. Amazingly, that Elder instantly caught on and called out someone else's sound during the very next clap. That other someone, however, just kept slapping and clapping and grinning.

I caught that grin only by accident. I was not looking at that Elder because I knew he was supposed to call out the next number. I just happened to be looking in his direction. I wouldn't have fared any better had it been my sound instead of his that was called out. After several more mistakes, we all caught on to the rules and played several rounds of the game. After that, we all knew the first ten numbers in Cantonese —for the moment anyway.

---

7. You can see a virtual picture of an MTC classroom, exactly like the one in which I learned Cantonese, at: www.mtc.byu.edu/main/tour.htm.

The other teacher then took the lead and pointed to his head, making another new sound. Then he touched both of his shoulders and uttered something else. He continued with his knees, toes, eyes, ears, mouth, and nose. After a few repetitions, he directed the eight of us to stand and point to these various parts of our bodies while singing these weird words to the tune of "Head and Shoulders, Knees and Toes."

That was my first lesson in Cantonese; not a word of English was spoken.

There is a Mormon joke about difficult languages such as Finnish, Navajo, and Cantonese: such languages can only be learned by babies and Mormon missionaries. This is taken more than half seriously by Mormons. And even outside of Mormon circles, LDS missionaries have a reputation for learning languages well.

One could assume, as Mormons do, that God helped us learn Cantonese (perhaps religious anti-Mormons think it was the devil's doing). But there was nothing unusual or outstanding about our linguistic performance. Our Cantonese-speaking abilities were exactly what one would expect considering the type and amount of language training we received, coupled with the type and amount of real-life exposure and practice we had. We started with eight weeks of very intensive language learning in the MTC, during which there was a Speak-Your-Language (SYL) rule that required us to speak only Cantonese. No English made for a rather quiet eight weeks, but it forced us to try and figure out how to say things in Cantonese, though naturally we cheated a lot or we would have gone insane.

The serious schooling started after we arrived in Hong Kong. We studied Cantonese a couple of hours a day, the SYL rule continued (in theory), and we were constantly forced to use Cantonese in real life. After eighteen months, we all returned home able to hold a fairly decent conversation in Cantonese. The same is true of all missionaries serving in foreign-language missions.

The Church transforms thousands of young men and women every year into the kind of bilinguals that are the envy of their fellow Americans, and are as common as sliced tomatoes to most people throughout the rest of the world. My brother learned Finnish for his mission, and my good friend learned Texan, the hard way. On his very first day knocking on doors in the Dallas, Texas Mission, a man greeted him and his companion by pointing a handgun at them at point blank range. Roughly translated, it meant: "Get the hell off my porch now, boy!" My friend's companion had been on his mission for a year, and was therefore able to respond with native fluency; he turned and ran as fast as he could, leaving my friend alone on the porch.

My friend, who was still new to the lingo, kept trying to explain to the man who they were, certain that the man didn't know. But it turned out that the man knew exactly who they were, and, speaking loudly and slowly like people always do to those who don't speak their language, the man said that he didn't like Mormon missionaries and that that was why he was holding a gun. My friend now understood and in no time caught up with his companion. Despite that first-day experience, my friend still requested, and got, a six-month extension to his mission.

Groundhog Day

More recent missionaries have described the MTC experience as being similar to Bill Murray's *Groundhog Day*—living the same day over and over. It is an appropriate description. Our unvarying schedule was as follows:

6:30 am	Up and out of bed
7:00	A "mandatory" regimen of vigorous calisthenics[8]
8:00	Breakfast in "the best cafeteria in the world"[9]
9:00	Scripture study
9:30	Three hours of Cantonese instruction in the classroom
12:30 pm	Lunch in the world's best cafeteria
1:30	Four hours of Cantonese instruction in the classroom
5:30	Dinner in the world's best cafeteria
6:30	Three hours of reviewing and practicing what we learned that day
9:30	Personal time
10:30	Lights out

---

8. We could skip this without getting punished or sent home; it wasn't the military.

9. The wife of the MTC president told us, in all seriousness, that the cafeteria in the MTC was the best in the world. She apparently never ate in my high school cafeteria because it tied for first place. There are now three best-in-the-word cafeterias in the MTC. You can see a virtual picture of one at: www.mtc.byu.edu/main/tour.htm.

The eight of us got to know each other extremely well. We were as busy as could be, but we were busy together. We socialized when we walked to and from classes, when we ate meals, during our hourly ten-minute breaks from learning Cantonese, and especially during our evening hour of free time. We were like-minded Americans (and one Canadian) of the same age, race, and gender with the same beliefs. It was only natural that we all got along with few difficulties.

The MTC is itself classified as one of the Church's many **missions**. The MTC Mission is the smallest mission physically but has the largest number of missionaries for an obvious reason. The MTC Mission is divided into branches. Our branch included missionaries going to the Hong Kong, Thailand, Taiwan, and Southern California (Vietnamese-speaking) Missions.

One of the only breaks we had from our regimented schedule was when we attended talks and Sunday church services. There were weekly devotionals in the MTC where visiting General Authorities gave talks. These were an advanced-level continuation of our lifelong indoctrination.[10] There were two purposes to this indoctrination—one was to strengthen our testimonies and the other was to turn us into obedient, God-fearing missionaries. They wanted us to believe in what we were doing and to fear the very thought of disobeying their rules.

Don't Play with Heavenly Fire

"Fear of things invisible is the natural seed of that which every one
in himself calleth religion."
—Thomas Hobbes, *Leviathan*, 1651

"Fear is the main source of superstition, and one of the main sources of
cruelty. To conquer fear is the beginning of wisdom."
—Bertrand Russell

Fear is an age-old tool of religion, and it is an effective method of social control. In the book *Contemporary Mormonism: Social Science Perspectives* (University of Illinois Press, 1994), there is a chapter by William A. Wilson titled "Powers of Heaven and Hell: Mormon

---

10. You can see a virtual picture of missionaries being indoctrinated at a devotional at: www.mtc.byu.edu/main/tour.htm.

Missionary Narratives as Instruments of Socialization and Social Control." Over approximately a twenty-year period that began in the mid-1970s, Wilson and a colleague collected oral narratives from returned missionaries (RMs) attending Brigham Young University. Wilson categorizes some of the stories heard in these narratives as "cautionary tales" that "deal . . . with the grievous errors of challenging or defying the powers of heaven and hell, engaging in sacrilegious behavior" that causes "the wayward missionaries [to] end up not only out of the Church but often dead." In some of the stories "missionaries foolishly seek a testimony of God by going through the back door, by first seeking a testimony of the devil."

I heard several such stories while on my mission. One was about a missionary in some remote part of the world at one time or another. (All the stories lack specifics.) This missionary told the other Elders in his apartment that he was going to pray to the devil and ask him to prove his existence. The missionary then went into his bedroom and closed the door. A few minutes later the Elders who lived with him heard a loud commotion coming from the daring missionary's room. They hesitantly opened the door to see what was happening, and what they saw terrified them: the Elder was being thrown about the room by an invisible force against the walls and even against the ceiling. When finally he stopped flying and flopping about like a blow-up doll that had sprung a leak, he lay dead on the floor, killed by Satan's power.

Other stories warned us not to abuse the power of God, a power that we were authorized to use, but only in necessary and righteous ways. One story described a missionary who performed the well-known ritual in which an Elder dusts off his feet in response to someone's rejection of him and his message. He did it in front of a laundromat because its owner had rejected him. A week later the Elder learned that the laundromat had burned down with its owner inside, just one day after the missionary had dusted his feet off in front of it. The dusting off of a missionary's feet in reference to any individual who has rejected him supposedly results in this sort of wrath-of-God consequence, and a similar story, described as typical, is related in Wilson's essay.[11]

---

11. Bertrand Russell eloquently and humorously criticized the attitude inherent in the vindictive ritual of feet dusting:

"Christ certainly as depicted in the Gospels did believe in everlasting punishment, and one does find repeatedly a vindictive fury against those people who would not listen to

Wilson's essay also mentions tales of missionaries being struck by lightning or dying in other ways as a punishment for using their priesthood power in sacrilegious ways, such as anointing and blessing a dog, or a fence post, in order to mockingly grant it the power of the priesthood. Mormon missionaries like to say that they hold more power from God in their little finger than the Pope does in his entire body. We were warned to respect this power and not to abuse it. Of course more than a little arrogance rubbed off on us because of this privileged status, but apparently that was all right.

As mentioned earlier, none of these stories are very detailed, and they are rarely if ever told by someone claiming to be an actual eyewitness. I never considered the possibility that such tales were purposely fabricated, so I assumed, as most missionaries must, that these stories were true. They are vivid, image-filled reminders of both the power of Satan and the power of God. The former power would kill me if I called upon it, and the latter would kill me if I mocked it.

One particular story designed to augment social control was especially startling to us, and, in retrospect, it provides a clue as to how such narratives begin. We heard the story during **priesthood meeting** one Sunday afternoon. It came from our MTC branch president, a portly, balding man in his late forties who had served a mission in Taiwan. The story was about an encounter he claimed to have had with a missionary just a few days prior. The missionary, who coincidentally was not from our branch and therefore unknown to any of us, walked into our branch president's office—rather than his own branch president's office—and said he wanted to talk. Our branch president invited him to sit down and asked him what was on his mind. The Elder began expressing second thoughts about serving a mission, wondering if maybe he shouldn't give up and go home.

The branch president was listening with an understanding heart when suddenly the Elder sat up straight, looked the branch president

(11. cont'd) His preaching—an attitude which is not uncommon with preachers, but which does somewhat detract from serenity. You do not, for instance find that attitude in Socrates. You find him quite bland and urbane toward the people who would not listen to him; and it is, to my mind, far more worthy of a sage to take that line than to take the line of indignation . . .

"You will find in the Gospels Christ said, 'Ye serpents, ye generation of vipers, how can ye escape the damnation of hell.' That was said to people who did not like His preaching. It is not really to my mind quite the best tone . . ."

square in the eye, and in a strange and powerful voice declared, "This is Satan! What do you want?!" I remember thinking at the time that this was an oddly nonsensical thing for Satan, a profoundly intelligent being—whatever one may think of his ethics—to ask. Nevertheless, I believed the story.

The branch president said he immediately raised his right arm to **the square** and used his priesthood authority—something we all had—to cast out the demon from the missionary. Addressing the evil spirit in a firm tone, he said something like this: "In the name of Jesus Christ, and by the power of the holy Melchizedek Priesthood vested in me, I command you to leave!" The missionary blanked out. After a moment of sitting still, the Elder slowly raised his head. He was obviously confused, and the branch president asked him if he knew what had just happened; he hadn't a clue.

After sharing this story with us, the branch president got straight to the point. He revealed the reason why this Elder had become possessed by an evil spirit, possibly even Satan himself. It was because the missionary had broken several mission rules. He was sleeping in late, for example, and even worse, he had been listening to rock and roll music. And that was the moral of the story. It was a warning to us: obey the rules or something like this could happen to you.

That night, the vivid story of the possessed missionary was fresh in our minds. The four of us who shared the same room talked about it as we lay in our beds. This naturally caused us to exchange stories about other possessions that we had heard about. We also shared typical "missionary narratives" that we had heard from RMs. Finally, one Elder said he had heard enough. We all had, but he was the first to speak up. "Let's not talk about it any more," he said. Everyone happily agreed, and we lay in our beds scared, knowing, as all Mormons and all Chinese do, that talking about evil spirits invites them to appear. We were much more like the superstitious people we had been called to serve than we realized.

* * *

During my time at the MTC, there were two especially meaningful talks given by visiting General Authorities (usually referred to as GAs by missionaries). The first talk offered yet another warning about missionaries engaging in sexual activities. The GA told us we were all attractive and desirable targets for people throughout the world, both members and nonmembers alike. He said it would be easy for us to turn and run from overt and obvious temptation, such as the sight of a prostitute. He said we would instinctively turn and run, just as Joseph had fled from the temptations of his master's wife (Genesis 39). It would be much more difficult, however, for us to escape the temptation of a pretty Church member who was attracted to us.

The second talk relayed a story about some missionaries who were repeatedly guilty of heavy petting. Several other missionaries knew about it, but it went on for a while before one missionary finally reported it to the **mission president**. This was unacceptable. The missionaries who were guilty of the serious sin of heavy petting were ruining the entire mission, which belonged to all the missionaries serving in it. The GA told us that all missionaries have a responsibility to keep a mission free of sin and therefore must immediately report the sins of other missionaries to their mission president.

I was reminded of what the worker on the pig farm had told me, but the purpose of this story was very different. The farm hand seemed to be trying to tell me that missions and missionaries aren't actually the way they're depicted to be by members and Church leaders. This GA, in contrast, was telling us it was our duty to try to make reality match the myth, to purge the mission field of missionaries who behave the way gentiles do. As a true believer in the myth, I was again surprised to be hearing about such behavior. I also assumed that it was extremely unusual, and that it was very unlikely that any of the missionaries in the audience that day would ever need to heed that GA's advice.

* * *

During our time at the MTC, we Hong Kong-bound missionaries were repeatedly told that missionaries assigned to serve in Hong Kong were extra special—the elite of the elite. I was almost convinced of it after the fifth or sixth time I heard it. Mormon culture traditionally propagates the concept of being a chosen race in a chosen place. I was a white, LDS male, who was born in the United States of America. That's as good as it gets. And now, topping it all off, I had been called to serve in Hong Kong. But it wasn't only me; all LDS children are made to feel like they are the chosen of the chosen.[12]

---

12. H. Clay Gorton used to have an "Ask Gramps" page at the Mormontown web site (www.mormontown.org). In one answer to a question, he quoted a talk given at an "Especially For Youth" conference. It clearly illustrates the creative (cont'd next page)

I was special because I was taking a golden message to my Chinese brothers and sisters across the Pacific. At the time, I was unaware of Apostle Mark E. Petersen's explanation of the wretched condition of those who were "born in China with a dark skin, and with all the handicaps of that race," and who had "little opportunity" because of "whatever they might have done in the pre-existence to justify being born over there as Chinamen." But because "the mercy of God [is] marvelous," we eight Elders of Israel—so called, even though none of us were yet twenty years old, and none of us had once set foot in the Middle East—had been commissioned to save their pitiful souls. For some reason, this made us more special than missionaries called to convert the people of other races and cultures.

Hong Kong

Through the miracle of rote memorization we could recite things like this: *Dong Simahtyeuksat faanyihk Momùhn Gingge sìhhauh, keùih* . . . We didn't understand everything we were saying, but we could say it nonetheless, the way a singer can learn to sing an Italian song without knowing Italian. Memorizing paragraphs, even pages, of words that we didn't entirely know the meaning of seemed to me to be a distraction from learning the language. I would later find out how wrong I was.

(12. cont'd) ability of church leaders to repeatedly drive home to Mormon youth the idea of being the chosen of the chosen.

> You, the youth of the Church today, were not just leaders, you were Generals in Heaven. Someday, when you are back in the Spirit World you will be enthralled by other souls who lived during the time of many great Prophets. You may ask one person—"When did you live?" and hear something like, "I was with Moses when he parted the Red Sea," or "I helped build one of the Great pyramids," or "I fought with Captain Moroni." And as you are standing there amazed at the people who you are with, someone will ask you during which Prophets' time you lived in; and when you tell them you lived during the time of President Hunter and President Hinckley, a hush will fall over every hall and corridor of Heaven and all in attendance will bow at your very presence.

This is a very important stewardship we have been given. We were held back six thousand years because we were the most righteous, most talented, most obedient servants of our Heavenly Father. (Note the fundamentalist assumption that the world is only six thousand years old.)

As busy as we were loading our brains with pages and pages of this mumbo jumbo, eight weeks flew by in no time and we soon found ourselves on a plane to Hong Kong. The flight from Salt Lake City to San Francisco was typical, but when we changed to a 747 flying from San Francisco to Hong Kong, we suddenly found ourselves in a different world. We were minorities. I had never seen so many Chinese people in one place as there were in the confines of that plane.

After more than fifteen hours of sitting on firm, narrow, economy class seats, we arrived in Hong Kong at night to experience one of the most spectacular shows on earth. Hong Kong's old Kai Tak airport required pilots to make a sharp right turn as they flew breathtakingly near to the rooftops of Kowloon's multi-storied apartment blocks. The vast and beautiful field of lit-up buildings was so close beneath us that I almost felt as if I could shout to the inhabitants and be heard. But instead of me, it was the plane that shouted, rudely blasting the people beneath with thunderous, highly stressful noise.

After we landed and passed through immigration, we gathered at the luggage carousel. We looked around at all the Chinese people, who all seemed to be moving about very quickly and talking very loudly. I listened to those who were standing next to us, but didn't understand a word they said, even after two months of very intense language training.

After we had collected all of our luggage and put it on trolleys, we walked past the customs check point with no questions asked. Then we exited the area that was restricted to departing passengers and entered the greeting area where everyone's friends and relatives were waiting to pick them up. It was like walking onto the stage at a concert. A blanket of black-haired heads filled the spacious room, and every one of them was staring at us. We were new arrivals and were therefore part of the show. The number of people was staggering. Although we had been initiated gradually, from the 747, to the luggage area, to this, it was still shocking for a white Mormon boy who had spent almost all of his days in Nebraska and Utah to suddenly be a tiny minority among such a huge crowd. Rather than being allowed to walk in slowly from the shallow end, I'd been thrown into the deep end of this icy pool that was going to be my home for the next sixteen months.

The mission president's two assistants were among the crowd and, not surprisingly, were easy to spot. The assistants to the president are sometimes referred to in missions as "APs," but more often as "apes."

The apes took us to the YMCA in a section of town called Yaumatei. At street level, the buildings were even more impressive than they had been from the air. The sights, sounds, and distinctive smells of Hong Kong mesmerized us. A continuous flow of commercial and residential skyscrapers towered over our gawking heads. Shops lined the nighttime streets on both sides, advertising themselves with a milky way of gaudy neon glitter—an unrivaled display of psychedelic, ancient Chinese script. I started recording memories of Hong Kong's distinct and numerous smells, the most vivid and lasting of all my mission memories.

During our stay at the MTC we had repeatedly heard stories about Hong Kong, but no amount of classroom description can equal the experience. Hong Kong, more than most places, is hard to put into words, because it shouts at all the human senses at once from every direction. There's nothing quite like the assault on your olfactory nerves of *chau dauhfuh* (smelly bean curd) wafting its way from a street hawker's cart. And Hong Kong is only fully experienced when you add to that the heat of a tropical summer day and a mass of people rushing in all directions alongside a dusty street full of noisy vehicles.

After we arrived at the YMCA and checked into our rooms, the apes told us to go to bed at ten o'clock and to lie there until we fell asleep, no matter how long it took us to do so. It was good advice for reducing jet lag, but it sounded more like an order than a suggestion.

We did our best to sleep through the night, which, as far as our minds and bodies were concerned, was daytime. The apes returned the following morning and took us to the mission home at 2 Cornwall Street in Kowloon Tong, an upper class neighborhood famous for its love hotels where relatively rich men and women break their wedding vows with high class, one night stands. Their cars and license plates are discreetly hidden within curtained-off parking spaces. The real purpose of these establishments is ingeniously hidden through the use of carefully coded names such as Romantic Hotel or ESsex Hotel, with the capital E in ESsex shaped like a sideways heart. Scattered among these hotels is an equal number of kindergartens and grade schools with the reputation of being the best in town.

The building that the mission home was housed in was torn down in 1996 and replaced with an expensive and elaborate Italian marble structure. This new building is not only home to the mission home and a chapel, as before, but now contains a temple as well. An east-facing statue of the angel **Moroni** stands atop the gold colored dome on the temple's roof with a horn to his mouth that looks a bit like the long plastic horns I remember blowing into at my high school football games. When the time comes, Moroni is going to blast away on his horn to announce Christ's second coming. Be prepared.

We entered the mission home, where we met President Smith, his wife, and his children. President Smith was a tall, charismatic man from Austrialia with dark hair. Like all mission presidents, and in fact all Church leaders, he kept his hair short and wore dark colored suits and ties, and a white shirt. He spoke with the confidence of someone who assumed his audience would never challenge him or question a word he said. He talked about the history of the mission and told us a little about what our lives would be like as missionaries. A local Hong Kong missionary, who was living in the mission home, was there and was listening to one of the apes translate everything President Smith said. At the time, I assumed the translation was thorough and accurate.

Born Again

After our brief orientation and a good home cooked meal, we went to the mission home lobby to meet our first companions, endearingly referred to in worldwide mission-speak as "dads." There we were, a living, breathing mass of dark, plain colored suits, white shirts, quiet ties, and black badges with the Church's name in Chinese and our names in both English and Chinese. It was a small scale version of what we experienced constantly in the MTC.

I was labeled Elder Worthy. Our first names were strictly off limits at all times throughout our mission. We all had a drastic new look and a new identity, which was, I suppose, a purposeful attempt to make us believe we were all different from the boys we had been back home, in the hope that it would cause us to behave differently as well.

One of the proud fathers who was there to claim his newborn son and take him to his birthplace (missionaries are "born" in the first district they are assigned to) said he knew my dad, and he told me that my dad spoke slow, clear Cantonese, and that that would be a great help to my learning the language. I was pleased to hear that.

I tried to act naturally and at ease, but I was understandably a bit nervous, realizing myself to be one of the ignorant newcomers that were being sized up by the veterans. Of course we were treated very politely. We were all "brothers" after all, and I was comfortable knowing that there would be no cruel initiations or hazings. Suddenly, the Elder I was talking to gently took hold of my arm and led me through the crowd toward an Elder who had just arrived. We were introduced. There he stood: Elder Brodie, my dad, a farm boy from Idaho who was going to take me, a country boy from Nebraska, by the hand until I learned enough Cantonese to survive.

Elder Brodie's English was slow and deliberate, so I assumed that what I'd just been told about his Cantonese must be true. He had dark hair and soft brown eyes set inside a strong, square-featured face. This matched his demeanor; he was soft spoken but acted quite sure of himself. After all of the newborns were matched up with their dads, we joined the missionaries from throughout the entire mission, who were all in the chapel waiting for the monthly mission conference to begin.

Elder Brodie and I sat at the end of one of the long wooden pews, halfway back from the stage. President Smith soon entered and took his place on the stage. Two Chinese missionaries were sitting on the stage off to one side at a table that had two microphones set on it, one for each of them to use. Their job was to translate from English to Cantonese. The Chinese missionaries who wanted to hear the translated version of the conference wore headphones. The rest of us listened directly to the speakers.

We sang a hymn. Then an Elder gave the invocation. After that, President Smith gave us a long, inspirational pep talk. He talked about moving mountains and walking on water, saying we could actually do it if we had faith, though he never said we should try—perhaps because he knew we'd fail; and swimming is strictly forbidden because Satan has control over the water. This reminded me of a man in my ward back home who had said he would not have failed the way Peter had when Jesus asked him to step out of the ship and walk on the water. Peter started out okay, but he became afraid and began to sink. Jesus said to him, "O thou of little faith, wherefore didst thou doubt?" (Matthew 14:31). The man in our ward claimed to have more faith than Peter did, saying he could have walked on the water for as long as Jesus wanted him to, and now we were being told we could do the same by our mission president.

After the conference I felt ready to go out, shift a few buildings around, and convert all their inhabitants.

Kwai Hing

My "birthplace" was Kwai Hing, a district located northwest of Kowloon. My dad took me there on the Mass Transit Railway (MTR), Hong Kong's subway. From the Kwai Hing station we walked a few blocks to a twenty-storey structure situated in a clump of tall buildings of various sizes, shapes, and colors. It was painted dark teal. All of these buildings were skinnier than any I had ever seen. They ranged from about twenty-five hundred to forty-five hundred square feet per floor, and went up to thirty stories high.

We passed a door watchman, whom my dad addressed as *a-suk* (sounds like "a soak"). This word can only translate into English as "uncle," but in Chinese it specifically refers to a paternal uncle younger than one's father.[13] The *a-suk* responded to my dad's greeting with a

---

13. Chinese culture is one of many in which kinship ranking affects how one is supposed to speak and behave. Therefore, Cantonese differentiates just about every possible variation of relationship. For example the word for a brother-in-law married to an older sister is different than for a brother-in-law married to a younger sister, and the word for a maternal grandmother is different than for a paternal grandmother. Kin terms are used to address family members much more often than in English-speaking cultures, providing a constant reminder of one's status.

Cantonese is, of course, a very convenient language for specifying exactly how people are related. If someone wants to refer to, for instance, a great uncle that is their maternal grandmother's brother-in-law (married to a younger sister), the average Chinese cannot remember the term. They can, however, refer to him as their *a-pòhge* (maternal grandmother's) *muìhfu* (younger sister's husband). It looks complicated in English, but notice that only two words, at a total of five syllables, are needed to name such a specific relation in Cantonese (and it can even be done with just one word: *yihgung*). Keeping in mind the lack of such terms in English, a comparison of similar conversations between Cantonese and English might go something like this:

CANTONESE:
"Who's that?"
"My *a-pòh's muìhfu.*" (or "My *yihgung*")
"Oh."

ENGLISH:
"Who's that?"
"My great uncle."
"Oh? Which side of the family?"
"My mom's."
"So he's your grandma's brother."
"Actually he's her brother-in-law."
"I see. Did he marry her younger sister or her older one?"
"How should I know, and what do you care anyway?"

deep, resonant grunt. We rode the elevator to the thirteenth floor. I didn't know at the time that 13 is a lucky number in Chinese. The swaying elevator was well worn and groaned with age. It stopped with a jolt when it reached our floor. The doors banged open and we entered a typical residential hallway—my first glimpse of thousands. Over a period of only sixteen months my mission would take me to many more homes in Hong Kong than most locals have ever seen.

The corners of the dimly lit hallway were full of dust cobwebs. The walls were stained by the smoke from the incense that burned daily in small red urns at three of the four doorways. Ours was the only apartment on the floor that didn't burn incense to our house god. The gray, inch-square tiles covering the corridor's floor were probably clean at one time. The walls looked as if they had been painted white decades ago. There were several hand-sized paint flakes that had separated from the walls but remained attached along one edge. Hong Kong's heat and humidity had curled them, making them look like giant flower petals. Our apartment, like the rest, was locked securely behind a foreboding metal gate.[14]

With a high pitched screech of metal against metal, my dad forcefully slid open our gate, swung open the front door, and welcomed me home. I stepped into the two hundred-square-foot living and dining room and found myself surrounded by the ugliest walls I had ever seen. A layer of faded turquoise paint covered a previous layer of pea green. There were several white, powdery patches where both layers of paint had worn off. They looked like fluffy white clouds with dark green edges floating in a sickly blue sky.

An oval dining table with a scarred, dented metal border and a gray Formica© top faced me. Its maker had cursed the Formica© with loathsome specks of black and gold. Accompanying the table were four metal-framed chairs upholstered in shiny plastic of the same cursed design as the tabletop. Their plastic upholstery had split open in several places, exposing synthetic stuffing that bulged out from within. Looking down, I saw that the dark wooden floorboards were in the

---

14. This is a standard accessory to almost every home in the city. Unfortunately, these make convenient babysitters, allowing busy people—and everyone in Hong Kong is busy—to lock their kids inside. The *South China Morning Post* reported that during a one-year period (1995–96) 113 of Hong Kong's children burned to death inside their homes because their parents had locked them inside.

process of shedding numerous layers of old wax, much like like a human body suffering the aftermath of a horrible sunburn.

It was a three-bedroom apartment. Two bedrooms housed a pair of Elders each. The remaining one served as a laundry room, complete with clotheslines and a chipped up washer/spin dryer with a plastic shell, the color of which closely matched the faded turquoise of the walls. Was that a coincidence?

The bathroom was just long enough for its tub, and just wide enough to also include a toilet. The tub was brownish yellow with plenty of blackened scratches. This made it difficult to tell whether it was clean or dirty.

The toilet's flush tank was located overhead. It used a pull-chain, something I had only seen in movies. It was rust stained along one side where water dripped out through a crack in the plastic. Based on that bit of evidence, I concluded that the building's plumbing system would supply me with all the iron I needed. Although that was probably true, the evidence I was looking at was unrelated; in Hong Kong the flush water for toilets comes from the sea and is separate from the potable water that Hong Kong gets from mainland China.

The bedrooms were small, about ninety square feet each. The one I shared with dad contained a desk, a wardrobe, bunk beds, and just about enough room remaining for one person to comfortably put on a suit jacket without accidentally punching something. Looking out the window, our view was of the building next door. It was my first glimpse of Hong Kong's version of Alfred Hitchcock's *Rear Window*. In Hong Kong's version, Jimmy Stewart could have played his role without binoculars. All that separated us from our numerous neighbors was a narrow alley, and if we strained slightly we could look into people's homes and watch TV, something that missionaries are prohibited from doing—watching TV that is, though peeping into other people's homes is surely frowned upon as well. I would later find out that TV wasn't the only thing visible from our rear window that was off limits to a missionary's eyes.

I examined the foam mattress on the top bunk where I was to sleep. Some of the fabric at both the foot and the head of the mattress had rotted away, exposing the foam inside. Where the foam was exposed it had oxidized and crumbled into crusty brown powder. The sight of that pleased me immensely. It gave me a deep sense of satisfaction to know that I would be sacrificing the luxuries I had enjoyed from the day I was born. My service to the Lord would thus be more difficult and, therefore, more meaningful. Such open-armed acceptance of sacrifice makes excellent fodder for faith-promoting mission stories.

I climbed the bunk bed ladder and lay down to ponder what was in store for me. I looked over at my dad who was in the middle of changing his clothes. A large Chinese character was scrawled onto the backside of the lower portion of his temple garments, appearing like graffiti on his derriere.

"What does that say on your rear end?" I asked.

"Leng," he said, which is Cantonese for "good looking." We both grinned.

Converting Mr. And Mrs. Fesik

"And now, if your joy will be great with one soul that you have brought
unto me into the kingdom of my Father, how great will be your
joy if you should bring many souls unto me!"
—*Doctrine & Covenants* 18:16
(Jesus Christ speaking to Joseph Smith, Oliver Cowdery, and David Whitmer)

The surname Brown is used in the English versions of the didactic discussions, which are memorized verbatim by missionaries. In fact, memorizing the missionary discussions is the main goal of MTC training. "Mr. and Mrs. Brown" refers to the imaginary people taught by the missionaries when they practice their lines. "How do you feel now, Mr. and Mrs. Brown?" a missionary will ask his companion, a wall, or a bedpost, when practicing the question that missionaries ask people after they have just said their first Mormon-style prayer. Our discussions used the name Mr. and Mrs. Wong instead of Brown, but when I practiced I said Mr. and Mrs. Fesik, which is the Cantonese word for brown.

Anyone willing to let us "teach" them more than once was called an **investigator**. Our purpose as missionaries was to turn as many people as we could into investigators, and then as many investigators as we could into members. We accomplished the first part (finding investigators) by proselytizing, which we did ten hours a day.

Proselytizing

I started off as a hard working missionary. Except for the occasional ice cream or soda break, all of my time was spent proselytizing. Mostly we **tracted**, which is door-to-door cold calling, but we also did the occasional **street display**, and we were sometimes in charge of running the **visitors' center**.

In Kwai Hing, we started each session of proselytizing by catching a sixteen-seater minibus to our area. Minibuses in Hong Kong don't have predetermined stops along their routes. They pick you up if you wave them down and drop you off where you tell them to. It's very difficult to ride a minibus if you don't speak any Cantonese and if you don't know exactly where you want to go. I therefore felt like a dependent child, and I admired the relaxed and confident way in which Elder Brodie led me around throughout our assigned area.

Most of the homes we approached during our tracting sessions were inside government housing estates, because there were no locked doors or door watchmen to keep us out. About forty per cent of Hong Kong's residents live in high-rise public housing, and the majority of the remaining live in high-rise private housing—tufts here and there of towering apartment blocks that commonly reach up to forty stories high.

Most of the older estates consist of buildings that look like they've been tipped over. They are seven to fifteen storeys high and ten to twenty households wide, making them all much wider than they are tall. They are only two-and-a-half units thick, having apartments on both sides separated by halls running down the center.

One estate we frequently visited was Kwai Shing Estate, built in 1975. It had ten big blocks with an average of over five hundred households in each one, housing roughly twenty-five thousand people in toto. It is difficult to exaggerate the crowded conditions of Hong Kong.[15]

---

15. According to *Social Life and Development in Hong Kong* (The Chinese University Press, 1984), in 1954 the minimum floor space allocated per person in public dwellings was twenty-four square feet. That increased to thirty-five square feet in 1970, enough space to fit a queen-sized bed, but not a king. Today publicly owned flats range in size from three hundred to seven hundred square feet, and the amount of space each person is guaranteed for their living space is at least a hundred square feet, which is still very crowded by American standards.

We concentrated our efforts on these easily accessible estates full of relatively poor people. It saved us lots of energy. Four to six people in a three hunded-square-foot household with up to forty flats per floor allowed us access to huge numbers of people in short periods of time.

We started each tracting session with a prayer. We would seclude ourselves in the stairwell of a building and ask Heavenly Father for guidance as to which floor we should begin tracting on. Miraculously, we almost never came up with the same answer. To solve this problem, we democratically took turns following the answers to each other's prayers. Starting with the floor that one of us was guided to, we knocked on each and every door. Then we would go to another floor, which was usually the next one down. "We're in the area sharing a message about Jesus. Can we come in and talk with you?" was one of our typical greetings.

Not surprisingly, people seldom invited us into their homes, but when we did get past a door they always gave us a drink, usually hot tea, which we always accepted but never drank because it was against the Word of Wisdom. We were invariably offered the best seats in the house. Even those people who rejected us treated us nicely on the whole, and verbal abuse was rare. People slammed the door in our faces only three or four times, and I only recall one time that such an act was preceded by loud expletives. Nobody ever threatened me, let alone pointed a gun at me.

I baptized seventeen people on my mission, an average of about one per month during my sixteen months in Hong Kong. That's pretty incredible if you think about it.[16]

Of all the buildings that we tracted through, the types that fascinated me the most were the twenty-five-storey square prisms. These structures, many still standing today, are comprised of two hollow, square-shaped towers that are connected at their corners. The fronts of the

---

16. Imagine a pair of Asians knocking on your door and asking in broken English to come into your home and talk to you about their Eastern religion. That makes seventeen conversions seem impressive. The analogy isn't completely appropriate, though, because Christian missionaries have been in Asia for a very long time, and Christian schools have been doing years of groundwork for today's missionaries as well. Nevertheless, I'm sure readers can imagine the difficulties we faced.

A former secretary of mine, a Hong Kong local, once asked me: "Did anyone ever let you inside their home?" She apparently thought it plausible that I knocked on doors for a year and a half in Hong Kong without getting through a single door.

homes face inward, towards the centers of the hollow squares, creating a very unusual frog-in-the-well neighborhood.

I enjoyed entering these buildings at the beginnings of evening shifts. We would walk to the center of one of the squares and look straight up at the tiny section of deep blue evening sky that could be seen through the top of the well, with an occasional cloud drifting by. The walls of the well consisted of twenty-five layers of balconies. The air inside was heavily flavored with the distinct smell of Chinese home cooking, heavy on oil, garlic, and ginger. The rice winners were just returning home to their children.

In these neighborhoods no sounds go unheard. There is the knocking and scratching of spatulas vigorously stirring the contents of woks, the clinking and clattering of bowls and chopsticks being set onto tables, and the chattering of children and parents, all joining together to create a bustling orchestra of Hong Kong domestic life.

We were invited into three or four homes a day. In the beginning it was fresh, exotic, and fascinating. Reciting my half of the first discussion was a tremendous challenge, and trying to understand any of what dad and our hosts were talking about during the warming-up session of small talk required enormous effort. Needless to say, I wasn't bored at all during the first few months of my missionary work. We proselytized ten hours every day; eventually it would get old, but for the time being it was mentally stimulating.

Another way we proselytized was by stopping people on the sidewalk and asking them if we could go to their home sometime. We occasionally planned a systematic session of doing this with a group of missionaries from one or two districts. For these street displays, we would set a sandwich board up on a street corner, which advertised who we were alongside some message aimed at attracting people's attention—usually something that pitched the Church's strongly promoted image of being an organization that produces healthy, happy families. Missionaries all over the world do these types of street displays.

We never liked doing street displays, so we didn't do them very often. We felt less comfortable approaching people in mid-stride on the sidewalk than when they were in the comfort of their homes. People were annoyed by our approaches because it forced them to publicly refuse to speak with us. That made them visibly uncomfortable, which in turn made us uncomfortable.

The visitors' center was a passive way to proselytize. Our district, Kwai Hing, was part of the Tsuen Wan **Zone**. Since the visitors' center was located in Tsuen Wan, all the Elders serving in that zone were on rotation to sit inside the center and wait for people who were inspired by the Lord to walk in and ask us to teach them about the Church.

The visitors' center was a welcome alternative to the monotony and the discomfort of tracting. It was quiet and relaxing, because nobody except members who wanted to chat with the missionaries ever walked in.

* * *

There were four Elders living in our apartment in Kwai Hing. We took turns cooking dinner and washing dishes. Every other day, my companion and I would cut short our afternoon session of proselytizing so that we could shop for dinner and then return home early to cook. We alternated cooking dinner and washing the dishes. Fried rice and spaghetti, featuring canned luncheon meat similar to Spam, were by far the most popular meals because they were easy to make. The fried rice was flavored with canned pineapple chunks, and the spaghetti was drowned in Ragu. Neither Chinese nor Italians would have recognized either dish.

Our only official break from proselytizing was on Monday mornings and afternoons. That was our P-day (preparation day), a necessary break, which, as explained by President Smith, did not belong to us. It was to be spent in a way that would make us more effective in our work; we were supposed to do something that would effectively charge us up for the next week. If we instead lay around the apartment, then, according to him, we "deserved to be depressed." Apparently there were enough missionaries doing this that President Smith felt it needed to be addressed. Hanging around the apartment all day is not something that many people in their early twenties like to do, so the missionaries who did so were probably depressed to begin with. Most of my P-days were spent acting like a tourist along with my companion.

* * *

The first month went quickly. My mind was overloaded with an unfamiliar lifestyle and an unfamiliar language. I had to concentrate hard to understand what people were saying, as well as to make myself understood. It was mentally demanding. It is frustrating for missionaries in English-speaking missions to convert people to their way of thinking, but for us the task often seemed next to impossible. In English I would have been thinking about my intonation, tone of voice, and which word choices might have sounded most intelligent and persuasive. In Cantonese, however, I was worried about whether or not people understood any of what I said. I became frustrated and discouraged.

The next monthly mission conference at the Mission Home didn't arrive a moment too soon. It gave me a pleasant high. My mission was not the non-stop series of spiritual experiences that I had expected it to be. It was nothing but hard work. Another pep talk full of pulpit-pounding, faith-building rhetoric from President Smith was just what I needed. I came away feeling once again like I was ready to convert the city *en masse*. After the conference, however, it took only a few hours of fruitless tracting to throw me unceremoniously back into reality.

Culture Shock

Being in constant contact with Hong Kong residents had a maturing effect on our young minds, just as exposure to any alternative culture does. However, because we were not allowed to watch TV, read books, or read newspapers, and because we were discouraged from talking to people about much of anything except the Church, we were not affected by Hong Kong culture nearly as much as we might have been. Most of my ignorance and ethnocentricity remained intact. I didn't learn until years later that in 1982, while I was in Hong Kong, Margaret Thatcher visited Beijing to discuss Hong Kong's 1997 handover to China. Her visit was one of the catalysts that caused an economic recession and a property crash in Hong Kong, none of which entered my awareness at the time, which is incredible if you think about it. Missionaries prove beyond any doubt that it is entirely possible to live in a place and not be at all "of it"—unfortunately.

Under such circumstances it was ironically and unfortunately our fellow American companions (rather than our locally born and raised companions) who provided us with our most lasting memories and deepest impressions. To a large extent we Americans relied on each other to "learn" about the local people and culture. In an essay titled "The Mormon Missionary Companionship," Anthropologist and

Mormon scholar Keith Parry wrote about a discussion that took place among a group of returned missionaries (RMs):

> Gary notes that "greenies not only learn to teach and be missionaries from their senior companions, they learn how to live in a new country and culture." Joanne agrees: "As a new missionary in a foreign country, I found it quite comforting to have someone always there who could tell me what was going on . . ."

As a greenie, I bought into that. I depended on my dad and other senior missionaries for insights into Hong Kong culture. About six weeks after arriving in Hong Kong, still unable to understand much Cantonese, I jokingly said to a more senior missionary, "I wonder if they have as difficult a time understanding each other as we do them?"

In all seriousness he replied, "I know they do for a fact. It's obvious. Why do you think they talk so loud to each other? They're always yelling and arguing. It's because they don't understand each other very well. It's not a very precise language."[17]

Divine Guidance

One evening dad and I entered one of those frog-well buildings, walked up a few flights of stairs, and secluded ourselves inside the stairwell. After a moment of reverent silence, we quietly discussed whose turn it was to pray. It was mine. We folded our arms, closed our eyes, and bowed our heads.

"Heavenly Father," I said, "thank you so much for all the wonderful blessings you've given us. We're grateful for the opportunity to serve you, and ask that you give us the strength and guidance to do so in a manner that is pleasing unto you. Please forgive us for any shortcomings we may have. We ask that you please bless us with the Spirit as we visit these homes this evening, that we may be guided as to what to say and do, that we may be instrumental in helping these people to accept the gospel and be baptized, so they can one day live with you again. We ask you, Father, to please inspire us to know which floor we should

---

17. Maybe that explains why China's immensely rich history of complex culture and profound philosophy never dominated the entire world: it's all been recorded and passed along using an imprecise language.

begin tracting on. And we say these things humbly, in the name of Jesus Christ, Amen."

As mentioned earlier, we prayed for inspiration as to which floor to begin tracting on before each and every tracting session. Sometimes a floor number would faintly pop into my head, but just as often my mind was a blank. And when the Spirit prompted us both, we nearly always came up with different floor numbers. On this particular evening our democratic process of turn taking meant that we would follow Elder Brodie's inspiration.

It turned out to be an especially successful session. We got into three homes, and the people in one of them said we could visit them again. I complimented my companion for being so in tune with the Spirit. He thought about what to say for a moment. Then, with a nervous smile, he admitted that he chose which floor to begin tracting on by counting the pairs of underwear that were hanging out to dry on the bamboo pole just outside the window where we prayed. That's the gospel truth. Apparently the Lord works in mischievous ways.

Another evening when we were tracting through one of the blocks in Kwai Shing Estate, we prayed for inspiration as usual, and again neither of us received any spiritual prompting. There was no underwear hanging in plain view, so we took the elevator straight to the top and began working our way down. Most people's doors in Hong Kong's government housing estates are kept wide open during the preparation of dinner. Chinese cooking generates a lot of oily smoke, so it makes sense to open the front door and a back window or two for ventilation. This causes the smoke to blow out of the house. When they finish cooking, the residents usually close the door and, if it's summer, turn on the air-conditioner.

At one of the first doors we approached, I reached through the grates of the locked metal gate and knocked on the open door. A young girl came to the door. She stared at us inquisitively but said nothing.

"Is your mommy or daddy home?"

"Mom!" she yelled, turning her head but remaining where she was.

Her mother emerged from the kitchen wiping her hands on her apron. "What is it?" she asked us.

"We're here in your neighborhood sharing a message about Jesus Christ. Can we come inside and share it with you? We won't take much of your time."

"I'm cooking dinner."

"No problem. We'll come back when you're finished eating. What's a good time?"

"That's not necessary."

"It smells really good. What are you cooking?"

She ignored us and walked back into the kitchen.

A large portion of all our evening door approaches were rejected with the excuses "We're cooking" or "We're eating." Most of the remaining rejections fit onto a short list: "We're watching TV," "No thanks," "Nobody's home" ("Aren't you somebody?" we sometimes asked the person with a smile, which, for some reason, never resulted in the person smiling back), and "We worship Chinese gods" (by far the most common excuse when dinner wasn't being cooked or eaten).

We were invited into one home during our long, slow door-to-door journey back down to the ground. We marked down the room numbers of several homes where people had said "Fine" in response to our offer of "We'll come back when you're finished eating." We tried each of those homes again later and, not surprisingly, not a single one of their residents had actually wanted us to return. We didn't really expect to be let in the second time around, but any serious and persistent salesman will try, and most missionaries are serious and persistent.

When we finished with tower number one, we walked to the center of tower number two. It was now dark and the rats had come out of hiding, and were scurrying around in the inevitable build-up of garbage that such a setup generates. I looked at them and imagined the fun that a kid with a slingshot could have. I looked up through the well and breathed deeply. We only had time to tract out four or five of the floors, but we could always continue the next day if we wanted to.

The Art of Persuasion

I started to feel that we weren't being led by the Spirit, that we were left on our own to find converts the hard way. I also began to question my companion's tactics. Elder Brodie had the habit of overstaying his welcome, and as his **junior companion** I felt compelled to comply. An example of this happened one evening when a teenage girl let us into her home just as her mother was setting dinner on the table. The girl apparently thought that inviting us in was the proper thing to do, but her parents disagreed.

"We're going to eat dinner now," her father said without offering us a seat. In the culture of Hong Kong, that is as direct as an American telling someone to leave.

"This will only take a few minutes," my companion assured him.

"It's not a good time," the father said. Anyone who at all understood the local culture and its use of language would have recognized that the patriarch of the house wanted us to leave immediately.

The girl's parents and a younger brother were seated at the dinner table. The fish, vegetables, pork, and rice were all steaming and smelled wonderful. The girl stood beside the television and we stood facing her, only four or five feet from the dinner table. (In Hong Kong government estates, everyone is always close by.)

We had crossed the threshold and were inside their home. My senior companion, whom I had no authority over, was not about to give up the ground we had won and insisted that we present the first discussion to this girl. I felt uncomfortable. Even with my limited knowledge of the language and culture, I realized that we were not at all welcome in that home.

Elder Brodie told me to take out the flip chart and start giving the first discussion. Considering that I was both a junior and a greenie, I didn't feel it was my place to take charge and insist on leaving. I did manage to muster up a little bit of defiance, however, and stated the obvious along with a suggestion: "I don't think they want us here. I think maybe we should go."

My companion looked at me firmly and said, "Hand me the flip chart." Reluctantly I took it out of my bag and handed it to him. He then started presenting the first discussion to the girl while she remained standing, and he ignored the rest of the family members who remained seated and waiting at the table.

Discussions are divided into sections, which are presented in turns by the two Elders in a companionship. After the first section, he handed me the flip chart and told me to continue. I did as I was told. Our audience of one was visibly uncomfortable and kept glancing at her impatient father, who once again said, "We're going to eat dinner now."

Elder Brodie assured him we wouldn't be long and told me to continue. The poor girl was torn between being hospitable to us on the one hand and obeying her father's wishes on the other. She didn't know what to do. She stood motionless and silent. Her father was too civil to throw us out, allowing us to finish the entire first discussion while the food grew cold. When we were finished, the wonderful smell of dinner had entirely faded.

We had victoriously said every word, but I don't think the girl, let alone the others in her family, heard a single one of them. When my companion asked her to pray with us, she politely refused. We thanked the family for their time and left. I'm sure we planted a seed, but not the one we had intended.

Elder Brodie did something similar another time when we were presenting the first discussion to a man in his early twenties. Halfway through the discussion the man asked, "Are you two ready to leave yet?" He didn't have to eat the whole sheep to know he was being fed bad mutton; he had allowed us to start, but he soon realized he didn't want us to finish.

"We're not done yet," Elder Brodie told him, and he continued without breaking his stride. The man interrupted three more times to ask if we were ready to leave, and each time that he asked, my companion said, "No." The first "no" was pleasant, but when the man asked the second time, Elder Brodie stopped smiling. The third time the man asked, Elder Brodie lost his patience. And the fourth time he asked, Elder Brodie responded angrily, obviously annoyed by our host's persistence in resisting the Word of God.

* * *

Like all door-to-door solicitors, we had a prepared and rehearsed routine. Once we were sitting inside people's homes, a major victory in itself, we would engage our hosts in a moment of idle chatter. After five or ten minutes of small talk, we would then casually and politely remind them of the message we were there to share. That is when we would take our flipchart out and begin presenting the first discussion.

We sincerely believed that we had the most important message in the world: information about God's only true Church, along with instructions on how to join. This information is vital because Church membership is a prerequisite to entering God's kingdom in heaven. Theoretically our only responsibility was that of message bearer.

Missionaries are not responsible if someone refuses to accept the message; the receiver of the message is held solely accountable.[18] We even believed that strongly rejecting the missionaries could put a person at risk of having a dusting-off-of-the-feet ritual, bringing tragedy, and perhaps even death, to his or her door.

We both believed that our only responsibility as missionaries was to present our message to as many people as we could; whether or not they converted was up to them.[19] The primary difference between me and my companion regarded our presentation. I believed we were responsible for convincing people to willingly listen to us, and then to give them a persuasive presentation. Elder Brodie, on the other hand, seemed to think that our only responsibility was to recite our scripted message to captive audiences.

* * *

The second month went by almost as quickly as the first. My dad, who was the district leader in our apartment, received the monthly phone call from the **zone leader**. These calls informed the **district lead-**

---

18. Everyone ever born on this planet will get a chance—either in this life or the next—to hear the message of Mormonism and choose whether or not to accept it and be allowed into the Celestial Kingdom. Those who never meet missionaries in this life will meet them in the afterlife (the spirit world) before Judgment Day. Because baptism by immersion is absolutely necessary, spirits (dead people that are all stuck without bodies until after the resurrection, which won't take place until the end of the world as we know it) need help from people who are still alive and have bodies. That is why Mormons perform proxy baptisms for the dead. The spirit person that the baptism is performed for can choose to accept it or reject it. Each baptism is done in the person's actual earthly name, and that is the reason why the LDS Church is famous in the field of genealogy for its massive archive.

However, it is infamous among some sectors of the Jewish community for posthumously baptizing victims of the Holocaust. The fact that Adolf Hitler was also baptized on December 10, 1993 in the Church's London temple doesn't help matters much. His endowments were done on the same day and he was sealed to his parents on March 12, 1994 in the same temple. People actually performed these ceremonies by proxy on his and his parents' behalf. I wonder what went through the mind of whichever unsuspecting Mormon walked into the London temple that day to perform rites on behalf of whichever dead person's name(s) that happened to be handed to them . . . and then read "Adolf Hitler."

19. Regardless of where the responsibility theoretically lies, it is obvious that the Church's leaders don't shrug their shoulders at low conversion figures. They spare no efforts in ensuring that lots of people are persuaded to willingly listen, and that lots of those listeners are then persuaded to convert.

ers throughout the mission about **transfers**, telling them which missionaries were going to be transferred to which districts. Elder Brodie was told that I would stay in Kwai Hing, but that he was going to be transferred somewhere else. Elder Tseng would replace him as my new senior companion.

We went to the Mission Home in Kowloon Tong. All of the more than one hundred thirty missionaries serving in Hong Kong and Macau gathered inside the church's large multi-purpose room behind the chapel, where I waited for my third mission conference to begin. I was introduced to Elder Tseng and we immediately became a pair of inseparable companions, which was something neither of us chose.

The Chinese Elders were, on average, shorter than those from America. Elder Tseng was one of the shorter Chinese Elders. The top of his head was about even with my nose. His unparted hair was short and thick and refused to lie completely flat against his head. He had a round face, tired eyes, and thin lips. He spoke softly with a kind smile and, because he was a native of Hong Kong, his Cantonese was lightning speed compared to Elder Brodie's.

We all moved into the chapel and seated ourselves, ready for yet another fiery pep talk. I was wising up to the process and therefore didn't allow myself to be filled to the brim with unreasonable expectations; I only allowed myself to get half full. I let myself get boosted, but told myself it was going to be just as hard to convert people after the conference as it was before. And, sure enough, it was.

Advanced Lessons in Cantonese

Cantonese is a dialect of Chinese, though it's worth noting that Cantonese and Mandarin are mutually unintelligible; they are roughly as different from each other as French is from Italian. Cantonese is spoken by tens of millions of people in Hong Kong, Macau, Southern China, and Chinese overseas communities around the world. Mandarin is spoken either as the main dialect, or as the *lingua franca*, everywhere in China except Hong Kong.

Cantonese is a relatively difficult language for English speakers to learn. One reason for this is because it is, like all Chinese dialects, a tonal language. That means that tones carry meaning. For example, in

English, the explicit meaning of the word "fun" will not change if you say it in a high tone, low tone, or rising tone. In Cantonese, however, there are several words that are pronounced the same as the English word "fun." If a high-level tone is used, then it means "to separate" or "distinguish"; if said in a mid-level tone, it means "to sleep"; if said in a low-level tone, it means "portion"; and if said in a rising tone it means "powder." Some Cantonese words are dangerously alike. For example, the words for buy and sell are articulated in exactly the same way using only slightly different tones; you can imagine the stress this must add to stockbrokers' lives.

The tones often caused us missionaries problems. One example of this was when my dad wanted to tell an investigator that he could eat candy as a substitute for smoking. Giving up smoking is a prerequisite to joining the Church, so it is the job of missionaries to make their smoking investigators kick the habit. With this in mind, my dad asked one of our smoking investigators if there was any candy in the house. After giving my companion a puzzled look, the investigator thought for a moment and then disappeared into his kitchen. He quickly reappeared with a can of Campbell's soup gripped in each hand. Because my level of Cantonese was still very low, I didn't get it, but my dad immediately realized his mistake. In Cantonese the word for candy is *tong* said in a rising tone, and the word for soup is *tong* said in a high-level tone. Elder Brodie had used the wrong tone.

To learn a language well it is essential to both study it and use it. We studied Cantonese every morning and then used it the rest of the day. Each day we spoke to large numbers of people at their doorways, asking them to let us in. A few always did, and each time that happened we had the opportunity to practice our small talk skills in Cantonese, as well as the opportunity to recite the memorized script known as the "first discussion." This frequent presentation of a large amount of memorized text helped us learn the language. (When I was in the MTC I thought that all of the memorizing was a distraction from learning the language. How wrong I was.)

It was some time before we understood the meaning of everything we recited in the first discussion. Of course we knew the English translation, but we didn't have a real understanding of many of the Cantonese words and sentence structures that we were constantly repeating. We learned a little more each day until—after several months and well over two hundred repetitions—we knew every word and phrase by heart.

By that time we had common sentence structures so ingrained in our minds that we had no trouble substituting new words for some of the memorized words. In this way we were able to express a tremendous number of new ideas with little effort. All we had to do was substitute new vocabulary into syntax structures that had become second nature to us.

Within the discussion, in Cantonese, I clearly remember saying, "Some people don't even know who Jesus is." I said it over and over without quite understanding how the grammar worked. To me it was just a memorized sentence that fit into a particular slot in the middle of the first discussion. The word order in Cantonese was this: "Some people *lìhn* Jesus is who *dou* don't know." Later, after I understood what it meant and how the syntax worked, I had it so well memorized that I was able to insert other words and phrases at will. I could say things like "That kid doesn't even know how to tie his shoes." (That kid *lìhn* tie shoe laces *dou* doesn't know.)

The way in which Mormon missionaries learn their languages would be extremely difficult, if not impossible, to duplicate. Study, day-and-night tutorship from companions, immersion in the foreign language environment, and constantly reciting large amounts of memorized text are the secrets to LDS missionaries' language-learning success. It is what makes Mormons believe that the Lord is helping their missionaries do what previously—as the joke goes—only babies could do: learn tough languages.

My routine with Elder Tseng was the same as it had been with Elder Brodie, but the experience was quite different. It didn't seem like he was capable of speaking slowly and clearly the way Elder Brodie could. And all the people we talked to weren't speaking as slowly, clearly, or loudly as they had been before. Suddenly everyone in Hong Kong was talking at lightning speed. They didn't need to slow down or repeat themselves anymore because Elder Tseng always, miraculously, understood them. Even when I was the one who said the door approach, people often looked at Elder Tseng when they responded. I felt both lost and left out.

As a result of all this, the foreignness of my whole experience multiplied. The novelty of the city's sights and sounds was wearing off by that time, which is usually when culture shock starts to set in. For me this was compounded by the fact that I suddenly lost the only piece of home that I still had: an American companion. I felt frustrated and mentally exhausted trying to understand what people were saying to me. Tracting became a dreaded chore.

I started to look forward to the visitors' center, where I could just sit and stare at nothing. I also looked forward to buying and cooking dinner. The visitors' center and cooking were both guilt-free escapes from proselytizing. And of course my favorite day of the week was P-day. Like most missionaries, I never wanted P-day to end, but it always did, and I was back knocking on doors that same evening.

Elder Tseng did his best to make sure I was able to play my role. It would have been very easy for him to answer all of the questions that were directed at me and treat me like a table lamp while he and our hosts chatted away. Instead, he repeated questions and comments for me whenever I required it, and he prodded me along without ever speaking for me entirely. Most of the time, I would have preferred to be left alone to wander around in the safety of my daydreams. That would have been much less stressful and demanding, but Elder Tseng didn't allow it. I knew that at any moment I would be required to contribute something to the conversation, so I focused as hard as I could on what was being said. I didn't appreciate it at the time, but now I do. That one month with Elder Tseng early on in my mission, the only month in which I was paired up with a local Hong Kong missionary, was by far the best Cantonese course I've ever had.

It wasn't only the language that was driving me crazy; it was a combination of all the things that made my experiences and my environment so Chinese. When Americans invite you into their homes, one of the politest things they can say to you is, "Make yourself at home." A good American host tries to put guests at ease and makes them feel like they can relax and act informally. An American host might ask some guests, "Would you like something to drink?" And if the guests say "No thanks," the host might follow that up with, "Are you sure?" That's usually the end of it. The host assumes the guests would have said "yes" if they had actually wanted something.

Chinese hosts are different. They don't allow their guests to sit wherever they want. The guests must sit in the seats that are considered by the host to be the best. If you choose the seat you like best and it's not the one that the host thinks is best, the host will probably think you are trying to be polite and insist that you move. If you say you prefer the seat you're on, you probably won't be believed. This was a source of real frustration, and sometimes it made me angry. I was denied my independence to do what I wanted, and my words were not taken at face value. I wasn't believed when I said that I didn't want anything to drink, or that I was very happy sitting where I was, or that I didn't want to eat whatever the host insisted on giving me.

One time Elder Tseng and I were offered a bowl of sugary soup containing gelatinous white balls. Elder Tseng refused when offered, but our host gave us each a bowl anyway. Elder Tseng happily took the bowl that was handed to him and eagerly bit into a ball. Dark purple paste oozed out from within and dripped over the edge of his spoon. "No, thank you," I said. The host laughed at my politeness and pushed my bowl of soup closer to me. No problem, I thought. I'll just ignore it like I always do the hot tea we're served. The host would have none of that, however, and kept insisting that I eat the sweet desert on the table in front of me. Elder Tseng was no help at all; he encouraged me right along with our host. The sense of obligation forced me to lift my spoon to my mouth. The balls were slippery and slimy on the outside and gooey on the inside. I had no idea what it was, and that bothered me. I gave up after half a bite, despite how unhappy that made our host feel.

Rather than looking at ease in people's homes, Elder Tseng always sat up straight and looked to our hosts for cues about how to act. He refused whatever was offered and always accepted it graciously with both hands when it was inevitably given to him anyway. His movements were slight and proper. If another member of the family came home while we were there, he instinctively and immediately stood up. I followed his lead in everything, but was always one or two beats behind him. I didn't know how to behave in this strange world, and I therefore used him as a model, mimicking him the best I could.

The month with Elder Tseng was miserable for me, and I was horribly homesick; but that month provided the best lesson in language and culture I could have asked for. And what I learned from that month-long lesson soon proved invaluable.

Kwun Tong

Elder Tseng was the district leader in our apartment. When the time came, he received the monthly call from the zone leader. He hung up the phone and told me I was being transferred to Kwun Tong. My new companion was going to be Elder Compton, a greenie from Utah who had been in Hong Kong for two months, a month less than I had. I was stunned. Here I was still a young toddler learning to talk, and the mission was making me a dad. I was frightened by the idea of suddenly, as a young senior companion, having to take the lead in tracting sessions. I would no longer have anyone to explain things to me. Instead, my companion would be looking to me for all the answers about what people were saying and how we were supposed to act.

Although I had been studying and using Cantonese every day for months, I was still far from being a proficient speaker. And I was just as far from fully understanding Chinese behavioral norms. Nevertheless, after two months in the MTC, and another three in the field, I was made a senior companion, which was, and still is, very unusual in the Hong Kong mission.

On the sixth of April, we went to the mission home for my fourth monthly mission conference. I was paired up with my new companion, Elder Compton, a medium-built nineteen-year-old with light brown hair. He maintained an unkempt, grungy look. I would later discover that his appearance was part of a larger package of eccentricity.

This time the mission conference didn't give me any sense of euphoria. These conferences were meant to motivate us and make us confident in our ability to convert the locals, but I was changing; I was becoming less easy to convince. I had just spent a month feeling lost with a Chinese companion and was now being tossed into a situation that I believed would be even worse. President Smith talked as if we should be able to find, through the promptings of the Spirit, people who were ready for the gospel, and then miraculously convert them. I didn't believe it was going to happen, at least not in the way or to the extent that he described it. He said our success depended on our obeying all the mission rules, but I was obeying them at the time, so I didn't understand why I was unable to do what he was claiming I could.

I didn't think he was lying, or even exaggerating. Instead, I felt I was inadequate for some unknown reason. I logically assumed I wasn't spiritual enough, but I didn't know how to change that. Obviously I lacked faith, but there was no instruction manual that explained how to build my faith up.

It was depressing.

The building that housed the Kwun Tong apartment was newer and cleaner than the one in Kwai Hing, and the elevators didn't sound or feel life threatening. The apartment itself was not only newer, but bigger as well. It had a metal gate, like almost every home in Hong Kong, but the gate had wheels that slid along two tracks, one in the floor and one above the door. This allowed it to open much more quietly and smoothly than the one in Kwai Hing. The veneer on the hardwood floors still shined. There was a worn but comfortable sofa in the living room upholstered in fake leather. The bedrooms were bigger than the ones in the Kwai Hing apartment, and the wardrobes, beds, and mattresses were all newer. All of this was a nice change. I no longer craved to have additional sacrifices thrown upon me in the form of poor living conditions. I felt that the life I was living was sacrifice enough. The apartment in Kwun Tong was still cockroach infested and far from luxurious, but it was a welcome step up from the conditions in Kwai Hing.

There were six Elders living in the apartment. One of them was Elder Larson, a thin young man who was confident and articulate. He was nearing the end of his mission and was obviously "**trunky**," a term used to describe missionaries who have psychologically packed their trunks and are ready to go home. He spoke irreverently about President Smith, whom he disliked.

As well, Elder Larson frequently talked at length on the phone with a local girl. He told us that he planned to return to Hong Kong shortly after his mission, pick up his girlfriend, and then take her back to America and marry her. For some odd reason he had told President Smith of his plans. He apparently didn't feel that there was anything wrong with his having gotten engaged while serving his mission, despite the fact that merely dating a girl is a serious infraction of mission rules. He told us that President Smith didn't believe he'd go through with it, and he talked gleefully of the time he would see the look on the president's face when he proved him wrong.

The whole situation was strange to me. It was hard for me to understand how an Elder could either end up engaged or dislike his mission president, let alone both. I couldn't comprehend why he was even serving a mission in the first place. It didn't occur to me at the time that perhaps he didn't start out the way he was when I met him, that perhaps he started out in a way that wasn't all that different from the way I started out. I also didn't realize, on a conscious level, the extent to which cultural pressure ensures that Mormon boys not only go on missions, but stay on missions, whether they want to or not.

Despite the slight discomfort he caused me, Elder Larsen didn't weigh too heavily on my mind. He wasn't my companion. He was neither my subordinate nor my superior. I therefore didn't spend much time with him, and I didn't feel very affected by his actions, because I didn't have to lead him or be led by him.

My life as a missionary continued as it had. The only significant difference was that I was now in charge of my companion, and the area where we proselytized was new to me. Dressed in slacks, ties, and leather dress shoes, we walked to and from our area. It was fifteen or twenty minutes each way, depending on how quickly we walked, and we made the trip twice a day—three times if we returned to the apartment for lunch. We walked on rough pavement that wound alongside a busy road filled with taxis, vans, trucks, and double-decker buses, all of them puffing diesel exhaust.

Rain or shine, we went in search of people willing to hear the truth about the origin and purpose of their lives. During rainstorms the wind would sometimes render our umbrellas useless. It played with us, attacking from one direction before suddenly coming out of another. It occasionally caught the undersides of our umbrellas and turned them inside out. On such days we stood at people's front doors with soaked clothes, matted hair, a smile, and a badge. "We're in your neighborhood sharing a message about Jesus Christ. Can we come in?"

More than once we wore rubber thongs to save our leather shoes from rain damage. We occasionally saw some locals wear thongs outside, and in the typical ignorance of people who observe another culture, we assumed that this was a normal and acceptable practice for anyone at any time in any place. Along the same lines of reasoning, we sometimes ventured outside in our pajamas to buy breakfast, or to make a quick run to the supermarket; a few locals did it, so surely nobody would think it odd if we did the same.

The neighborhoods we tracted through in Kwun Tong were similar to the ones in Kwai Hing. We spent most of our time in government housing estates. Once in a while, however, we visited temporary housing areas. These were single-storey, terraced houses covered with sheets of corrugated steel. The Hong Kong government built them as temporary homes for people who were on the waiting list to get into housing estates. Each temporary housing community had one public bathroom that we missionaries used only when absolutely necessary. The toilets in these bathrooms, like most public bathrooms in Hong Kong, were pear-shaped porcelain bowls set into the floor. The bottoms of the bowls were ill designed. They were too large and flat so, when the water flushed into them from the tanks overhead, not everything washed down the hole. This resulted in residents and visitors alike being assaulted by the sight and smell of human excrement nearly every time they went to the bathroom.

The homes in temporary housing areas consisted of a single room of about one hundred fifty square feet, often housing an entire family. There was water and electricity, but the water supply came from taps outside the homes. The lifestyle in those communities, and in fact in all the communities in Hong Kong, was so foreign to us that we were naturally fascinated by it. Things as simple as seeing people getting a haircut under a bridge, or seeing the occasional elderly women squat while waiting at a bus stop made us happy.

The Green Leading the Green

As interestingly exotic as Hong Kong was, sticking to a highly regimented schedule was still monotonous. We welcomed anything unusual in our lives, the more unusual the better. During my two months with Elder Compton, it was he, my new green companion—new to me and green to Hong Kong—who kept my life interesting.

One of the most strictly enforced mission rules is the requirement that missionaries stay by their companions' sides. Being half of a Mormon missionary companionship is a unique experience. Missionaries spend more time per day with their companions than couples in love do. It wasn't so unpleasant in the MTC, because our district was almost always together as a group. That meant we had a choice of whom to interact with. Out in the field, however, I was alone with my companion hour after hour, day after day, week after week, month after month. The only break was when one of us went to the bathroom.

There is a very low probability that a missionary will end up paired with a companion whom he or she would choose, someone whose personality is so compatible with their own that he or she would actually want to spend every waking hour by that person's side.

I made some good friends with Elders on my mission, a couple of whom I still keep in touch with to this day. I think back fondly of Elder Compton, but I didn't appreciate his uniqueness as much as I should have at the time. When I was made his senior companion, after only three months in the field, I was still dead serious about the work I was there to do. Elder Compton's personality and behavior sometimes seemed to get in the way, and under the circumstances of my mission it was a source of frustration. When it didn't affect our work, however, his unusualness was preferable to the boredom and loneliness that hover over silent companionships like depressing grey clouds.[20]

Elder Compton told me he wanted to be a music composer. He had never studied music, nor did he plan to do so, but that didn't matter because it wasn't necessary. He planned to work with people who could write music by ear. He said he would hum tunes of inspiration trapped inside his head, and the songwriters would write them down. Although this meant he would only be required to hum, he still worked on learning to play makeshift instruments. To my amazement, he figured out how to play portions of songs by Pink Floyd on a touch-tone calculator. Most of those who play this "instrument" can only manage "Mary Had a Little Lamb."

Elder Compton's composing was going to make him famous, which was a goal that he obsessed about. He spoke fondly of an experience that he had had just a month prior. He and his companion were walking alongside a primary school when they walked past the open door of a classroom full of students. As they passed, they heard a loud, excited clamor—apparently a reaction to their presence. They were curiously amused, so they popped their heads inside the door. The students loved it, and the classroom erupted in noisy chatter. Elder Compton stepped inside and basked in this flood of commotion, invigorated by the idea

---

20. The way Elders usually deal with personality clashes is through silence and by being together yet separate; this is done by one man walking several paces in front of the other, rather than either side by side or one right after the other. Humans crave companionship, but only with the right kind of companion. The wrong kind just increases the craving.

that his mere presence could cause such a thing. His vivid imagination turned the students into a hoard of screaming fans. He said it was the best experience of his life.

He talked proudly of the day when he would return to Hong Kong after becoming famous. Those students would tell their family and friends that they had actually seen Elder Compton in person years ago: "He walked right into our classroom!"

Elder Compton also said this about any youngster who ever laughed or sneered at us: After his glorious return, those kids would be too embarrassed to admit to anyone what they had once done to Elder Compton; instead, they would dwell on it with feelings of shame and guilt. This seemed to satisfy Elder Compton.

Not only did he and I have rather different predictions about the level and type of impressions that he might have on people in the future, but we also had very different interpretations of the type of impressions we made on people in the present. For example, one evening after we finished proselytizing in an area that was too far to get to on foot, we went to a bus stop to catch a bus home. The only other people at the bus stop were a woman and her young son, who appeared to be about three years old. Elder Compton approached them and told the woman who we were. He asked her if she'd like us to come to her home sometime and teach her about Jesus Christ. Her method of rejection was quite typical by the standards of Hong Kong culture. She shook her head, giving us only an instant of eye contact, and said nothing. When Elder Compton continued, she remained silent and kept looking determinedly off to the side. I interpreted that as a clear "no" and moved away, but Elder Compton stayed where he was and kept talking to her for a few minutes while she stood rigid and looking to the side. The child looked back and forth from Elder Compton to his mom, probably wanting to know who this strange man was and why his mother was reacting to him in this way.

Elder Compton eventually gave up and joined me where I was standing, about ten yards away so that the woman could have some space. After the mother and son were left alone, they started talking, laughing, and playing a local version of patty cake. I assumed that the woman wished she'd never seen us that night, or any night, and that she was extremely relieved when we finally left her alone. My companion didn't see it that way. With a contented look on his face, Elder Compton said we had planted a seed: "Some day she's gonna look back and remember that time when some Mormon missionaries gave her that special moment with her son." He had concluded that we were the cause of that woman's special patty-cake moment with her son, and he believed that the woman also thought we had caused it.

Another Promotion

Another month passed. The phone call came, and with it another surprise; I was promoted to district leader after only four months in the field. It was like a shot of adrenaline. Leading five other Elders meant I had to be especially righteous and faithful. I therefore soaked up all of the mission president's rhetoric at the next mission conference, my fifth.

President Smith gave an especially fiery talk. Emphasizing the word "nothing" with pounds of his fist on the pulpit, he told us that we were just that: nothing. We were as the dust of the earth, and the only way we could accomplish anything was with God's help. Tapping into that source of help required faith, of course, but once we had enough of that, we could do anything. This made me as determined as ever to perform miracles, to convert lots of people quickly and easily through the power of the Spirit.

I had always known that such miracles were possible because I was a product of Mormon culture. I believed everything the mission president said, which was very much in line with what I'd been told my whole life. I believed I hadn't been guided by the Spirit up to that point because of some unknown fault of my own. I thought that could change if I just had enough faith—if, in other words, I believed strongly enough that it would change. After all, I knew that if I wasn't sufficiently worthy of spiritual guidance, I would never have been called by the Lord to be district leader.

Predictably, the reality in the streets and doorways of Hong Kong shattered my illusions. But the extra buildup this time made me fall significantly harder.

A week after the conference I was feeling quite disillusioned, and then something happened to make things even worse. Our zone leader arranged a switch so that he could spend the day proselytizing with me. (A switch, also called a **split**, refers to one pair of Elders swapping companions with another pair. Zone leaders throughout the mission periodically did this with the district leaders under them as a form of top-down leadership training.) On this particular switch, the zone leader felt inspired to share a "faith-promoting" story with me.

Church leaders do not overlook the fact that most missionaries expect an unrealistically high level of spiritual guidance while on their missions. Therefore, in addition to narratives that warn missionaries of the dangers of heaven and hell, there are also stories that "prove" that spiritual guidance exists, if only one is faithful enough to receive it.

My zone leader was approaching the end of his mission, so he was able to tell me this inspirational story with the confidence of a wizened veteran. His manner and tone of voice gave every indication that he himself believed the story to be true. On the hill to our immediate left was a fifteen-storey, thirty-unit-long residential block. Along the face of the building laundry was hanging out to dry on bamboo poles that protruded horizontally outward from most of the windows. It was a vertical field of underwear ready to harvest for inspiration.

"There used to be a missionary in Hong Kong that never had to tract," the zone leader said. "He spent all his time teaching."

"How'd he find investigators if he didn't tract?" I asked.

"He'd look at the side of a building," he said, pointing up at the building on the hill, "and he'd wait for inspiration to know which home was the right one to go to. When it came, he'd count the number of windows up and number across. Then he'd go to that floor and count the doors 'til he got to the right one."

"How often did it work?"

"Every time."

I stared at the grassy hill beside us and thought about what I'd just heard. The hill dissolved into a blurry swirl of green as the implications of the zone leader's words sunk in. Stories like this are meant to be "inspiring," but of course they don't inspire missionaries for long, if at all. When viewed against reality, stories like this make missionaries feel inadequate, unworthy, and guilty. The *Church Handbook of Instruc-tions* tells "[b]ishops and stake presidents [to] teach prospective missionaries that to qualify for the needed guidance of the Spirit, they must resolve transgressions . . ."[21] Linking spiritual guidance to spiritual

---

21. *The Church Handbook of Instructions, Book 1: Stake Presidencies and Bishoprics*, published by The Church of Jesus Christ of Latter-day Saints, Salt Lake City, Utah, 1998, by Intellectual Reserve, Inc. (p. 80).

purity puts the blame of failure squarely onto the shoulders of the missionary. If a missionary doesn't receive guidance from the Spirit, then it's because he or she is unworthy. What was I doing wrong?

Missionaries don't expect to perform as miraculously as the nameless, fictional missionary in the zone leader's story. They merely expect to get better results than one would expect to get from knocking on door after door, and trying one's best to be as likable and persuasive as possible. In other words, missionaries expect to get better results than if they were salespeople relying solely on the art of persuasion with no help from Heavenly Father.

As missionaries, my companions and I believed that spiritual inspiration was our true guide to finding receptive souls, so we prayed constantly for floors and room numbers. I thought back on all my failed attempts at getting inspiration. Ironically, I was also able to consider the lack of success I had just experienced with my zone leader. He and I prayed before beginning our session of tracting, as was the norm, but we didn't come up with the same answer about where to begin. We followed his lead, but it didn't take us directly to people who let us in. We did get invited into a home eventually, but that was nothing unusual, and the people we talked to didn't want us to return.

Here was a zone leader near the end of his mission, and he didn't appear to have any more spiritual guidance than I did. In previous months I'd been disillusioned by the fact that my results seemed equal to my own human efforts. I contrasted the zone leader's story with my past failures as well as our failure that afternoon. Then, like an epiphany, I realized that the zone leader didn't think our failure was in the least unusual; in fact it seemed to be just what he expected. Unlike me, he wasn't bothered by the contrast between his story and our reality. It dawned on me that this same lack of guidance was the norm for all the missionaries in the field, both green and veteran. The only difference was that some could accept it while others couldn't. I was one of those that couldn't.

It was a strong dose of disillusionment. Before that switch with the zone leader, I had already known that my mission, up to that point, was not the experience I'd been led to believe it would be from all the inspiring stories I had heard growing up. After the switch, however, I now also knew that it was very unlikely that my mission would ever change. I hadn't seen any miracles, and the only ones I'd heard about were from stories about nameless missionaries long ago. The idea that this is all I could ever expect depressed me, and it affected my morale. Not long afterward, I wrote to a friend back home and asked him to send me some music. Choosing to break the very rule that caused a missionary in the MTC to become possessed by Satan was my first step towards apathy.

A Career Change

Elder Compton changed his mind about wanting to be a music composer. He chose to become a writer instead. He bought a paperback called *My Book*, which was filled with blank pages. He carried it with him at all times, and between doors, as we tracted, he would add a verse to a poem, a line to a story, or a lyric to a song.

"Are you going to take classes after your mission to improve your writing?" I asked him one evening. We were relaxing in the living/dining room at the end of yet another long day.

"I won't need to write good English," he said, "'cause I'm gonna write about inner-city kids."

I sat sideways on a chair at the dining table with my right leg draping over the chair adjacent. My left elbow rested on the table and my chin was fit snugly in my palm. I thought about what Elder Compton had just said, but I didn't get it. "What do you mean?" I asked. "Why wouldn't you have to write good English if you write about inner-city kids?"

"Inner-city kids don't have good English," he explained. "My books will be mostly dialogue." He was cleverer than he looked. Just as he had done with composing music, he had figured out a way to become outstanding and famous in a field without having to acquire the skills of the trade.

At some point during a foreign mission, missionaries inevitably feel a proud sense of accomplishment from having learned to converse in another language. This feeling came to Elder Compton much earlier than it does to most. He was also incredibly proud of having learned to use chopsticks. He said that after he finished his mission and returned home, he planned to use chopsticks all the time and to talk to his friends constantly in Cantonese. "I don't care that they're not going to understand," he said.

One day after a tracting session Elder Compton did something rather embarrassing as we passed by a group of high school girls. About ten steps before we reached them, he starting speaking very loudly and slowly in Cantonese: "Do . . . you . . . speak . . . Cantonese?" He kept looking straight ahead, indicating that he was talking for show rather than in an attempt to communicate. When we were right next to the girls, he started speaking very quickly and continued to look straight ahead: "Hi! How are you? Have you eaten yet?" He must have assumed that these common Cantonese greetings, spoken quickly, loudly, and without looking at anyone, would impress his female audience.

One other evening while lounging at the apartment, Elder Compton recounted another high point in his life, which took place during a meal in the MTC one day when the best cafeteria in the world was serving green jello cubes. After settling himself down at one of the high school-style cafeteria benches, Elder Compton pulled out his personal pair of wooden chopsticks, which was something he did for every meal he ate in the MTC. It was self-motivated training. He was contemplating which food item to begin with when an Elder sitting across from him asked, "Do you really know how to use those things?"

It was a challenge.

Without thinking, Elder Compton went straight for the jello. He swiftly, and ever so delicately, squeezed his chopsticks onto the sides of a green cube. Without even breaking the jello's skin, he lifted it high in the air towards his challenger's face. He then popped the lime-flavored treat into his mouth, raised his chin, and gave that Elder the smug look of victory.

Elder Compton was helplessly incapable of stopping his grin, which was probably complemented by green gel oozing out from the cracks between his teeth. He knew he couldn't have successfully chopsticked another jello cube the way he had just done, even if his life depended on it, so he felt very relieved when his challenger, who was already finished eating, reacted by nodding approval and leaving without saying, "Let's see you do that again."

Elder Compton shared this story with me while we were still sitting at the dining table after dinner, not yet having cleared away the dishes. The telling of the story apparently gave him the urge to demonstrate his chopstick proficiency. Lifting up his chopsticks, he snatched up some grains of rice that were stuck to the edge of his bowl. He moved too quickly, though, and with too much confidence. As a result the bits of rice dropped onto his chest before he could get them into his mouth. His eyes darted downward for an instant and then locked onto mine, trying to decipher if I had noticed. I pretended not to.

Elder Compton was a topic of conversation among many missionaries. One story claims Compton came out of the bathroom one day shouting, "I just saw an angel!"

"Shut up," said one of the other Elders.

"No, really, I did! I just saw an angel!"

Every time he repeated it, that same Elder would yell, "Shut up, Compton!"

Elder Compton eventually relented and said, "No, I didn't really see an angel." After that he tried to engage the Elder who had been yelling at him in a pseudo-philosophical discussion. "Could you imagine what it would be like if you really saw an angel? I mean think about it." (Having a vision is a hypothetical that Mormons can easily discuss in all seriousness. For example, "Can you imagine what it would be like to have an Angel appear in your room the way Moroni appeared to Joseph Smith?") But only moments before, Compton had irreverently acted as if he'd actually had a vision, while sitting on the toilet no less, so the other Elders in his apartment were understandably unwilling to discuss hypothetical visions with him at that time.

I almost always welcomed Elder Compton's idiosyncrasies because they spiced things up. However, I was frustrated whenever I thought his behavior had an adverse effect on our work. The fact that I had begun to equate the fruits of my labor with my own efforts was a difficult enough thing to take on its own, but when that was coupled with the behavior of a companion who sometimes sabotaged my efforts, it was infuriating.

As with any cold-call approach, the number of people that we could convince to let us into their homes depended on three things: our technique, the number of approaches we made, and the degree to which the host culture accepted us. In Hong Kong in the early 1980s, poor technique would get missionaries into less than one percent of the doorways they knocked on. On the other hand, good technique might have gotten a missionary into as many as three out of a hundred doors. The way to win at this numbers game was to never stop knocking on doors and to develop a successful door approach.

It was all about standing straight, wearing a pleasant, friendly smile, and saying things in the right way. The most difficult part was figuring out how to make our message sound appealing. It only made sense for us to be honest about the purpose of our visit, but the problem was that it wasn't a message that appealed to many people in Hong Kong.

"How are you?" I would say with a pleasant smile. "We're missionaries from the Church of Jesus Christ of Latter-day Saints. We're in this area sharing a message about Jesus Christ. Can we come in and share it with you? It will only take about ten minutes."

The reactions were almost always as expected: "We're busy," or "We're eating," or "Nobody's home," or "We worship *sàhn* (a generic name for various Chinese deities)." Occasionally we'd be yelled at or told that we were crazy, but usually people were quite civil, although abrupt.

Rejection after rejection made me desperate to see someone reach down and slide open the accordion-like metal gate that always stood between us and them, forcing us to look at everyone through a grid of diamond shapes. I felt worn down if, after three or more hours of knocking on doors, we weren't invited into a single home. This happened one afternoon when I was tracting with Elder Compton. We had spent four hours tracting through six floors of a government-subsidized housing estate. Each floor had forty-eight apartments. After we finished, we had knocked on two hundred eighty-eight doors in all, and there was someone at home in roughly half of the apartments.

Elder Compton and I walked to a corner store and bought ourselves two bottles of Green Spot, a brand of orange soda that was popular in Hong Kong at the time. We picked a position on the curb to rest a moment before heading home. I went over my approach in my mind. Was it my wording, my foreign accent, my smiling too much or too little? It could have been any or all of these things, but I didn't feel I had done anything differently than I usually had. I looked at my companion. As his senior I felt responsible for consoling him and helping him maintain a good level of morale, even if my own was low.

I was just going to say something when Elder Compton spoke first. "That was fun," he said. I didn't understand what he was he talking about. He couldn't have been referring to our tracting session. I had never heard of any missionary ever refer to tracting as fun. Was he talking about buying our sodas?

"What was fun?" I asked.

"When you were doing your door approaches," he said, "I was practicing my acting. Sometimes I would act really sad." He drooped the sides his mouth and slumped his shoulders. "And sometimes I would act happy . . ." His face brightened and his eyes doubled in size. ". . . or angry." He bunched up his forehead and tightened his lips.

Now I understood the reason for our complete failure. In the four hours that we had just spent asking people to let us into their homes, my companion had been standing next to me making exaggerated facial gestures. I took a deep, hard swig of Green Spot, trying to dilute the impact of what Elder Compton had just told me. I didn't know how to react or even what to think. Acting? I thought he wanted to be a writer. I said nothing. I stared at some children who were running around in a small playground in front of us.

I knew there would be challenges to doing the Lord's work, but this was a challenge I had never anticipated. I couldn't make sense of it. If my companion hadn't made those facial gestures, would we have gotten into someone's home, eventually converted them, and thereby ensured their eternal salvation? Had he destroyed someone's chance to go to the Celestial Kingdom with his acting practice? Was it possible that by merely manipulating the muscles in our faces for fun, we missionaries could sabotage the outcome of people's existence throughout all eternity, destroying their opportunity to learn about the test they were required to pass? And was I responsible for what my junior companion had just done? After thinking about it, I concluded that at the very least I was responsible for doing my best to prevent it from happening again.

"Don't ever do that again!" I said angrily. The shocked look on his face told me he had no idea why I was bothered by what he'd done.

I didn't have to endure Elder Compton's uniqueness for long. A couple of weeks after his tracting act, I was assigned a new companion.

The Boy Scout

I was paired with Elder James from June to August. Being assigned to a new companion was always like another new beginning, and with it I committed myself to working harder. There were two additional factors that worked as catalysts to my renewed commitment: the mission conference and my new companion's disposition.

At the mission conference, my sixth, President Smith told us we were baptizing far more females than males. We were instructed to focus our efforts on baptizing more men because there weren't enough priesthood holders in the local church community to fill all the positions that only males can fill. (The Church is a patriarchal society from top to bottom, so virtually every decision-making position is a male-only position. The Church simply cannot function without enough men to tell the women what to do.)

The mission conference also included a dire warning about listening to music, a rule I had been breaking at the time. During President Smith's talk, he pounded his fist on the pulpit to dramatize his words: "Every beat of the drum takes you one . . . step . . . closer to hell!" He said, "Missionaries who listen to music are definitely going to hell."

After the conference he instructed the district leaders and zone leaders to remain seated in the chapel and told everyone else to wait outside. He asked each of us leaders two questions: "Do the Elders in your apartment wake up on time?" and "Does anyone in your apartment listen to music?" I was one of the last Elders to be asked. Everyone before me had answered "Yes," and "No," respectively. I answered "No," and "Yes." In the end, I was the only one who gave those answers.

President Smith was pleased with me. He said he knew there were others who were breaking those rules but that I was the only one to admit it. On the train ride home I complained to other missionaries that I hoped he wouldn't make me a zone leader. I didn't want any more pressure than I already had. I later found out that one of the missionaries I was talking to developed a very bad impression of me that day, because he assumed I was saying the opposite of what I actually meant. He assumed I had ratted out the Elders in my district precisely for that reason: I *wanted* to be made a zone leader. He, like many missionaries, apparently couldn't comprehend that some Elders don't have ambitions to climb the mission political ladder, dreaming of one day reaching the highest rank—that of an ape. This is understandable. Mormon culture idolizes authority to a much greater degree than most.

* * *

Elder James, my new companion, was of medium height with dirty blond hair and a strong build. He always stood straight, almost as if at attention. Another Elder in my apartment accurately described Elder James as looking out of place without a Boy Scout uniform on. I got the immediate impression that he was going to be very obedient and dedicated. This, along with President Smith's warning of ending up in hell if I didn't stop listening to music, inspired me to turn myself around.

That night at the apartment, as we knelt down for evening prayer, I pulled out a cassette tape of Pink Floyd's *Animals* and destroyed it in front of everyone. I encouraged the other two Elders in the apartment who were listening to music to do the same with their music tapes, but they didn't take heed, and I didn't use my authority as district leader to force them. I was never a strict leader, probably because I would have felt like a hypocrite forcing others to keep rules I myself had broken at one time or another.

Tracting with Elder James was the same as it had been with Elder Compton, but it was much hotter in June and July. The diesel exhaust and dust added to the misery of Hong Kong's tropical heat. We were constantly sweaty, making the dust stick to our arms, necks, and faces.

Psychologically, proselytizing with Elder James was different. Whereas Elder Compton had been in his own personal fantasy world that I couldn't relate to, Elder James was in the collective fantasy world that I was a part of. I perfectly understood his way of thinking. He was serious about the work and ready to follow my lead. He wasn't a mindless follower looking to me for all the answers. He was assertive and made lots of suggestions, walking by my side as an equal. However, he always made it clear that I was ultimately in charge, and if I made a stupid decision, he would faithfully follow it even though he knew it was stupid. It made me feel like I needed to work hard and be serious.

Elder James helped to change my attitude about missionary work. Instead of constantly looking for miracles, I felt that my job was to put my shoulder to the wheel and push along. Despite being told that we could perform miracles, I concluded that missionary work was ultimately about knocking on doors and asking as many people as was physically possible to listen to what we had to say. Elder James's relentless, let's-go-knock-on-some-more-doors enthusiasm helped me to accept the idea that this busy work was what constituted a mission.

By now the first discussion was chiseled deeply into my brain. It had become boringly repetitious. While reciting the words and flipping through the pictures, I could now even watch a television that was running directly behind the person to whom I was speaking without missing a beat.

* * *

My seventh mission conference was a very different experience. A new mission president arrived to take Elder Smith's place. His name was President Clark, and he was a much kinder, gentler version of a mission president. The Asia **area representative** was there to announce the transition. He praised both Smith and Clark in very lofty terms, saying this transition was like Moses replacing Abraham. Both men were called of God, and were inspired directly by Him to guide the mission.

President Smith got up and gave his final speech. He said he was proud of us all, and that he would miss us terribly. He praised our efforts and said we were all doing a wonderful job. Throughout his talk, he spoke softly and kindly. In short, he didn't sound at all like himself. His behavior was entirely different in front of those two men sitting on the stand behind him.

President Clark then got up and spoke in the same way. We would later find out that this reflected his actual personality; he wasn't putting on a show. He really was a nice man. He told us to go about our business as usual, that he had a lot to learn, and that he looked forward to working with us. It was nice to sit through a mission conference without being belittled and told to perform miracles. President Clark could have been even more intimidating than President Smith if he had wanted to. He had a strong voice and stood a couple of inches over six feet. He looked liked a man who played football in college. But he never used these things to intimidate. He never pounded the pulpit or told us we were nothing. He always spoke to us softly, kindly, and with respect.

A large component of my new definition of missionary work included my own contributions. I no longer felt that I needed to witness spectacular miracles. I just needed to work hard, and any miracles that Heavenly Father decided to work through me would be subtle, perhaps in the form of a person deciding to open his or her door and invite us in. I no longer felt guilty or frustrated about not seeing obvious signs of His hand throughout my daily grind.

The message that we got in that first mission conference with President Clark was very different from the one we got in all of the previous conferences. It was much more in line with what I had come to realize from experience, which was that I couldn't expect to walk out of a mission conference and start walking on water. I knew that tracting would be as hard the next day as it had been the day before. At the same time, however, merely working hard and ending up with the predictable results of my labor was never going to be enough to satisfy me. I had to see at least little signs of the Lord's hand in my work.

* * *

We continued proselytizing, and, as expected, people reacted to us the same way they always had. Our own reactions varied at times, depending on the type of person we came in contact with. Early one afternoon, for example, we knocked on the door of an attractive girl in her early twenties. She answered the door wearing silk pajamas. Elder James told her who we were and what we were doing. To our surprise, the girl opened the door and let us in—a miracle perhaps. Her hair was unkempt and she looked as if she had recently woken up. I thought about how late she must have been up the night before to cause her to sleep until so late in the day.

After we presented the first discussion, we taught her how to say a simple Mormon-style prayer, which included four things:

1) Address God as "Heavenly Father" because he is literally our father in heaven.
2) Thank Him for what He has given you.
3) Ask Him to help you with something.
4) Finish by saying, "I say these things in the name of Jesus Christ, Amen."

This is something we always taught people after presenting the first discussion. Using this formula for communicating with Heavenly Father, people could ask Him if the things they had just heard were true. For those who felt too uncomfortable saying a prayer, we did it for them.

We explained all this to the girl, showing her the page in our flip chart with the four simple prayer instructions. We asked her to pray. Agreeing, she prayed to God and asked if the things we just said were true.

We had told her before the prayer, as we always told everyone, that the answer would come in the form of a good, comfortable feeling. After she finished her prayer, we waited for a moment in reverent silence with our heads bowed and our eyes closed. Then we slowly opened our eyes, lifted our heads, and calmly looked at her.

"Do you feel anything?" I asked.

"I'm not sure," she said. "Do you?"

You would think that those two words—Do you?—would be something that people often thought to ask us, but it was the first time anyone had ever thrown the question back at us. It threw me off balance. I wasn't sure how to respond. I knew that the correct answer was a confident "yes," but I hadn't felt anything out of the ordinary, and it seemed like an ironic thing to lie about, so I hesitated a moment.

Before I could respond, Elder James said, "No," admitting that he had not felt the Spirit. Then he asked her, "Do you know what 'worthy' means?" We often asked people if they knew what the word meant, because in Cantonese the religious term "worthy" is not in common use.

I knew exactly where he was going with that. We were commanded not to have lascivious thoughts, but we were nineteen-year-old boys. Genetically, we were no different than any other human boys. Obviously this girl was causing Elder James to have thoughts similar to those that were crossing my mind, and he realized that such thoughts prevented him from feeling the Spirit.

I wasn't sure exactly how he was going to explain his unworthiness, but I knew I couldn't let him proceed. The reason I knew this is because I very clearly understood something that all Mormons understand: as members, and especially as missionaries, we were public relations officers for The Church of Jesus Christ of Latter-day Saints. It was our duty to portray it in as good a light as possible, and a large part of that is done by presenting its members and missionaries as the cream of the human crop. That isn't done by admitting that an Elder is unworthy to feel the Spirit because he's fantasizing about a pretty investigator.

"I felt it," I said, cutting off Elder James. It was a lie, but it was something I instinctively knew I was supposed to do. I explained to the girl that sometimes answers don't come after a single prayer. I encouraged her to continue praying for an answer and asked if we could return. She wasn't interested, which was typical, so we left and never saw her again.

That experience made me think about the predicament we missionaries were in. We were supposed to be examples of righteousness and purity to the entire world's nonmember population. We therefore felt guilty if we were not righteous enough to feel the Spirit, and especially if we felt guilty of a sin. Yet we were put into situations under which any nineteen-year-old male would find it almost impossible not to have at least a flash of an impure thought, and all it takes is a flash to make one unworthy of the Spirit, and therefore to ignite guilt.

More significantly, this experience made me wonder about my testimony, which was based entirely on what I had been taught to believe were feelings from the Holy Ghost. I started asking myself uncomfortable questions. What had I felt after all those prayers that I had guided people to say after presenting the first discussion to them? Why was my testimony ("I know these things are true") written into the memorized discussions? My testimony was supposed to be real, personal, and expressed with conviction from the heart; it wasn't supposed to be a piece of memorized text. And regarding all the people I had converted up to that point on my mission, why did their socially based reasons for joining the Church seem far more evident to me than any sign of them actually knowing that the Church was true? For example, one of my converts was the elderly mother of a recently baptized member. The elderly woman was going senile and showed no indication that she comprehended what her baptism into the Church really meant.

Despite the fact that I saw no miracles in my work, I did not conclude that the Church was false. I still believed, at some level, that it was what it claimed to be. I didn't see it for what it truly was until many years after my mission. My questions didn't set me free even though they had the potential to do so. Instead, they made me miserable because I couldn't reconcile my beliefs with reality. There was a huge mismatch, and that depressed me. Because I was depressed, I started listening to music again. And that depressed me even more.

My Testimony is Further Challenged

A Mormon missionary's one and only purpose is to baptize (or "to dunk") as many people as possible. To become a member of the Church, a person has to be baptized. Therefore, "getting baptisms" is equated with getting people to join the Church. At the time I was a missionary, the Church spent a very small fraction of its income, probably less than a quarter of one percent, on humanitarian aid; and while I was a self-paying missionary in its service, I spent none of my time on humanitarian efforts, though I would have gladly and obediently done so were that to have been my assignment.[22]

---

22. In fact, the degree to which virtually every active Mormon is willing to perform any Church-assigned humanitarian project—called a service project—is quite impressive. Service projects are understandably considered to be a great missionary tool. If Mormons are willing to do good things so eagerly, even if it's for a combination of the right and wrong reasons, it's difficult to criticize them for it.

I knew I wasn't being sent to fight for justice or to help the poor, but that was all right. Simply converting people was good enough as long as the Church was true, and it had to be true. And because of what I had been taught all my life I expected to see some evidence from above, rather than just the results that one would expect from one's own labor. I couldn't help but notice, however, that after months of continuously trying, our prayers didn't get us into any more doors than one would expect without superhuman intervention.

If this was caused by my lack of faith, then why hadn't any of my companions fared any better? And if it was because they were hindered by my unworthy presence, then why did none of them say there was a difference in success between tracting with me and tracting with their previous companions? Also, if my unworthiness was the cause of our entirely unremarkable results, then why did I end up with the better-than-average success rate of one baptism per month?

Other signs occasionally appeared that forced me to see the fruits of our labor in very natural, humanistic terms. For example, President Smith had previously announced that we were baptizing too many girls, and that we therefore needed to focus our efforts on converting more men. I thought back on that in the light of seeing my mission more and more as a product of human efforts. It seemed to me that a larger number of female converts is exactly what one would expect from a group of missionaries comprised mostly of nineteen-to-twenty-one-year-old boys. The fact that the mission president told us to focus on a certain sector of the population made me think that mission strategies were nothing more than a man-made marketing plan.

I did not at all expect my mission to be what it was: a sales job. I knew that a missionary's success was based on the number of baptisms he or she was able to get, but the official story was that those baptisms were the direct result of a missionary's ability to tune into the prompt-ings of the Holy Ghost. Missionaries who are obedient and worthy will be guided by the Spirit to find people who are ready to hear about the gospel, the end result being a large number of baptisms. I therefore expected my mission to be one spiritual experience after another, at least during the times I was keeping all the mission rules. That was the official view of the mission experience, and that was the view I bought.

Needless to say, my way of thinking was naïve, but it was typical of missionaries. Instead of experiencing the envisioned year and a half of non-stop spiritual events, I experienced rejection at one door after another. It was a sales job that literally wore holes in my shoes. It was nothing but hard work, with no evidence of inspiration guiding me or any of my fellow missionaries.

I came to realize that our plans of action were not guided by divine intervention. They were guided by marketing strategies and goal setting. Very little of what we did and said was left to chance. Even our testimonies, proclaiming that we "knew" that the Church was true, were a written part of the memorized lessons that we taught to people. This ensured that everything was presented just right. We were using polished techniques to sell our product. The product was club membership. The selling price was one baptism, ten per cent of one's income, and a lifetime of commitment. Comprehending the realities of my mission work challenged my testimony.

The long, drawn out process of questioning what, to that point, had been a given—that the Church is true, and that it explains our existence and purpose—was heart wrenching, and it dragged on for a very long time. The core of my world view was challenged and threatened throughout my mission because I never saw any sign of the inspiration that I had assumed was going to constantly guide me as a missionary. All I saw in the way of "conversions" were the predictable results of standard sales efforts and friendly socializing—what the Church calls fellowshipping, a very calculated form of befriending people for the sole purpose of converting them.

My testimony was battered and weakened, but its roots were strong. It would never again be what it was from the age of sixteen (my personal conversion) through the first half of my mission. Nevertheless it would not die off completely for at least ten more years. The Church's mind-molding techniques are indeed very effective. John and Marjorie Hasler were right when they concluded that "[y]ears of [indoctrination] had laid a foundation that [I] could reject, perhaps, but not ignore. Once truth is etched in the heart by the Spirit of the Holy Ghost, it becomes an integral part of a person and must be dealt with. A child so taught will never be the same!"[23]

---

23. "Train Up a Child," by John W. and Marjorie E. Hasler, *Ensign*, April 1999, p. 50.

A Sales Job

"Although the research department at LDS Church headquarters has carried out a number of research projects on the conversion process in the United States and other countries of the world, findings from this research remain outside the public domain."

—Marie Cornwall, Introduction to *Contemporary Mormonism: Social Science Perspectives*, p. 3

Just like all sales cultures, the mission field strives for maximum results. To this end, our lives were extremely regimented. This was to ensure that we were in contact with potential converts as much as was humanly possible. Our daily routine was as follows:

6:30–9:30 a.m.	Wake up; exercise; shower and dress; eat breakfast; study Cantonese; read scriptures
9:30 a.m–12:30 p.m.	Proselytize
12:30–1:30	Eat lunch
1:30–5:30	Proselytize
5:30–6:30	Eat dinner
6:30–9:30	Proselytize
9:30–10:30	Unwind; tell jokes; reminisce about life back home; go to bed

Under both Presidents Smith and Clark, we were trained to both expect miraculous guidance and to be effective salespeople. The difference between the two presidents was one of emphasis. Under President Smith, I saw a huge discrepancy between the miracles he promised us and the miracles we saw. Under President Clark, there were no discrepancies. He didn't talk much about miracles, and the ones he did talk about were the ones that were so subtle and after the fact that they were easy to see. For example, each time someone chose to be baptized, it was a miracle that proved we had been guided to that person's door, and also proved that the Church was true.

President Clark emphasized sales tactics rather than miracles, and because the miracles he talked about were not really miracles, there were no contradictions with reality. It made life simpler, but it also made it easier for me to see my mission for what it was: a sales job.

Few people are born salespeople, but most people can be made into salespeople with proper training. In addition to the mission conference pep talks, we had a mission-wide retreat that July that included training seminars. The best missionaries—those with the highest numbers of baptisms—taught the rest of us how to improve our results. My baptism rate was only slightly better than average, one baptism per month, and I had been on my mission less than a year, so I was not qualified to train other missionaries.

One missionary in particular reminded me of a typical sales trainer. He spoke quickly, loudly, and authoritatively. In his training session, he didn't talk about prayer or learning to recognize Heavenly Father's guidance. He and the other trainers all talked about the wordings of door approaches, the way to stand, how to effectively engage people in idle conversation as a lead-in to presenting the first discussion, how to get them to commit to a return visit, commit to attending Church, and commit to getting baptized. The training sessions were all about the art of persuasion.

One constant throughout my and my fellows' missions was a continuous regimen of goal setting: how many *Books of Mormon* we were going to sell during a particular week or month; how many investigators we were going to generate during the week or month; how many people we would "challenge" (an interesting choice of terminology) to get baptized that week or month; or how many people we would actually baptize that week or month.

We learned all the standard goal-setting techniques. We learned how to set practical goals so as not to discourage ourselves, but yet to choose goals that would stretch us, ensuring that we worked hard. Our district and zone leaders would help us to evaluate our goals, judge our success at achieving them, and then discuss with us how to refine our goal setting so as to improve future performance. Everything we did was very practical and well organized, and consisted of time tested sales techniques.

Tied in with all of this were motivational programs. Hunger is always a good motivating force, so one program had us refrain from eating lunch until we had sold at least one *Book of Mormon*. (*Books of Mormon* were sold inexpensively for "the cost of publishing." I assume that was to create a psychological incentive in people to read it since they had made a token sacrifice to get it.)

One motivational program took the concept of hunger to a rhetorical and metaphorical level. President Clark decided we should be "hungry" for baptisms. He concluded that yelling "I am hungry!!" at the top of our lungs would be a good way to start off each day. He apparently believed that such an act would give us a psychological charge.

District leaders were in charge of directing the motivational programs. That meant me, so every morning during the "hungry" phase of my mission, I gathered the Elders in the Kwun Tong apartment together before proselytizing and led them in an "I am hungry!!" yell. Good yells were accompanied by clenched fists, inflated chests, and bared molars. It was a great way to take us back to our primitive roots.

A fellow missionary told me an "I am hungry!" story about two Elders in the Kwai Hing apartment, the first apartment I lived in. The two Elders were an interesting match. Elder Hanes was a hefty six-foot-two Californian who weighed in at about two hundred thirty pounds. Elder Hanes's companion was Elder Ng from Hong Kong. Elder Ng was about five foot four and weighed roughly one hundred ten pounds.

Yelling such motivational phrases is not something the average Chinese person would feel comfortable doing, but Elder Ng always gave it his best. Elder Hanes, on the other hand, thought that the whole idea was dumb and refused to participate. He stood motionless and silent while the rest of the Kwai Hing Elders scared their next door neighbors. Such non-participation in these types of programs was not unusual. We were all self-paying "volunteers," so none of us felt at risk of being fired.

One morning Elder Hanes yet again rolled his eyes while the other three yelled, "I am hungry!" The four Elders then left the apartment together to begin their day. The elevator serving the odd-numbered floors had been out of order for a few days, so they had to walk down one flight of stairs to the twelfth floor to use the elevator that served the even-numbered floors.

When they were about halfway down in the elevator, Elder Hanes was overcome with a mischievous urge to do something he thought would be incredibly funny. He dropped halfway into a squat and then catapulted himself into the air. "I am," he bellowed in mid-flight, "hungry!!" he roared as he crashed onto the elevator floor. The elevator jerked violently and jolted to a stop.

They all stood there for a moment in stunned silence as the elevator gently swayed and groaned within the confines of the elevator shaft.

Elder Ng looked up into Elder Hanes' eyes and in broken English said, "I am dangerous!"

They managed to pry open the elevator's inner doors. There was a three-foot gap between the floor of the elevator and the top of the sixth-floor elevator doorway, so Elder Hanes knelt down and pried the doors open. They climbed through the gap and, hanging from the floor of the elevator, dropped one by one onto the floor of the sixth-floor hallway. There were now no working elevators in the building, forcing them to take the stairs the rest of the way down, slapping the dust from their trousers as they went.

When Elder Hanes and Elder Ng returned for lunch a few hours later, the elevator that served the odd-numbered floors still displayed an "out of service" sign, just as it had for several days. Next to it, inside the shaft of the even-numbered elevator, were two repairmen trying to figure out what had caused it to break down that morning.

Elder Hanes was embarrassed and ashamed to have broken the only working elevator in the building. He felt bad about the inconvenience he had brought to the lives of everyone who lived there. He didn't fully realize how bad a person could feel, however, until he had walked up the first flight of stairs and had rounded the corner to the second flight.

Looking up, he saw a frail woman who appeared to be in her seventies. She was scaling the stairs backwards. Each step she took was exceedingly strenuous work because she had to lean forward each time to dead lift a fifty-pound bag of rice from the step below up to the step she was standing on. She then back-stepped up another step and repeated the process. The instant Elder Hanes saw her, his heart fell straight to his belly and his jaw dropped. What had he done?!

He sprang his huge frame up the stairs toward her and offered assistance. "Let me help you, grandma," he said, which is the standard way to address an elderly woman in Chinese.

"Thank you. Thank you very much," she said. "Thank you." She was understandably very grateful.

Elder Hanes hefted the bag of rice over a shoulder. Using the handrail to steady himself, he wondered how the old woman had possibly gotten as far with the heavy load as she had. "Which floor do you live on?"

"The twenty-first," she said with a large smile and a look of relief.

Causeway Bay

At the next transfer, after my eighth mission conference, I was moved to Causeway Bay. I was the district leader over the six Elders in that district's apartment. I was quite disillusioned by this point, and I felt terribly homesick. I had started counting the days until I could go home. Boredom, mild depression, and twenty-year-old hormones were all taking their toll. My twentieth birthday came a week after the transfer, and a birthday is not usually a happy event for missionaries; it makes them think about where they are in life, and few are satisfied with the progress of their missions. A mission birthday is spent away from family and friends and, unlike all previous birthdays, is spent doing exactly the same things that are done every other day. On top of all that my parents sent news that they were moving away from my hometown, which meant that I wouldn't be returning to my friends back home.

For my birthday, I received a box of goodies from home, which included a bag of Nacho Cheese-flavored Doritos®. The monosodium glutamate and artificial flavoring spread over my tongue like processed manna from heaven. It is amazing how much you miss the simplest things when you haven't had them for a long time. It was wonderful, but a bag of chips can only improve one's life so much.

My new companion, Elder Roberts, had a very pleasant, easygoing personality. He laughed gently at everyone's jokes, even when they were at his expense. He was intelligent enough to understand everyone's humor and mature enough to never take anything personally. This was a helpful trait, particularly with another apartment mate, Elder Laughlin, who was bright and witty and loved to poke fun at other people. Elder Laughlin was very tall with blond hair and baby-face features. He had started his mission at the same time I did. Like many Elders, he occasionally broke the rule against reading things not published by the Church. His choice of reading material was an American history textbook, and he couldn't seem to understand why anyone would think that was odd.

Elder Laughlin's own companion, Elder Stans, was not so mature. He misinterpreted any joke that could possibly be misinterpreted. He always felt insulted and couldn't bear the thought of someone having a better time than him. This made splits a sensitive issue. I didn't mind being with Elder Roberts at all but, as is normal in missionary life, I had to go on splits occasionally. It didn't matter whether I paired myself up with Elder Laughlin (which I enjoyed because of his intelligent humor), or with Elder Stans. In either case, Elder Stans complained. He always assumed that the pair of Elders that he was not a part of was going to do something fun.

Elder Roberts' compliant nature led him to willingly go along with all of my suggestions. This was different than it had been with Elder Compton, who went along with everything I said out of a sense of duty. Elder Roberts did so because he was good at going with the flow. If I felt like slacking off, which was becoming more of a temptation for me, Elder Roberts was happy to comply. Interestingly, he could both work hard alongside me without slowing down, and he could blow off a session of tracting without any noticeable sign of guilt. That made it easier for me. If I believed I was causing a reluctant but compliant companion to feel guilty, I would have felt bad about what I was doing to that companion.

Every morning we rode the tram from Causeway Bay to our area in North Point. At the end of the tram's journey, the tracks looped around a block so that the tram could turn around and make its return trip. Every time it made this loop, and before we got off, the tram drove through the middle of a block-long street market. We enjoyed this part of the journey, and we therefore always sat on the upper deck of the tram in the front seats so that we could look down at the mass of heads shifting to and fro throughout the market. The market was always so crowded, and the crowd always surrounded the tram so completely, that it literally looked as if we were floating above a sea of black-haired people as the tram crept along at a snail's pace, ringing its bell to warn people off the track.

Sitting on the upper level put us even with the second-floor apartments on either side of the street. Clothes hung out of people's windows to dry, some on bamboo poles, and some on hangers that clung to window frames. We saw people living their lives—cooking, cleaning, or perhaps lounging in front of the TV.

This was fascinating to us, and after exiting the tram, we never got tired of walking back through the market before we began tracting. Compared to tracting, just about anything in the world is interesting. There were shops along both sides of the street, as well as tables set up along the edges of the road itself. Each vendor specialized in some variety of food. Some shops were filled with dried fish, dried fish bladders, pickled vegetables, and an assortment of Chinese herbs and seasonings. Other shops were filled with fresh lettuce, bak choi, tung choi, Chinese broccoli, and other vegetables.

There were shops with fresh cuts of meat. Large slabs of beef and pork, along with tongues, hearts and intestines hung from hooks above the butchers' cutting boards. A truck would drive through each morning with its bed full of gutted pig carcasses. The truck would stop at the shops that sold pork and deliver their orders, two pigs here, three there. Each time it stopped, a couple of shirtless deliverymen would hop out and scurry around to the back of the truck. A third man on the truck bed would push a pig carcass onto the open gate of the truck so a delivery man could heft it onto one of his shoulders. The delivery man then carried the carcass, blood dripping down his back, into a customer's shop.

A market-sized pig must weigh well over a hundred pounds, even after being gutted. To set down his heavy load, the delivery man would squat slightly, then quickly straighten his legs and lean forward, pulling the head of the pig downward. The carcass's back legs would spring over his shoulder and arc up, around, and down towards the ground. With a loud slap, the pig would strike the cement floor and jiggle violently like a dish of peach pudding tossed onto a kitchen counter. It would then lie unceremoniously in this pitiful state, ignored like every other perfectly normal part of Hong Kong life, until it was set on a hook and hung face down, where it would wait to be cut into edible bits.

The smells changed with every few paces, from that of salty pickled vegetables, to raw meat, to freshly baked bread, to fish, to barbequed pork, to braised goose, to live chickens. The fish stalls displayed swimming fish alongside flailing, dying ones and freshly killed ones.

Our proselytizing in this area was all done in private buildings, which included the ones that lined the two sides of the market. In between the shops, stairwells led to homes. To their residents, the bustling market we were so intrigued by was simply the street in front of their house, no more unusual to them than the street in front of anyone's house is to the people living there. The taller residential buildings in Hong Kong have elevators, but most buildings with eight floors or less don't. The stairwells of these short buildings are narrow, usually dirty, and seldom well lit. Tracting in buildings like these was much slower going than it had been in the government housing estates, because there were only two to four homes per floor.

Mandy

On my first Sunday in Causeway Bay, Elder Roberts and I stood at the entrance to the chapel to greet everyone as they arrived. "Hello brother. Hello sister," I said, shaking their hands. "Welcome to church." A strikingly pretty girl named Mandy and her mother were nearly the last to arrive. The girl shook my hand firmly and held onto it just long enough to start me thinking. She then lingered and talked, paying a lot of attention to me. Without warning, my evolutionary imperative rushed to the surface like a leak-proof basketball that had been forced to the bottom of a swimming pool, held there for more than a year, and then suddenly released.

If that had been the extent of our contact and I had never seen her again, I might not even remember her now. But that didn't happen. I went to church three more times during my one-month stay in Causeway Bay, and so did she. Not only did her interest in me not fade, it grew. And I was much too polite to ignore the attention of an attractive girl.

There was a Chinese Elder named Elder Tang living in our apartment. I paired myself up with him a couple of times during the month that I was the leader of the Causeway Bay District. One of those times we were let into an apartment by two T-shirted girls in their early twenties who were obviously not wearing bras. I had progressed, digressed, or whatever one chooses to call it, significantly by that time and allowed myself to look—discretely of course—without feeling terrible about myself. After all, I had no control over what those girls chose to wear. The former prophet, Spencer W. Kimball, may have sympathized. He once said that he wondered "if our sisters realize the temptation they are flaunting before men when they leave their bodies partly uncovered or dress in tight-fitting, body-revealing, form-fitting sweaters."[24] He obviously had a vivid imagination.

On the way back home on the tram, I could see that the Chinese Elder looked extremely unhappy. There was a very noticeable differ-

24. Kimball, Spencer W. *The Miracle of Forgiveness*. Salt Lake City: Bookcraft, 1977, p. 226.

ence between how he looked on the way out and how he looked now, on the way back. I asked him what was wrong. He said that even after so much effort over such a long time, he still had bad thoughts. Obviously his thoughts were not clean when he saw the outlines of those girls' breasts so clearly through their T-shirts, and he felt terribly guilty. I didn't feel guilty for having had the same kinds of thoughts; it just made me think how interesting it was that he could be so much like a typical American Mormon. The belief system of Mormonism apparently translates itself into other languages and cultures very effectively.

Aberdeen

One month after my arrival at Causeway Bay I was transferred to Aberdeen, located at the southern tip of Hong Kong Island. My ninth conference was delayed a day, because the day that the transfer was supposed to take place a number 10 typhoon hit Hong Kong.

I later learned that Elder Compton had befriended a homeless man who slept on a sidewalk near the apartment that Compton lived in at the time of the typhoon. He had given the homeless man an English name: Henry, with a silent "H." He would chat with Henry going to and from his proselytizing area, and frequently bought things for him from the bakery.

When the typhoon hit, Elder Compton was worried about Henry, and he wanted to go out and see if he could find him and bring him back to the apartment. Elder Compton's district leader stood in front of the door and physically prevented him from leaving the apartment. The district leader felt responsible for Compton and wouldn't risk letting him go out in a number 10 typhoon where he could easily get hurt. He probably also felt it would be a serious breach of the rules to allow some stranger to spend the night in the apartment. We were proselytizers, not humanitarians. Elder Compton resented what his district leader did. He never saw Henry again after that, and wondered if perhaps he didn't survive the typhoon. I think Elder Compton basically had the right idea about what something called "a mission" should be.

Thou Shalt Not Leave Thy Companion's Side

The mother of all rules—the one that helps to ensure that all the others are kept—requires missionaries to remain in the presence of their companions every second of every day. Being in different rooms while at the apartment is acceptable, but rarely is it considered acceptable outside the apartment. The function of this rule is obvious: anything a missionary says or does will be witnessed by his or her companion. To make this rule as effective as possible, companionships are chosen carefully to avoid the pairing up of two notorious rule breakers, or even two missionaries who get along too well.

The natural result is that a lot of companionships are social disasters. This creates the desire, more likely the need, for switches. These are arranged by either a zone leader or a district leader, so obviously leaders can use switches to their advantage if they want to; they can pair themselves up with missionaries they get along with.

There were only two pairs of Elders in Aberdeen. I got along quite well with Elder Sharp, a large, strong Elder who not only admired, but also exemplified, the American macho male. At the sales training retreat, Elder Sharp wrestled with his closest match, another large brute who was a wrestling star in high school. With their ties removed and shirt sleeves rolled up, they pushed, pulled, grabbed and rammed each other's bodies in an attempt to flatten their opponent face-up on the grass. A crowd of Elders surrounded them and cheered them on. After they finished, an Elder who had arrived too late said, "Oh, I missed it. I wanted to see a fight." When Elder Sharp walked out of the circle, he drove a clenched fist into that Elder's stomach, leaving him hunched over and groaning. The Elder got to see a fight after all, though it was probably shorter and much more one-sided than he would have liked.

Elder Sharp was one of the best story tellers I'd ever met, and he had done enough crazy things growing up to provide a long list of fascinating tales, like the one where he wrestled with two policemen and managed to get their heads under his arms, one on each side, and bashed them together. Needless to say, he also had a story or two to tell about visits to jail. Some of his stories were rather hard to believe, but he gave enough colorful detail leading up to the unbelievable parts that one couldn't help but be entertained. One was left either believing the story or not caring whether it was true or not.

Unfortunately my companion was Elder Metcalfe, whom I didn't find entertaining because he was far too serious. I couldn't relate to him. He was one of those boys that girls seem to like and other boys can't understand why. He was tall, slender, and well proportioned. His seriousness and his round-rimmed glasses gave him the appearance of a university professor in the making.

Elder Sharp's companion was Elder Bird, a lanky boy who stared intently at Elder Sharp every time they were in the elevator together. Elder Sharp was so annoyed by it that one day he suddenly yelled at Elder Bird, telling him to cut it out. Elder Bird went wide eyed with shock. He told Elder Sharp that he hadn't realized it bothered him. A few hours later, when they had returned from proselytizing and were riding the elevator again, Elder Bird stood in silence, staring at Elder Sharp.

One day Elder Bird received a letter from his father. It was a very emotional thing for him. He told Elder Sharp it was the first time in his entire life that his father had ever written a letter to him. At dinner that evening, Elder Sharp said, "So what did your father say?"

"Oh, the usual," said Elder Bird.

I arranged splits as often as I could, keeping in mind that my companion, Elder Metcalfe, did not like being paired up with Elder Bird. Occasionally I mixed up the splits to camouflage my intentions, spending a few tracting sessions with Elder Bird. It was difficult to keep a straight face when Elder Bird was presenting a discussion. He struggled with the tones of Cantonese. In an apparently conscious effort to differentiate the high tones from the low tones, he used a very wide tonal range. He set his high tones at a pitch that was uncomfortable for him, so that every time he spoke, it was like someone singing a song that is beyond their range. The tendons in his neck tensed and protruded as he told people in a strained and cracking voice about Joseph Smith being visited by Heavenly Father and Jesus Christ. It was all I could do to keep myself from bursting out laughing, even though I knew that doing so would be sacrilege.

Pray with Me

One night Elder Metcalfe and I returned home a little early from our evening proselytizing. We got out of our uncomfortable suits and sat and talked in the living room while we waited for Elders Sharp and Bird to return. As we talked, Elder Metcalfe shared an experience of his from a few months prior that involved a local church member. Apparently the member had become possessed by an evil spirit and was flailing around on the floor and drooling. Elder Metcalfe's companion at the time, a local Chinese, was happy to cast the spirit away, but he needed help. In order to facilitate the exorcism for his companion, Elder Metcalfe held the flopping Church member down.

There was poor Elder Metcalfe, in the foyer of one of Hong Kong's LDS church buildings, sitting on top of a local member's chest. It took all of his strength to hold the possessed man's arms down. Surrounding this spectacle was a crowd of curious churchgoers. The Chinese Elder stood with his right arm raised to the square and loudly commanded the evil spirit to leave. This was done in Cantonese "by the power of the Holy Melchizedek priesthood," the branch of priesthood power vested in all male missionaries, giving them the authority, among other things, to cast away evil spirits.

Elder Metcalfe was too preoccupied to notice the crowd. Understandably, struggling to hold down a possessed man was scaring the living daylights out of him. Eventually the evil spirit departed and the man calmed down. After a while the two elders escorted him home.

I thought it was a pretty decent story, especially considering that it came first hand. I figured it was only fair that in return I share with Elder Metcalfe a few of the fourth- or fifth-hand (more likely the hundredth-hand) stories that I had heard. They were the standard missionary narratives described earlier. Elder Metcalfe shared some of the same types of stories that he had heard as well.

All of a sudden, he urged that we change the subject, because we were inviting evil spirits to appear by talking about these things. I agreed, and we sat for a moment in silence. Then, without warning, Elder Metcalfe knelt down with his arms leaning on the couch and began to pray. I thought that was a very odd thing to do. Although it was getting close to bedtime, and missionaries are supposed to pray nightly before retiring, it is not normal practice to suddenly kneel down in the living room next to another missionary without warning and begin to pray. He looked up at me after a minute of silent prayer. His face was ghostly pale, and he looked utterly terrified. He asked me to pray with him.

I knelt beside him and listened as he offered an unconventional prayer. Actually it wasn't a prayer at all by Mormon standards. It was more of a declaration: "God is good. God is powerful. Satan has no power over me." After saying this a few times he stood up, removed his glasses, and began pacing the room. He repeated those few sentences over and over. He walked straight and tall with a look of studied determination. He had a scholarly appearance, tapping the air with his glasses to complement the rhythm of his utterances. His attire, however, made it impossible to take him nearly as seriously as he was acting. He was wearing only his temple garments, which look like loose-fitting polyester long johns with a short-sleeved top and knee-length bottoms.

I didn't know how to react to his behavior. I was uncomfortable, not because I was afraid that Satan was going to get us, but because he was breaking the rules of normal social behavior and I didn't know how to respond. He wasn't doing any harm, so I just looked on with interest. He decided he needed a longer place to pace, so he opened the door of our apartment and walked out into the hallway. This concerned me because our neighbors could have seen him. Being keenly aware of how important image was to the type of sales-oriented mission we were serving, I persuaded him to come back inside.

He eventually calmed down enough to sit still and to stop verbally reassuring himself that Satan had no power over him. It was then that we heard the rattling sound of our front door's gate being opened. It was the other two Elders returning home later than usual. "I'd like you to give me a blessing," Elder Metcalfe said quickly in a soft whisper, "but I don't want them to know what it's for."

I immediately understood that he was embarrassed about what had just happened. I had to think quickly. He wanted me to give him a blessing that would help him resolve his problem, yet I couldn't specifically mention his problem in the blessing. But what exactly was his problem? Was it merely the fear of becoming possessed by an evil spirit, perhaps Satan himself, or was it that he was actually at risk of becoming possessed? Even at the time, I concluded it was the former.

I tried to act natural so that Elders Sharp and Bird wouldn't suspect anything unusual. After they had removed their jackets, ties, shoes, and badges, I told them that Elder Metcalfe wanted me to give him a blessing, but I didn't say why, and out of respect to both my authority and Elder Metcalfe's privacy they didn't ask.

In preparation for the blessing we positioned one of the dining chairs at the center of the room for Elder Metcalfe to sit on. We followed the proper procedures that all blessings must strictly adhere to in order to be official. The three of us gathered around Elder Metcalfe.

From a small vial, I poured a drop of previously consecrated olive oil onto my index finger. I rubbed it into the crown of Elder Metcalfe's scalp and then laid my hands upon his head. The other two Elders both placed their hands upon mine. Then I blessed Elder Metcalfe "in the name of Jesus Christ, and through the power of the Holy Melchizedek Priesthood," a power that I, a twenty-year-old "Elder of Israel," had. In the blessing, I said that he would soon feel better and that the Holy Ghost would comfort him and help him overcome the adversities he was presently experiencing.

My benign blessing made no mention of his fear of becoming possessed. The other two missionaries who helped me with the blessing, therefore, had no idea what it was about and they didn't ask. I was their district leader and they were instinctively respectful of my right to secrecy regarding sacred matters.

Elder Metcalfe had always been too serious for my taste, and now he was becoming a little spooky. Splits with Elder Sharp were becoming more and more of a pleasure. When I received the call from the zone leader that month, he told me that no one in my apartment would be moving, that everyone was to remain in Aberdeen with no changes. As soon as the zone leader said this, an idea for a practical joke popped into my head. After hanging up the phone I announced that none of us would be moving, but that we were to switch companions. I said that Elder Sharp was going to be my companion, and that Elder Metcalfe and Elder Bird were to be each others' companions.

I thought they might believe it for a second or two, but no longer than that. As their district leader, however, I suppose I was believable and, therefore, believed. My keeping a straight face also helped. Elder Sharp tried not to appear too happy. It was obvious, though, that he was suppressing a smile. At the same time Elder Metcalfe was very unhappy about this new setup. After a few minutes of sitting on the sofa staring into space, he asked who would sleep in which room. I said it didn't matter, and he and Elder Sharp quickly came to an agreement on their own and started moving their things from one bedroom to the other.

This was going much further than I expected, and I was tempted to try to get away with it. But the chances of getting caught were high, and I have always hated practical jokes that go too far, so I told them it was only a joke. It's interesting that by this point of my mission I was actually tempted to override an arrangement that came from above, supposedly originating from God himself. I was a different missionary from the one who first arrived in Kwai Hing, happy to have an old crumbling foam pad for a bed, ready to accept any kind of suffering the Lord wanted me to endure.

I didn't allow myself to arrange a permanent split, but I still arranged as many daily splits with Elder Sharp as I thought I could reasonably get away with. Over the next few weeks we became less and less missionary like. One Sunday evening Elder Sharp and I decided to go to a movie. Even regular members are not supposed to break the Sabbath by watching a movie on Sunday, let alone missionaries.

We laid our money on the counter and asked for two movie tickets. The girl behind the counter looked up and said, "Elders, it's Sunday!" She was a member working at the cinema and reproached us for breaking the Sabbath. Her remark startled us so much that we immediately scurried away without saying a word, like little children caught in the act of stealing some candy.

Before long, I started breaking much more serious rules. One P-day that month, I went to the mission home with Elder Metcalfe to pick up the letters for our apartment. Among the small pile was a letter from Mandy. After I read her simple letter that said nothing very interesting, except for the sentence that expressed a desire to see me, I wrote her back.

The next phone call from the zone leader scared me. I was transferred to the mission home. President Clark wanted me to be his personal secretary. I didn't want to work with the president so closely on a daily basis. My mother saw it differently. When I wrote home about it, she was incredibly proud. The bishop in our ward back home told her that my new calling was even more important than that of assistant to the president (ape), because I would be working even more closely with the president than an ape does. Perhaps she thought I was still on my way to becoming a prophet. I'm sure she must have told lots of members in her new ward about my being assigned as secretary to the president.

Kowloon Tong

I was the president's secretary for four months, with three different companions. My mornings and afternoons were spent typing and arranging appointments, and each evening was spent proselytizing. At first I was a little intimidated about being around the president so much, but I quickly got used to it. The relationship became very much like a working relationship, which made it hard for me to see him as a man of God. He was just a typical man.

I was privy to all the information that officially went out of the mission. I typed a letter to the parents of every missionary who was about to go home. It was a form letter that raved about each missionary's accomplishments. It talked about his or her spiritual growth and said that he or she had learned to speak Cantonese almost like a native speaker. When I typed these exact same words to Elder Bird's parents, it made me realize that nothing in any of the letters was sincere. But they made all the mothers proud, I'm sure. (After I returned home from my mission, my mother refused to listen to me when I told her it was a form letter. She wanted to believe that her son was especially good at learning languages.)

In the mission home, my companion and I slept in a large bedroom with the apes. Six Elders slept on three bunk beds. There were never any sisters living in the mission home because sisters never hold positions of authority. I felt as at home there as anywhere else, and felt much less pressure since I was no longer the most senior in the apartment, despite my mother's opinion about the superiority of my new position.

During each mission conference I had chances to talk to the missionaries that I had befriended during my mission. We would swap stories with each other, and in the process I heard about two separate instances in which Elders got too friendly with local girls. One Elder put his hand up a girl's shirt and another Elder down a girl's pants. Both Elders confessed to the president. Of course they were reprimanded, but they were both allowed to continue their missions.

It was becoming clear that the things I'd been warned about before my mission, and in the MTC, were not as rare as I'd thought. The degree to which missionaries engage in this kind of behavior is certainly only a tiny fraction of the degree to which average nineteen-to-twenty-four-year-old boys engage in it. But Mormon Elders are normal human beings, so it is naïve to think that sexual activity could somehow be entirely wiped out of their lives. My world view had never included the idea that Elders were just average boys, however, so I was shocked to find this out. It was what the farmhand on the pig farm had tried to tell me. It was what my sister-in-law and the GAs at the MTC had warned me about. But it wasn't until I saw it for myself that I was able, or more likely willing, to believe it.

From the night I gave him a blessing onward, Elder Metcalfe regularly feared that he was in imminent danger of becoming possessed by an evil spirit. When I was still his companion in Aberdeen, we slept each night with the light on in our room. During especially stressful evenings he called the mission president, no matter what the time of night. This continued after I moved into the mission home, and in an effort to eliminate this annoyance, the mission president created a new position in the mission home especially for Elder Metcalfe. This caused some contention because Elder Metcalfe wanted to sleep with the lights on and the other Elders who slept in the mission home apartment refused.

Serving a mission is accurately described as excellent preparation for marriage. An Elder spends more time with his companion than any husband ever does with his wife. One cannot possibly go through the experience without learning at least something about the art of compromise. Living with Elder Metcalfe was especially helpful to me because my wife has also insisted a couple of times on sleeping with the light on to keep away the same kinds of nasty spirits that Elder Metcalfe was fearful of, those that are afraid of light.

Tsuen Wan

Assignments in one district rarely lasted for more than four months, so after four months as secretary to the president it was time for a change. Apparently there were no positions for district leaders anywhere in the mission, so I became just an ordinary senior companion, which was fine with me.

My new companion was Elder Shipps, a slightly gaunt Elder with brown hair. He wore a brown suit and a brown tie every day. He was nice and easygoing, but he didn't say much, even when you wanted him to. President Clark told me that Elder Shipps needed a lot of help with his Cantonese and said that that was why he was pairing him up with me. Elder Shipps' Cantonese didn't actually seem that bad to me; he'd only been in Hong Kong for three months. It was probably a little below average, but that may just have been because he was such a quiet person. Maybe people like that take a little longer to acquire a second language. Whether the help I gave Elder Shipps had any effect, I don't know. In fact I doubt it, but at the end of the month President Clark was thrilled with Elder Shipps' improvement and praised my success.

* * *

During my time as secretary, I had written a couple of letters to Mandy each month. Now that I was out of the mission home and in no position of responsibility, it was easier for me to develop my relationship with her. In the evenings, after all the other missionaries in the apartment had gone to sleep, I would call her on the phone and have long meaningless conversations. I had turned into the disillusioned missionary who I couldn't comprehend a year prior. I was now breaking the same important mission rule that he had been when I was living with him in Kwun Tong, and it would lead to my breaking other, much more serious rules.

A Match Made in Heaven

There was only one more call from the zone leaders that would affect me. It came a month before I was to return home. In my last mission conference, I gave a brief farewell talk along with the other seven Elders with whom I arrived in Hong Kong. I wasn't moved to a new district, but I was given a new companion. Elder Thompson was a lazy Elder with acne and a large head. He carried a picture of his dream girl in his wallet: Olivia Newton John. His plan was to get married at the earliest possible moment after finishing his mission. He knew he couldn't marry Olivia, but it didn't sound like he cared who he married. It was the timing that mattered: the sooner the better.

Our regimented schedule was as boring as it looks on paper. We could vary our lives in minute ways by sleeping in, or skipping our morning exercises or language study. But getting out of proselytizing, the major portion of our lives, wasn't quite so easy. Doing so required the consensus of both members of a companionship.

A typical missionary will look the other way if his or her companion sleeps in or listens to music (despite the risk of having to deal with a companion possessed by Satan), which was demonstrated very clearly months earlier when every district and zone leader except me said that all the Elders in their apartments were getting up on time and never listened to music. There aren't quite so many missionaries who are willing to give up their proselytizing, however, in order to accommodate a lazy or disillusioned companion who prefers to sit on the sofa or a park bench. For whatever reason, perhaps partly because he was lazy, Elder Thompson was willing to accommodate me.

It takes some time in the mission field to become disillusioned, but laziness is a trait that can be brought from home. This occasionally creates a match made in heaven. The same missionary who couldn't believe I wasn't interested in mission politics ended up becoming a classic example of the disillusioned senior companion. He spent the last three months of his mission dragging his junior companion to a park bench near the old Kai Tak airport where they sat and watched airplanes come and go—for hours on end, day after day.

It sounds boring, but no more so than knocking on door after door, repeating the same script over and over. For a disillusioned missionary, the choice is simple. Unlike tracting, a park bench offers comfort, support, and, in this missionary's case, a clear view of his ride home— "What a beautiful airplane . . . ninety more days, eighty-nine, eighty-eight, eighty-seven . . ." Looking to his recently arrived junior companion he might have asked, "How far away do you think that plane is?"

"I don't know, maybe half a mile."

"Wrong, eighty-six days for me, and almost two years for you."

* * *

In the fall of 1997, after my return to Hong Kong, a pair of missionaries came to our house for spaghetti. One of them said that he had previously had a disillusioned senior companion who was a local Chinese. They spent two months sitting at home like prisoners in self-induced confinement. They only left occasionally to buy food, and once to travel out of their assigned area—a serious infraction of the rules—to buy a pellet gun.

That same evening, the Chinese Elder went into the bathroom while another Elder in the apartment was showering. He threw back the shower curtain and peppered the showering Elder's naked body with little white plastic pellets. The artillery easily penetrated the Elder's armor of soap bubbles, sinking into his soft flesh. Rebounding weakly and leaving red marks, the pellets made dull clinking noises as they landed in the tub.

The weeks that that Chinese "assassin" and his junior companion spent sitting around their apartment doing nothing demonstrates, once again, that disillusioned senior companions, when paired up with lazy (or disillusioned) junior companions, will frequently choose to do nothing as opposed to subjecting themselves to doing missionary work.

The reason junior companions will often allow their senior partners to keep them from doing their work is likely rooted in one simple fact: they can justify it. A junior is technically subordinate to his or her senior companion. They know that they are not doing what they are supposed to, but because it is so much easier than the hard task of door-to-door selling (even the boredom of imprisonment is preferable), they allow themselves the luxury of placing the blame on the person that is ultimately in charge: their senior companion. This probably explains Elder Thompson's willingness to not only do very little proselytizing, but also to break a few rules.

* * *

I met Elder Thompson, my last companion, at my last mission conference. All of these "lasts" were blessings to me. I had been counting down the days to the end of my mission for a while. At the conference I also saw Elder Metcalfe, who was looking much better than I had ever seen him. He was extremely pleased to tell me that he had been diagnosed with an ulcer, and that whenever he didn't get enough to eat he experienced a nervous reaction because of it. He was relieved to know that this was the feeling he had been confusing with the symptoms of an oncoming possession. He also said he had found out that the local member whom he had helped "exorcise" suffered from a mental condition that made him act "possessed." My blessing appeared to have worked for Elder Metcalfe.

* * *

My phone calls to Mandy continued. With Thompson as my companion, I was even able to go on a date with her. As senior companion, I arranged for Elder Thompson and I to go to a movie with Mandy. (Sending my companion off on his own somewhere would, ironically, have seemed even worse to both of us.) Elder Thompson sat on my left, while I sat with my arm around Mandy, who sat at my right. Elder Thompson pretended not to notice. He was so convincing, in fact, that I'm not sure to this day if he did or didn't.

Then I took things a step further.

Lying motionless in bed one night, I stared anxiously at the underside of the bunk above me. I looked once again at the clock on the nightstand. Twenty minutes had passed from the time Elder Thompson had climbed to the top bunk, and I hadn't detected any movement for nearly ten minutes. I sat up slowly and strained to listen. His breathing was slow and steady.

I had gone to bed wearing my jeans and my pajama top. Carefully and quietly I slipped out of my pajama top and into the T-shirt that I had hidden under the covers next to me. As quietly as a spider I left the room, moved down the hall past the open door of the other Elders' bedroom, and out the front door. Once I was outside the apartment, I put on the pair of tennis shoes I had been carrying in my left hand.

After I was inside the elevator my heart rate slowed and I took a deep breath. The subway ran until midnight and would get me to where I was going. I had just enough money in my wallet to hire a taxi back to the apartment. About forty minutes later I arrived at the Causeway Bay subway station. Mandy was waiting for me. That night, my life changed forever.

Second Only to Murder

It was a romantic evening. We cuddled, we kissed, and we explored. But we remained virgins in the end.

An important, ever present part of Mormon culture is guilt and confessions. This could be what caused me to share the details of my experience with Elder Sharp a few days later on the phone. More likely, though, I think it was probably just that foolish and infamous desire boys have to brag to one or more of their male counterparts about sexual conquests. I thus stupidly put my story out there to be added to the list of stories that most members refuse to believe.

You'll recall that when I was at the MTC we were instructed by a General Authority to be informants, to tell our mission president about any serious infraction of mission rules by other missionaries. What I had done with Mandy certainly fit into this category; in fact it was the exact example the General Authority had cited: heavy petting. (Elder Sharp started his mission only one month after I did, so he was in the MTC with me when that General Authority gave his talk.)

A week later I arranged to meet Mandy again at the same time and in the same place.

Elder Sharp called me up the night I had arranged to rendezvous with Mandy for a second time. He said he had been brooding over my experience with Mandy since the day I told him about it. He couldn't sleep nights, he explained, and had discussed it with his companion. His companion was Elder Laughlin, who was part of my group in the MTC, and who therefore had also heard that same talk. They both felt that they had no choice but to turn me in. They decided to give me the option of confessing my own sin, but that if I didn't, they would do it for me.

I sensed Elder Sharp's sincere concern and didn't doubt for a moment that he and Elder Laughlin were doing the only thing they believed they could do. In fact, I even appreciated their giving me the choice, because I preferred doing my own confessing. I understand perfectly why they did what they did, and have never held a grudge about it. They did what they had been indoctrinated to do, and they did it out of love and concern for me—as well as for their own eternal salvation, of course. It's difficult to blame people for acting according to their beliefs.

"I want to go see her before I go," I said. "I want to say goodbye and tell her I'm gonna confess to the President. I owe her that."

"I can't let you do that," Elder Sharp said. "If you don't promise me you're gonna stay home tonight, I'll have to call the Mission President right now."

"Please," I begged, "just let me say goodbye. Nothing's gonna happen."

We argued back and forth until finally I convinced him I would only say goodbye, that nothing would happen, and that I would confess to the mission president the next morning. It was ten days before I was scheduled to go home with honors. I realized that wouldn't be happening now. I would instead get the equivalent of a court martial, and I had no idea how my dutifully patriotic family would to react.

I knew I would be confessing to the mission president the next day. Earlier that night, therefore, the experience of lying in bed waiting for my companion to fall asleep had been very different from the first time, and I was keenly aware of the eternal implications of what I had done on my first date with Mandy. On top of that, I was actually planning, in fact anxiously waiting, to meet my accomplice in sin again. I was a serious sinner and was undoubtedly under Satan's influence.

Mulling over these disastrous realizations depressed me profoundly. I suddenly hated myself much more than usual, which was no easy feat since I had become expert at despising myself for every infraction of Heavenly Father's numerous commandments. I even hated myself for things I *hadn't* done. A Mormon can never do enough of what he or she is supposed to do. I hated how pitifully weak I was. I hated my dirty, worthless soul.

People don't care for those they hate, so I no longer cared for myself. I no longer cared about anything at all. But such a state of mind isn't necessarily dangerous if it comes right before one goes to confess, although it can make driving there risky. Feeling that way about oneself creates a deep sense of humility before God, and causes the sinner to gratefully soak up the bishop's, priest's, pastor's, or mission president's expressions of understanding, love, and concern. It turns God's mouthpieces into heavenly angels with remarkable healing powers, most notably the power to promise sinners that they will once again become whole and worthy of self-respect, even self-love.

My self-loathing and self-disrespect were severe, and what made it dangerous was that I didn't feel that way just prior to confessing, rather I felt that way before my next encounter with Mandy, the source of my sin. This was a problem. A boy who hates and disrespects himself is not going to respect his date. I had entered a vicious cycle: my feelings of despair and my "sinful" acts were feeding on each other. I had defined myself as a loathsome sinner, and therefore I longed to sin. The more I hated myself, the more I wanted to make myself worthy of that hate.

Increasingly "sinful" behavior often happens simply because a person *believes* that he or she is a "sinner." "Sinfulness" often becomes a self-fulfilling prophecy. Harmless behavior, if believed to be sinful, can lead to harmful behavior. It did in my case. I was caught up in the you-might-as-well-sin-since-you're-already-a-sinner mindset. So I sinned.

Despite all the warnings from Church leaders about possibly becoming possessed under the influence of rock and roll music, I was breaking the important mission rule against listening to music. As I lay there that night, drunk with sin, waiting to date Mandy again, and waiting for my companion to fall asleep, I listened to the Talking Heads' tape *The Fear Of Music*. The title couldn't have been more appropriate.

I had already listened to the album several times on my mission, but on this night it turned to pure evil. I lay there listening to it while the room pulsated and I feared for my eternal life. I expected at any moment to be possessed by an evil spirit. Elder Metcalfe's experiences were no longer funny.

My departure that night was the same as a week prior, as was my money situation. This time Mandy met me at the subway station next to our apartment and rode with me to Causeway Bay. From there we went to Victoria Park, the location of our previous encounter. On our first date we saw a peeping Tom, an Indian man who spied on us before I chased him away. This act of chivalry gained me a great deal of respect from an easily impressed Mandy. That, along with our intimate moments, had set the mood for our second date; and these things have natural progressions of their own. To avoid being spied on again, we went to an even more secluded area—something that is extremely difficult to come by in Hong Kong.

On the subway on the way over I had tried to explain to her the predicament that I was in. I assumed that she would understand the seriousness of it all since she was a member of the Church. But for some reason she focused on one minor detail, the one about my telling a fellow missionary what we did on our first date.

Her reaction was quite natural; she was shocked and upset. I didn't understand this, however, because my unnatural Mormon mindset couldn't comprehend why she was fixating on something that was so insignificant when compared to what was ultimately at stake here. Why couldn't she understand that the only thing that mattered in the world right now, more important than war or famine, was my having to confess this to the mission president the very next day. I was on the road to eternal damnation and all she could think about was her own embarrassment. What was wrong with her?

Despite all of this, the mood wasn't destroyed. We sat on a bench in the moonlit park looking into each other's eyes. The long silent invitation to act made my mind reel. I was confused by a flood of hormones and indoctrination. The priest inside my brain (like the one in the final skit of Woody Allen's *Everything You Always Wanted To Know About Sex But Were Afraid To Ask*) was himself seduced by what he saw through my eyes. The fact that a priest, an Elder even, was consenting to an immoral act, multiplied the degree of the sin tenfold.

* * *

Mandy was not dating the same person she had been a week before. I was caught up in a religious daze. Submitting to the evil influence guiding me, I switched to autopilot and accepted the invitation I read in her eyes.

Because Christ's side won the War in Heaven, I had free agency. I could choose to do whatever I wanted. Unfortunately, I was choosing the wrong path, and I had gone so far astray that I was at risk of coming under the influence of Satan. The Church teaches members to feel guilty when they sin, and that the degree of guilt should correlate to the severity of the sin. Sins are ranked very clearly: first and worst is the denial of the Holy Ghost, making one a son of perdition; second is murder; third is sex outside of marriage. This ranks premarital sex very high, right after murder—and ahead of lesser matters such as aggravated assault and armed robbery—and heavy petting is near the top of sex offenses. This is why I believed my behavior was serious enough to give Satan influence over me. The state of mind that Mormonism had put me in was not conducive to clear thinking and mature, responsible decision making. Influenced by the logic of my indoctrination, my self-disgust and sinful actions fed on each other.

I kissed Mandy passionately. Thinking that I was being led into the abyss by Satan, I took her with me, tricking myself into believing it was perhaps beyond my control—regardless, I didn't care anymore. All was a blur. My brain was mush. I was blind to her welfare; I only thought of my own, which was already beyond repair. She soon realized where this was leading and took me to a two-storey boat that was docked at the pier. She led me by the hand . . . or was I leading her . . . or was Beelzebub leading us both? We lay down in the darkness of the upper deck. Slowly and awkwardly we undressed. After situating ourselves somewhat, we unceremoniously exchanged virginities.

And that was that.

The awkward experience was decidedly unromantic. More importantly, it was dangerously unprotected. It was a stupid thing to do. It was, in fact, something I believe I would not have done had I possessed a clear head. If I had carried an iota of self-respect with me that night, I would have respected my date at least enough to care whether or not she got pregnant.

She did not, but that's not the point. The point is that the idea of whether or not Mandy might get pregnant didn't even cross my mind, let alone whether or not it would hurt her psychologically to lose her virginity to someone who was about to walk out of her life forever. Ironically, the very same culture that had influenced me to remain a virgin until the age of twenty had also influenced my decision to lose it in a foolish, irresponsible manner.

I dwelt on the seriousness of my sin as I exited the boat. I was a sponge, and my painful thoughts were water, filling me up until I was almost too saturated to move. It weighed me down and made each step an effort. The skin of my face hung like dough on a rack. "You're going to hell," I said to myself. "You're going to hell." I repeated it over and over again.

* * *

I returned to the apartment, changed into my pajamas and got into bed. A few minutes later the alarm clock rang. After the other missionaries in the apartment had completed their morning rituals and left to proselytize, I called the mission president.

"I need to talk to you," I said. "Can I come see you right now?"

He surprised me by asking if it could wait until the next day. Wasn't he in tune enough with the Spirit to receive a message from God regarding the seriousness of my request? (Most members actually believe such things.) Obviously he didn't understand that I was in serious trouble. Although the mission president's reaction surprised me, it didn't stop me from proceeding. Soon I was sitting in his office while Elder Thompson waited in the mission home's reception area.

"I had sexual intercourse," I confessed to the president. He was visibly surprised and quickly began asking questions. First he asked where my companion was at the time. I gave him an overview of the previous night and he quickly judged my companion to be innocent. His questions were then aimed at assessing my level of guilt. He knew he would have to hold a Church court and sit in judgment of me, so he needed enough specific information to make an informed ruling.[25]

He asked if I had ever done anything like it before, either before or during my mission. He wanted to know the entire history of my rela-

---

25. These days a Church court is referred to more benignly as a "disciplinary council" or the Orwellian-sounding "court of love."

tionship with Mandy, how I met her, how many times I had seen her and where, and everything that had happened between us. He asked if I had masturbated on my mission, and if I had read any pornography.

I wasn't the least bit surprised by any of his questions and honestly answered each one. Then he surprised me with a question about someone other than myself. "Is there a possibility she'll get pregnant?" I actually had to think for a moment.

"Yes," I said, realizing for the first time the earthly consequences of what I had done. The thought stunned me briefly, but it didn't make the situation seem any more serious to me.

I was placed under house arrest. I was not allowed to leave the mission home or make any phone calls. My companion was sent back to the apartment. Two missionaries from the mission home accompanied him. This was the only way to ensure that no missionary would ever be alone: three left and two returned. For the time being—until the next monthly shuffle of missionaries from one district to another—my companion was made part of a threesome. Other than spending a lot of time in the bathroom, I had discovered that the only way to get around the sacred rule, "thou shalt not leave thy companion's side," was to quietly sneak out at night. Of course I was not the first, nor the last, missionary to make this discovery.

Judgment Day

I had already lived in the mission home for four months as secretary to the president, so the mission home environment was neither strange nor intimidating to me. None of the missionaries living there were told why I was staying there that night. The financial secretary that had been my companion during my stint as secretary was still there; he and I had become close friends. Like everyone else, he could sense that something was seriously wrong.

The next morning was awful.

On several occasions I have woken from nightmares, relieved to find out that my unfortunate predicament was only a dream. In these dreams I had committed a terrible act of one kind or another that would adversely affect the rest of my life. Each time after waking, I suddenly realized that I wouldn't need to suffer the terrible consequences of that act after all, because I had not actually committed it.

The next morning was the only time in my life that I have woken from a dream and thought, "Oh no! It really happened!" Rather than waking from a nightmare, I had woken into one. Everything came flooding back into my mind when I awoke. I had committed an act that is, according to Mormon doctrine, second only to murder, and an act that ensures a fate worse than death.[26]

Later that morning I witnessed the only convincing evidence that the mission president may have been truly inspired. I was pushed to the front of his schedule and was soon talking one on one with him in his office again. The first question he asked was "Are you sure what you told me yesterday wasn't all just a bad dream, and we can go on just the way things were before?"

I was taken aback by his question. It didn't occur to me that he was possibly offering me an escape route, that maybe he was reaching for some way out of dealing with this problem that I had so rudely thrown in his lap. But how could I possibly explain everything away as a bad dream? I judged his question to be a rhetorical one.

"No, it really happened," I said.

Before "convening a [Church court] for a full-time missionary," according to the *Church Handbook of Instructions* (p. 91), President Clark was required to "review the matter with a member of the Area Presidency and . . . receive authorization from a General Authority in the Missionary Department" at Church headquarters in Salt Lake City. I don't know if he did that before asking his "rhetorical" question or after.

I went back to the mission home apartment and waited. A couple of hours later I was called back into President Clark's office. This time his two apes were sitting next to him, one on each side, and the court quickly commenced. I had never had my peers sit in moral judgment of me before that day (or since) and it felt strange. Only an indoctrinated prisoner would willingly allow such a thing. Just twelve hours earlier I

---

26. The *Aaronic Priesthood: Manual 2* is a priesthood meeting handbook aimed at teenage Mormon boys that was published by the Church in 1993. On page 91 of the manual, Aaronic priesthood teachers are instructed to explain to the boys in their classes "that sexual sin has very grave consequences for them. In the eyes of the Lord it is second only to murder in its seriousness because it tampers with the sacred powers of procreation . . ." If sex outside of marriage is "second only to murder," then logically it is worse than things such as arson, armed robbery, or treason. That is a bizarre lesson to teach teenage boys.

had confessed the most intimate details of my life to the mission president, and doing so seemed as natural and as right as can be. Now I was admitting my sins to fellow missionaries, not as friends and confidants, but as judges.

The mission president related an abbreviated version of my story for the record, periodically asking me to confirm specifics. In this way I was merely required to admit my sins, saving me the embarrassment of describing them. He never spoke to the apes, nor did he ask them to speak.

Before he handed down the judgment, he offered me the chance to speak for myself. I fully realized where this was headed, so after expressing the incredible amount of guilt I felt I made it clear that I didn't want to lose my Church membership. I was sincere, and my mumbled, choked-up presentation attested to that fact.

The mission president made his judgment. After explaining that he understood I had never done such a thing before, and had no history of sinful behavior, he recommended that I be disfellowshipped. He asked the apes what they thought, which was the first time he asked them anything. They of course agreed—what were they going to do, challenge the mission president?—and my fate was sealed.

I was surprised by the outcome. I had assumed that I would be excommunicated and lose my membership. It was my understanding that the act I had committed as a missionary was automatic grounds for excommunication. My father, a former bishop, later told me that he had thought the same thing. Therefore we were both surprised that I had instead been disfellowshipped, which is the most severe form of probation, disallowing a Church member from participating in any Church activity. A disfellowshipped member cannot hold a Church calling or partake of the sacrament, and is not allowed to speak or pray during Church services. I would still be a member, however, and this would make it easier to return to the life I had lived before my mission began.

Excommunication is a cancellation of membership and includes the same restrictions as disfellowshipment, plus two additional ones: excommunicated people are forbidden to wear their temple garments and are not allowed to pay tithing (although it is invariably explained to them that they can pay tithing through another Church member if they wish—hint hint). It takes a long time for an excommunicated person to prove that he or she has fully repented and is worthy of being re-baptized. A disfellowshipped member, by comparison, can return to full participation status much more easily and much more quickly (usually not sooner than one year, though, according to the *Church Handbook of Instructions*).

So I was better off than I thought I would be, but I had still done something terribly unworthy of a missionary, and I wasn't going to return home with honors. Even though I retained my membership, I knew my parents were going to be devastated. My parents had moved to a new ward and my mother was no doubt anxious for all the members to meet and fall in love with her humorous, brilliant, good looking, well-behaved son. "Brilliant" and "good looking" could remain part of her highly biased view of me, but the definition of "well behaved" was something she had to look to the Mormon Church for, and it had already made its judgment: guilty—which in turn would greatly diminish anything remotely "humorous" about my disposition.

My trip home was not going to be an easy one.

At the end of the court, in a very compassionate tone, President Clark said, "Elder Worthy, this doesn't erase all the good that you did on your mission. You were a good missionary, with lots of success, and the Lord will remember that." Somberly and sadly he added, "It will take me a long time to get over this, if I ever get over it." I tried to fight back the tears, but couldn't. I only nodded, unable to speak.

President Clark apparently did get over it eventually. A few years later, while serving as the bishop of his ward, he was excommunicated for immoral behavior. He has since repented and returned to the fold. I chose a different path. I wish him the very best and will always be grateful for the compassionate way in which he carried out his duty as my ecclesiastical judge. The ordeal itself was disturbing, but that was not his fault. He was a fellow victim playing his role and reading his lines from the same script I was.

That afternoon, one of the apes escorted me to my apartment to collect my things, and President Clark's wife booked a flight for me. I left the next day, just one week before the official end of my mission. (My flights to and from Hong Kong were the only part of my mission the Church paid for: "The Church pays the expenses of full-time missionaries to travel to and from the field."[27] And that's it.)

---

27. 1998 *Church Handbook of Instructions*, p. 83.

I spent the remainder of that day with nothing to do but sit and ponder how painful my return home was going to be. I had already packed, so the next morning dragged on as well. More time to think. More time to dread.

I stood in the lobby a few minutes before it was time to leave. The mission president's wife walked in and stood across from me. She asked nicely, and matter of factly, if I was waiting to be taken to the airport. I confirmed that I was and we shared an awkward moment of silence.

I wondered what she knew.

The financial secretary suddenly walked out of his office. He knew that I was about to leave, and he had a very strong hunch as to why. I smiled at him as best I could. He stood there looking at me for a moment. Then he walked over, wrapped his arms around me and did something I will never forget. He wept.

At the time I felt as if I desperately needed to be comforted. Suddenly, though, I was comforting someone else, and it made me feel good. It was encouraging to know that I was still able to do so in my condition. I told him not to worry about me, that I would be fine.

I think he gave me what I needed more than anything else at that moment. I needed to be convinced that I was still worth loving, and he did it in an irrefutable way: by empathetically crying over my situation. Friendship doesn't get any better, or stronger, than that. I will always be grateful to him for that show of compassion.

The mission president's wife watched the whole thing. She said nothing. I again wondered what she knew.

Better Dead and Clean than Alive and Unclean

It may be hard for nonmembers to comprehend just how serious Mormons consider my sin to be. Former prophet Spencer W. Kimball said that "[e]ven mortal life itself, when placed upon the balance scales, weighs less than chastity."[28] In his 1969 book, *Miracle of Forgiveness*, President Kimball quoted two other Mormon prophets: David O. McKay said, "Your virtue is worth more than your life. Please, young folk, preserve your virtue even if you lose your lives" (not at all a pleas-

---

28. *The Teachings of Spencer W. Kimball*, edited by Edward L. Kimball, 1982, p. 265.

ant thing to believe for rape victims who are overpowered but not killed); and Heber J. Grant said, "There is no true Latter-day Saint who would not rather bury a son or a daughter than to have him or her lose his or her chastity" (both quotes on p. 63). Apostle Bruce R. McConkie, in the 1966 version of his classic *Mormon Doctrine*, put it bluntly: "Better dead clean, than alive unclean. Many is the faithful Latter-day Saint parent who has sent a son or daughter on a mission or otherwise out into the world with the direction, 'I would rather have you come back home in a pine box with your virtue than return alive without it.'" (p. 124)

Many members take all this very seriously. One example is the story mentioned in this book's preface about Brother Borden's reaction to his son Bradley having been stabbed while serving a mission in Russia. Bradley suffered knife wounds to his upper intestines, liver and pancreas. An article in *The Arizona Republic* (October 19, 1998) reported the incident. It describes the reaction of Bradley's mother, Myrna Borden, as follows:

> [W]hen the 20-year-old recovers from the stabbing, his mother said Sunday, "I know he'll want to go back to Russia" . . . "Being a missionary is the best thing a young man can do," Myrna Borden said. "It's what the prophet of our church has asked our young men to do."

The article said this about Brother Borden's reaction:

> [T]he young man's father added that there are worse things for a Mormon missionary than wounds or even death.

That must have put a tremendous amount of pressure on Bradley to overcome any fear he may have had of returning to Russia after his recovery. Then the article said this about the family's reaction:

> [Mr. Borden] said that when their church president came to their home Saturday and said, "There has been a problem with Bradley," the family was "worried that he'd done something unworthy."

They were apparently relieved to find out that Bradley hadn't done what I had done, but had instead merely been stabbed by drunken Russians. Quoting from Apostle Bruce R. McConkie's *Mormon Doctrine*, Brother Borden explained why they were so glad to hear this:

"You see, we'd rather have him come home in a pine box than do something unworthy," Dale Borden said, battling to hold back tears.

Tears coursed down Borden's cheeks as he explained the importance of his missionary son "choos[ing] the right, do[ing] what is right, return[ing] with honor."

[Bradley's brother] Christopher said he recently had come home from a mission in New Zealand.

[Christopher] related how he and fellow missionaries were told that in ancient Greece, Spartan mothers told their sons to come home carrying their shields or carried on their shields—to have fought well or to have died fighting well.

"We want Bradley to return with his shield, or on it," Christopher said.

That's pressure. If Bradley was frightened enough by his experience to not want to continue his missionary work in Russia, his family would probably not have been supportive, especially after having gone public with their views. And if, instead, Bradley had succumbed to the tempting invitation of a pretty Russian girl who fell madly in love with him, and he with her, his family might have actually preferred that he were dead.

Quoting from the article again, we learn:

Bradley Borden was stabbed once in the stomach, and his fellow Mormon missionary, José Manuel Mackintosh of Nevada, was killed.

We are left wondering what the Mackintosh family thought of the Borden family's preference that Bradley come home in a pine box rather than "do something unworthy." Perhaps the Mackintoshes would rather have seen their son come home outside of a pine box, even if he had done something so human as to commit a "sin" as defined by the leaders of the Church of Jesus Christ of Latter-day Saints.

Excommunication and Life After Mormonism

Returning Without Honor

It's not hard to guess what my twenty-four-hour trip home was like: lots of time to think, lots of time to shudder at the thought of facing my parents. Lots and lots of time, but still not enough. I didn't want the trip to end. I wanted it to last forever. I didn't want the plane to land. Ever.

When the trip finally did end, I sat on the plane and waited until everyone else had exited. I couldn't keep the flight staff waiting, so I forced myself up and dragged myself off the plane. When I neared the end of the exit tunnel, just before rounding the final corner where I would be in view of the people waiting in the reception area, I stopped. I set my luggage down and leaned against the wall. I didn't want to walk around that corner where I knew my parents were waiting—I didn't feel I could take it. I wanted to lie down, close my eyes and vanish.

I knew I couldn't stay inside an airplane exit tunnel forever, so I walked past the corner to face what lay ahead. I immediately saw my parents standing there all alone. Everyone else had left. This meeting was terribly hard on them as well, and my making them wait so long had made it even worse.

Dad forced a little smile. I know mom wanted to, but she couldn't. It was obvious she'd been crying, and I'm sure she had shed many tears during the previous two days.

Unlike some other missionaries, I was blessed with wonderful, loving parents, both of whom welcomed me home with open arms, glad to see me return to them alive and healthy. We exchanged big hugs and then they took me home. They certainly still loved me, and they made sure I understood that. They never once said or did anything to make me doubt it. But my mother's dreams had been shattered. I would later discover that she wrote in her journal that it was the saddest experience of her life. Nevertheless, her love and concern for me had not diminished in the slightest.

An example of how closely my mother stood by my side was the fact that she was angry about my being disqualified from returning to Brigham Young University, and therefore had to forfeit the academic scholarship that BYU had previously awarded me. That was because excommunicated former members and disfellowshipped members are not allowed to attend BYU. She was also frustrated and disappointed by my treatment as a disfellowshipped member of the Church. Many Mormon families would have stood by the Church in all its "righteous" judgment and ostracization of an "unworthy" son, but my parents stood by me as much as could be expected of active and devoted members. I will always be grateful to them for that.

The Unpleasantness of Church

The first thing a missionary does when he or she returns home is to give a homecoming talk. I didn't. I wasn't even allowed to pray in church, let alone give a talk.

My mother no doubt had been talking excitedly to people in the ward about my return. I'm sure the fact that I would soon be returning was announced to everyone at church. (I wonder how many noticed that I returned a week earlier than I was supposed to.) The ward members were no doubt all expecting to hear me speak on the first or second Sunday after my return. Instead, my return was merely announced by the bishop during sacrament meeting.

I stood up for everyone to see, then sat down without saying a word. Minutes later the sacrament was passed around for all worthy attendees. Because I was a disfellowshipped sinner I was unworthy to partake, and the fact that I merely passed the trays of bread and water on to the person sitting beside me was a physical manifestation of my unworthiness.

All of these obvious signs sent a clear message to everyone in the ward: the newly returned missionary had sinned. Every time I attended church, I was wearing the figurative scarlet letter I had stitched in Victoria Park with Mandy.

People at church were nice and I made some friends, but on the whole it was socially awkward and I hated going. I only went to make my parents happy. I knew I had hurt them enough. I didn't want to do any more to them than I already had. So I went through the motions.

None of this did my self-esteem any good.

Excommunication

Before long I met a girl and we started to date steadily. The relationship developed, and sex became a regular part of it. I was sinning while on probation.

My probation period involved regular interviews with the bishop and stake president. For a while I lied to them and said I was doing fine. Before long, though, I decided I had had enough. I no longer wanted to lie just so I could continue to participate in a charade that I wanted no part of. I wanted to end it all. So I confessed.

It is probably hard for nonmembers to understand, but at the time I had absolutely no harsh feelings against the Church. I had been programmed to blame myself for my unhappiness, and that's what I did. I wasn't angry at the Church or any of its members, but I hated my life, and wanted to stop play acting. Something had to change and confessing was the only way I knew to change things. Asking to have my name removed from Church records and my membership cancelled never crossed my mind. I was still following the programming from my lifelong indoctrination and was ready and willing to accept whatever judgment the Church pronounced on me.

I had not yet concluded that the Church was false, but I was very unhappy in it and I wanted out, at least for a while. In the back of my mind I still felt that if any church were true, then it was certainly the Mormon Church. I believed it was the most rational and logical of all religions, offering better, more thorough answers to all the deep theological questions. It explained very clearly where we came from, why we are here, and where we are going after we die. At that time, though, I needed a break. I decided to step away from religion entirely, believing that if I ever went back to religion, it would definitely be to the Mormon Church.

* * *

I now look back at my belief about the Church and laugh at it for two reasons. First, I had not studied other religions, so my assumption that the Mormon Church possessed the best answers was based on what I had been told by the Mormon Church itself. Second, I hadn't even studied Mormonism (which is typical of the vast majority of Mormons), so I believed it to be logical and rational—again, based on what it said about itself. So I allowed myself to remain in confusion for years regarding a belief system that is anything but logical and rational, a belief system that is in fact very easy to refute.

I foolishly postponed investigating the Church. For the time being I just wanted out, and as long as all my unconscious baggage remained, confessing seemed like the most natural thing to do. Unfortunately, I waited ten years to do my investigating; I say "unfortunately," because recovering former believers of a particular belief system must come to terms with the question, "Is it true?" Until they do that, they will always carry around a ball and chain—of various weight and size depending on their experience with the organization in question, and the nature of that organization. When I finally did my studying and saw how easily the Mormon Church can be seen for what it is, I kicked myself for not doing it years earlier. The truth really does set one free.

* * *

When I told my stake president I had had premarital sex, he asked me who the girl was. I was surprised that he asked and wondered aloud if I was required to tell him. He said I was. The fact that he knew I had taken his daughter out to dinner didn't cross my mind at the time, but it would be tempting for a father in his position of power to want to convince an indoctrinated confessor that God required him to say who it was he had slept with. The only reason I took his daughter out on a date was because he had encouraged me to date Mormon girls.

This may have been one reason for him to ask me who the girl was, but it certainly wasn't the only one. The *Church Handbook of Instructions* states that "[d]isclosure of the identity of others who participated in a transgression should be encouraged as part of the repentance process, especially when this can help Church leaders encourage the repentance of those participants . . ." It goes on to say that "[i]f a bishop learns that a Church member outside his ward may have been involved in a serious transgression, he informs that member's bishop confidentially. When members of different wards transgress together, and when one has disclosed to his bishop the identity of the other transgressor, the bishop to whom the disclosure was made consults with the bishop of the other member."[1]

---

1. 1998 *Church Handbook of Instructions*, p. 92.

As if that weren't enough of a violation of privacy, bishops are instructed to advise "the ward Relief Society president in confidence when a member of the Relief Society has been disciplined or was a victim."[2] So even female "victims" who have chosen not to share an extremely personal matter are not shielded.

In addition to spreading gossip in the name of love, Church leaders also gather dirt: "If [a] member denies an accusation that the bishop has reliable evidence to support, the bishop . . . gathers further evidence . . ." He may do so himself or "assign two reliable Melchizedek Priesthood holders to do so . . . instruct[ing] them not to use methods that . . . could result in legal action."[3] (Is Salt Lake City's Temple Square really all that different from Red Square?)

I told him who the girl was because I believed I had to. I regret having done so, even though it wasn't the stake president's daughter, and even though nothing at all happened to the girl, because she wasn't a member. I regret having done so for the same reason I regret having confessed anything to him at all: it was none of his business.

A Church court was quickly arranged and I received a letter informing me of the time and date. I arrived at the chapel with my parents. They were not allowed to attend the court so they waited outside in the lobby. My bishop escorted me in. I wasn't prepared for what awaited me. Filling the small room to capacity were fifteen men in suits and ties, standing around a conference table. This was standard procedure: "All three members of the stake presidency and all twelve members of the **high council** participate in a stake disciplinary council."[4]

My court was a stake-level event, rather than a more local, ward-level event. That is because I was a Melchizedek Priesthood holder, and I was a likely candidate for excommunication. The Melchizedek Priesthood is held by virtually every Mormon male over the age of eighteen. A member of the Melchizedek Priesthood can only be excommunicated by the stake president. Everyone else, namely all women and children, can be excommunicated by their local bishop.[5]

---

2. Ibid.

3. Ibid.

4. Ibid., p. 96.

5. "[B]ishops normally administer Church discipline unless evidence indicates that a person who holds the Melchizedek Priesthood is likely to be excommunicated" (1998 *Church Handbook of Instructions*, p. 90).

I was escorted to the end of the table and stood there looking at all those men, and they at me. It was the most intimidating moment of my life.

The first counselor of the stake presidency led the hearing. He instructed everyone to sit. He explained the charges, after which he asked me to confirm my guilt. After going over what I had confessed, I was then subjected to questions from all of the men, as if I were at a press conference. The questions involved actions going back even before my mission and were mostly related to masturbation, pornography, and sex. I went through the robotic motions of the indoctrinated and answered them all, which is something I now regret very much. My hearing was a perverted and bizarre expression of power by some men over another—in this case, me.[6]

When asked, I chose to say nothing on my own behalf and did not plead to keep my membership. My bishop, a good man, sat beside me throughout the hearing. I found no mention of a bishop doing this in the *Church Handbook of Instructions*, but the bishop appeared to be acting as a character witness in my defense. He spoke admiringly of my parents, saying they were a wonderful asset to the ward, but, oddly, the only thing he seemed to be able to say in my defense was that I was very intelligent—something he repeated three times during his presentation. I appreciated the compliment but wondered how that particular characteristic (putting aside the question of its validity) was supposed

---

6. Mormonism is a patriarchal society with very strict moral codes pertaining to sex. To ensure that members adhere to the rules, they are frequently interviewed by their male bishops in face-to-face, one-on-one meetings, and detailed questions about their sexual lives (including masturbation) are asked of both sexes beginning at the age of twelve. (It should be noted that not all bishops do this.) In *The Demon-Haunted World*, Carl Sagan writes about the perverted aspects of the Inquisition that I think are relevant, although much more extreme: "There were strong erotic and misogynistic elements—as might be expected in a sexually repressed, male-dominated society with inquisitors drawn from the class of nominally celibate priests. The trials paid close attention to the quality and quantity of orgasm in the supposed copulations of defendants with demons or the Devil . . . 'Devil's marks' were found 'generally on the breasts or private parts' according to Ludovico Sinistrari's 1700 book. As a result pubic hair was shaved, and the genitalia were carefully inspected by the exclusively male inquisitors. . . ." Of course I'm not saying that modern-day Mormonism is the equivalent of the Inquisition. There certainly isn't any examination of genitalia going on in disciplinary courts. However, questioning young girls about masturbation is still a form of perversion, albeit more subtle and less harmful. But unquestioned power often leads to harmful actions, and a patriarchal society such as the Mormon Church lends itself to instances of abuse, including sexual abuse.

to help me in this type of court, one where my eternal soul was on the brink for the grave act of having had consensual sex with another unmarried adult.

I was judged guilty based on my confession to the stake president. The sentence was excommunication. I was never told that "[i]nformation received in a member's confession cannot be used as evidence in a disciplinary council without the member's consent."[7] Even had I known that, I would probably have kept quiet and allowed information from my private confession to stand as evidence. But it only seems fair that a defendant should know the rules of the game before it starts.

In closing, the officiator said he was not asking anything of me that was not also required of him. He, after all, was required to maintain a monogamous relationship with his wife. Masked behind his indignant tone, I detected what seemed to be some resentment. I felt as if he was taking the opportunity to vent a little self-righteous frustration at my expense.

Not only did his tone of voice surprise me, but I was puzzled by his statement. He certainly knew I was well aware of the fact that the Church required him to live a monogamous marriage. Why state something so obvious? Perhaps the law of chastity, which required him to remain monogamous, may have been causing him some frustration. Or perhaps he just felt compelled, as the officiator, to say something that would emphasize the moral gulf between me and my ecclesiastical judges.

It is interesting to note that his analogy equated premarital sex between two consenting adults with an extramarital affair. And it is even more interesting to consider the fact that, if he had held me up against Joseph Smith, I would have looked pure as snow. Joseph Smith was a man with sexual morals that would shock most people who would approve of my having had consensual premarital sex. He had "sexual relationships with polygamous wives as young as fourteen, polyandry of women with more than one husband, [and] marriage and sexual cohabitation with foster daughters."[8]

Considering the behavior of the Church's founder, it is ironic that I was judged unfit for membership because I had sex outside of mar-

---

7. 1998 *Church Handbook of Instructions*, p. 92.

8. D. Michael Quinn, *The Mormon Hierarchy: Origins of Power*, p. 89.

riage. But I'm not complaining. It is much more interesting and rewarding to sit among the audience outside the dome of The Mormon Show than it ever was acting on the set.

What Might Have Been

After my mission I met an eighteen-year-old boy who, before going on his mission, had regular sexual relations with his girlfriend. He lied through all his interviews and went on his mission unworthily. Several years later, he told me that after he had been on his mission for about a year, he couldn't take the guilt any longer and confessed to his mission president. Instead of getting sent home as he expected he would, his mission president told him that he appeared to have repented and had suffered enough through his year-long guilt.

In order to contemplate a "what if" scenario, I don't need to go as far as wondering how I would have turned out if I had never had sex with Mandy. All I have to wonder is, What if after I had had sex with Mandy I didn't confess to my mission president? What if I had instead waited a year or two and then confessed to my bishop? It's possible that by then I would have regained a strong testimony.

After returning home, I would have immediately begun to lie about my mission, which is something that all active RMs do publicly. The post-mission process of an RM reverently speaking about his or her mission as a wonderful, humbling experience made up of a sequence of spiritual events is not initiated by the RMs themselves. It is a cultural requirement. The first thing any RM has to do after returning home is to stand up in front of the entire congregation and give a homecoming talk in his or her ward, usually addressing several hundred members.

The *Church Handbook of Instructions* tells bishops to invite "newly called full-time missionaries to speak in a sacrament meeting before they depart." These "talks . . . should be worshipful, faith promoting, and gospel oriented. The missionary should have sufficient time to deliver a spiritual message" (p. 86). It is understood that this applies equally to RMs, and the same section of the *Church Handbook* suggests that a sacrament meeting include both a newly called missionary and an RM. RMs are expected to include at least one or two spiritually uplifting stories from their mission experience.

In my homecoming talk, I would have been expected to bear my testimony, and I would have done so. "One of the most important com-

"What was fun?" I asked.

"When you were doing your door approaches," he said, "I was practicing my acting. Sometimes I would act really sad." He drooped the sides his mouth and slumped his shoulders. "And sometimes I would act happy . . ." His face brightened and his eyes doubled in size. ". . . or angry." He bunched up his forehead and tightened his lips.

Now I understood the reason for our complete failure. In the four hours that we had just spent asking people to let us into their homes, my companion had been standing next to me making exaggerated facial gestures. I took a deep, hard swig of Green Spot, trying to dilute the impact of what Elder Compton had just told me. I didn't know how to react or even what to think. Acting? I thought he wanted to be a writer. I said nothing. I stared at some children who were running around in a small playground in front of us.

I knew there would be challenges to doing the Lord's work, but this was a challenge I had never anticipated. I couldn't make sense of it. If my companion hadn't made those facial gestures, would we have gotten into someone's home, eventually converted them, and thereby ensured their eternal salvation? Had he destroyed someone's chance to go to the Celestial Kingdom with his acting practice? Was it possible that by merely manipulating the muscles in our faces for fun, we missionaries could sabotage the outcome of people's existence throughout all eternity, destroying their opportunity to learn about the test they were required to pass? And was I responsible for what my junior companion had just done? After thinking about it, I concluded that at the very least I was responsible for doing my best to prevent it from happening again.

"Don't ever do that again!" I said angrily. The shocked look on his face told me he had no idea why I was bothered by what he'd done.

I didn't have to endure Elder Compton's uniqueness for long. A couple of weeks after his tracting act, I was assigned a new companion.

The Boy Scout

I was paired with Elder James from June to August. Being assigned to a new companion was always like another new beginning, and with it I committed myself to working harder. There were two additional factors that worked as catalysts to my renewed commitment: the mission conference and my new companion's disposition.

It was all about standing straight, wearing a pleasant, friendly smile, and saying things in the right way. The most difficult part was figuring out how to make our message sound appealing. It only made sense for us to be honest about the purpose of our visit, but the problem was that it wasn't a message that appealed to many people in Hong Kong.

"How are you?" I would say with a pleasant smile. "We're missionaries from the Church of Jesus Christ of Latter-day Saints. We're in this area sharing a message about Jesus Christ. Can we come in and share it with you? It will only take about ten minutes."

The reactions were almost always as expected: "We're busy," or "We're eating," or "Nobody's home," or "We worship *sàhn* (a generic name for various Chinese deities)." Occasionally we'd be yelled at or told that we were crazy, but usually people were quite civil, although abrupt.

Rejection after rejection made me desperate to see someone reach down and slide open the accordion-like metal gate that always stood between us and them, forcing us to look at everyone through a grid of diamond shapes. I felt worn down if, after three or more hours of knocking on doors, we weren't invited into a single home. This happened one afternoon when I was tracting with Elder Compton. We had spent four hours tracting through six floors of a government-subsidized housing estate. Each floor had forty-eight apartments. After we finished, we had knocked on two hundred eighty-eight doors in all, and there was someone at home in roughly half of the apartments.

Elder Compton and I walked to a corner store and bought ourselves two bottles of Green Spot, a brand of orange soda that was popular in Hong Kong at the time. We picked a position on the curb to rest a moment before heading home. I went over my approach in my mind. Was it my wording, my foreign accent, my smiling too much or too little? It could have been any or all of these things, but I didn't feel I had done anything differently than I usually had. I looked at my companion. As his senior I felt responsible for consoling him and helping him maintain a good level of morale, even if my own was low.

I was just going to say something when Elder Compton spoke first. "That was fun," he said. I didn't understand what he was he talking about. He couldn't have been referring to our tracting session. I had never heard of any missionary ever refer to tracting as fun. Was he talking about buying our sodas?

ponents of a successful welcome-home sacrament meeting message will
be [the returned missionary's] testimony. . . . From the depths of your
heart and soul, share what you feel. Let there be no misunderstanding
of where you stand when it comes to a testimony of the truth."[9] I would
have received praise for the spiritual portions of my talks, and would
have been increasingly praised each time my reports of divine guidance
increased in number and vividness. If I had gone through this process,
perhaps today, more than twenty years after my mission, I would truly
believe that my mission was filled with miracles.

Members are taught to believe that God plays a hand in helping
missionaries to learn their particular language, and in guiding them in
their quest for souls receptive to His message. Missionaries therefore
begin their missions believing that there is a direct correlation between
a missionary's faith and obedience on the one hand, and language skills
and number of baptized converts on the other. Reality on the streets
quickly shows them that this is not the case. Instead, missionaries see
that language skills are associated with diligent study and innate ability,
and that the number of baptisms achieved is related to a missionary's
efforts and sales ability—an ability based on things such as charisma,
appearance, and the gift of gab.

The vast majority of missionaries must see these obvious facts. And
even for those who are somehow able to blind themselves to it all, these
inconvenient truths undoubtedly exist to one degree or another in
their minds. But they exchange the reality based on evidence for a reality based on fabrications. This is done through a process that begins
immediately upon the missionary's return home. Missionaries who have
lost their testimonies during their missions have to lie:

> The stake president counsels returned missionaries to teach the
> gospel in talks they give. As they speak in sacrament meetings, they
> should share experiences that strengthen faith in Jesus Christ, build
> testimonies, encourage members to live and share the gospel, and
> illustrate gospel principles. They should avoid travelogues, inappro-
> priate stories about their companions or others, disparaging remarks
> about the areas in which they served, and other matters that would be
> inappropriate for a servant of the Lord to discuss in the sacred setting
> of a sacrament meeting.[10]

---

9. Christensen, Joe J. *Welcome Home! Advice for the Returned Missionary.* Salt Lake City:
Bookcraft, 1989, p. 18.

10. 1998, *Church Handbook of Instructions*, p. 86.

There are two choices for those who literally don't have any spiritual, faith-promoting material, or, for that matter, a testimony: 1) give talks in church void of any spiritual, faith-promoting material, and without bearing one's testimony; or 2) begin the process of emphasizing and exaggerating some facts, while de-emphasizing and omitting others, and then adding, "I know the Church is true." They must choose between feeling uncomfortable about lying, or feeling uncomfortable about not living up to their families' and ward members' expectations. It is not hard to guess what virtually all RMs choose to do. Can you blame them?

RMs need a supply of spiritual experiences that they can share with other Church members. Good stories of a spiritual, faith-building nature are an essential part of fitting the mold of a successful RM. So, "Mission stories" are fabricated to strengthen the testimonies of other members—especially youngsters and newcomers. Elder Christensen, former president of the Mexico City Mission, put it this way: "[I]f you are not careful, some harm could be done to the younger members in the congregation."[11] The fabrications are slight at first, but grow with each telling. An RM will very likely judge these lies as not only harmless, but in fact helpful: "If you focus on the experiences that strengthened your testimony of the restored gospel, in the process you will likely strengthen others."[12]

On my mission I lied to a pretty girl wearing a silk nightgown. I told her that I felt the Spirit when she asked, because I knew it was the right answer to give. I'm sure I was not unique in this regard. All missionaries have no doubt exaggerated the strength of their testimonies in order to instill testimonies in their investigators. The talks RMs give in their wards are just extensions of that.

A person can't lie for long, though. Continually lying within a pressure-ridden religious context, and under the pretext of doing good, is especially hard, so RMs soon start to believe their own stories.

Church members also help RMs to believe their own stories. RMs receive positive feedback from the Mormon community every time they tell a good story. The strength of members' reactions is generally correlated to the degree of inspiration that a story conveys. RMs will "note that the congregation's attention level will greatly increase when [they]

---

11. Christiansen, op. cit., p. 17.
12. Ibid.

include a personal interest example that also includes a gospel message."[13] This works as a very powerful positive reinforcement, causing RMs to believe they are doing the right thing, and most likely encouraging them to believe their own stories.

Missionaries focus on the one or two times over a two-year period in which the answer to their prayer for guidance actually seemed to lead to a person who opened the door and then went on to be baptized. The idea that this could have happened by chance disappears after telling the story often enough and then being praised. Other spiritual events are "remembered" and told, and, after enough years go by, along with enough tellings of the stories, missionaries end up believing firmly in them. At the same time, they forget all the examples that undermine this faith-promoting view of reality.

This consistent, long-term distortion of the facts works like the gelatinous, insatiable monster from the 1950s horror movie, *The Blob*. In the end, all recollections of what actually happened are ingested by, and become part of, the new reality. Rule-breaking missionaries are either forgotten, or they are digested and transformed into obedient missionaries. They become like the forgotten, inconvenient facts described by George Orwell:

> To tell deliberate lies while genuinely believing in them, to forget any fact that has become inconvenient, and then, when it becomes necessary again, to draw it back from oblivion for just so long as it is needed, to deny the existence of objective reality and all the while to take account of the reality which one denies—all this is indispensably necessary.[14]

What Orwell described is necessary for an RM's new reality to withstand the occasional reminders of his actual mission experiences. He may be reminded of reality by other RMs who tell stories privately, or by seeing how missionary work takes place within his own ward back home. But he'll quickly manage to bury such reminders.

The process of changing reality thus begins as soon as RMs return home. After giving their homecoming talk, many members of the ward will approach them with warm compliments and comforting praise.

---

13. Ibid.
14. George Orwell, *1984*, p. 163.

Their slight exaggerations, or outright lies, are thus positively rein-forced, making the RMs feel good about what they said.

RMs are given numerous opportunities to tell mission stories and bear testimony in front of large groups of members. After the home-coming talk, RMs who have served in foreign countries will likely be asked on occasion to give a fireside talk about the country where they served—suddenly they are the resident expert on that country's food, language, culture, climate, and more. During such presentations, RMs know full well that they will be expected to tell at least one inspirational story, and to end by bearing their testimony.

There is a conscious process in the Church that turns good story-tellers into cultural icons. Local Church leaders have been instructed to ensure that good storytellers speak often. The *Church Handbook of Instructions* says, "[e]xemplary returned missionaries should also be invit-ed to speak about missionary work in sacrament meetings and other meetings" (p. 78). It is clearly understood by all RMs that each one of them is expected to be "exemplary." There is no middle road to happi-ness in Mormondom.

Fast and Testimony meeting is held on the first Sunday of every month. During this meeting, members of the ward are encouraged to stand and bear their testimony voluntarily. This monthly event is always a welcome opportunity for all RMs to once again tell a mission story, whether they are already considered to be exemplary, or whether they want to use the opportunity to work toward becoming exemplary. Each time a testimony is publicly borne, the person's belief in it grows. This process not only helps to alter the memory of the RM, it also works to teach children—the missionaries of the future—to believe in these types of stories.

Needless to say, mission stories improve with time. And just like fish stories describing the one that got away, there is a relationship between the length of time that RMs have returned from their missions and the quality of their stories. Most, but not all, storytellers probably grow to believe in their own storie. A few are able to live with the fact that they are lying, publicly repeating their "white" lies enough times to make their presentation smooth, entertaining, and believable. They think that the end justifies the means. And it is easy for them to get away with it, because it is inappropriate for Mormons to question other members' faith-promoting stories. In addition, most inspirational stories are of a personal nature involving few if any witnesses. The stories seldom include facts that are known to anyone but the speaker, let alone facts that can be researched and verified. "As [RMs] share these experiences, [they] can feel great confidence because, of all people, [they] are the only real authority in reporting what [they] personally experienced and felt."[15]

There is a famous case on record, however, that did include verifiable facts, and it is a good illustration of what I have been talking about. As a youth I used to love to listen to talks given by Elder Paul H. Dunn, one of the Church's General Authorities. On February 16, 1991, the *Arizona Republic* published the following about Elder Dunn:

> Among Mormons, Elder Paul H. Dunn is a popular teacher, author and role model. As a prominent leader of the Church . . . for more than 25 years, he has told countless inspirational stories about his life:
>
> Like the time his best friend died in his arms during a World War II battle, while imploring Dunn to teach America's youth about patriotism.
>
> Or how God protected him as enemy machine-gun bullets ripped away his clothing, gear and helmet without ever touching his skin.
>
> Or how perseverance and Mormon values led him to play major-league baseball for the St. Louis Cardinals.
>
> But those stories are not true.
>
> Dunn's "dead" best friend isn't dead; only the heel of Dunn's boot caught a bullet; and he never played baseball for the St. Louis Cardinals or any other major-league team.
>
> Dunn acknowledged that those stories and others were untrue, but he defends fabrications as necessary to illustrate his theological and moral points.

One example of how Dunn used fabrications to illustrate his theological points is found in an article in the August 1975 *New Era*, an LDS magazine for the Church's youth:

> A testimony was born . . . I've had verification upon verification that this church is true, that Joseph Smith was called and ordained to restore the gospel of Jesus Christ . . .
>
> Before I went into combat experience, I had . . . a patriarchal blessing given to me . . . that patriarchal blessing stated in a number of paragraphs that I would live . . . to a ripe old age . . . And one of the paragraphs indicated divine intervention in time of combat.

---

15. Christiansen, op. cit., p. 17.

Now there were 1,000 of us in my combat team who left San Francisco on that fateful journey, and there were six of us who came back 2-1/2 years later. How do you like that for odds! And of the six of us, five had been severely wounded two or more times and had been sent back into the line as replacements. There had been literally thousands of incidents where I should have been taken from the earth by the enemy and for some reason was not.

Regarding this story, the *Arizona Republic* article reveals the following:

[Dunn] has since acknowledged that only 30 soldiers in his unit died during the entire war, but he said the exaggeration of numbers is unimportant.

It is unimportant because the end, without question, justifies the means. So unimportant, in fact, that a member was excommunicated from the Church for challenging Elder Dunn's stories before these "exaggerations" had become public knowledge.

What if I had continued to participate in this culture that successfully shaped and molded a popular role model such as Paul Dunn? What if I had experienced a period of normal Church life before confessing my sin? What if, before confessing, I had spent a year or two telling faith-promoting mission stories to large numbers of people eager to stroke my ego every time I did so? What if I had had children with a Mormon wife that I loved dearly; and what if I believed that I would lose them if I rejected the Church?

I like to think that I still would have seen the Church for what it is, that I would not have changed my mind about the facts I witnessed on my mission. But who knows? Perhaps today I would be playing my part in The Mormon Show as a local Church leader, doing my best to live a "noble and blessed life" by convincing young boys to save money for their missions. Church leaders are instructed to tell "[m]issionaries and families [to] make appropriate sacrifices to provide financial support for a mission."[16] I would no doubt tell those young boys, therefore, to start saving early, because making such a sacrifice would put them in tune with the Spirit, making their missions all the more miraculous.

"Boys," I'd say, "it's going to be the best two years of your lives."

---

16. 1998 *Church Handbook of Instructions*, p. 81.

What Happened Instead

I'm glad I served a mission to Hong Kong. If I hadn't, I wouldn't have the wife and daughter I now have, and I wouldn't be living in Hong Kong and getting a PhD in Chinese linguistics. I like my life and wouldn't trade it for anything. Although I'm glad that I suffered through my mission because of what it ultimately helped me to accomplish, I still have mixed feelings about some of the consequences. For example, I could have spent eighteen months doing something productive. If I had, though, I never would have learned Cantonese and I probably never would have experienced another culture to the extent I have experienced Hong Kong culture.

If I hadn't served a mission, I could have avoided all the mental anguish that my mission caused—not only the pain of being labeled a sinner, but the pain of losing my testimony. However, if I hadn't experienced that anguish, I may very well have remained a Latter-day Saint, which, according to my present world view, would be a sad thing.

The worst consequence of my mission was that I spent time on it that I could have spent with my mother. She was diagnosed with liver cancer less than a year after I returned, and passed away three months after that. It is paradoxical, of course, because she would have been very disappointed if I had chosen not to serve a mission. That would probably have been true even if she'd known that she didn't have much time left. The culture would have required me to go on a mission, anyway.

An example of this is Elder Maurey Johnson, whose picture can be seen on page 60 of the January 1996 issue of *National Geographic*. The emotional pain that shows on his face is powerfully moving. He is bidding goodbye to his family before he leaves to serve his mission in India. It was the last time he ever said goodbye to his mother, who was terminally ill at the time and has since died. It is very likely that I would have done the very same thing that Elder Johnson did.

Had that happened to me, I would now be extremely resentful of Mormon culture. But, all things considered, I feel fortunate; I have suffered less mental anguish than many former Mormons. All too many of the hundreds of stories written by ex-Mormons at www.exmormon.org illustrate how LDS culture has harmed innocent people.

Since I was not allowed to return to BYU, which was actually a blessing in disguise, I went to the University of Texas in Austin. I attended church to make my parents happy when I lived with them, but as soon as I moved to Austin I stopped attending.

If I had decided to attend a ward in Austin, I would have had to tell that ward's bishop that I had been excommunicated. The ward members would have noticed that I didn't partake of the sacrament, and I wouldn't have been able to do anything other than sit and listen. The bishop probably would have felt obligated to have regularly scheduled interviews with me. The only reason anyone would choose to suffer such an uncomfortable situation would be if he or she were determined to regain membership and be re-baptized. I was happier out of the Church than in, so I had no incentive to go through such a socially awkward and humiliating process.

While attending UT I lived and hung out with students from Hong Kong. I met them at the all-you-can-eat university cafeteria, where some of them regularly ate four platefuls of food while somehow remaining thinner than me. I had learned to converse in Cantonese fairly well and had been initiated to Hong Kong culture, so I was naturally attracted to the cafeteria table where these students sat. They were a little wary at first, but once they realized I genuinely wanted to be their friend, and nothing more, they welcomed my presence. One of them told me years later that, in the beginning, he was sure I had some ulterior motive for befriending them, and that he racked his brain in vain trying to figure out what it could possibly be.

Although I was living in Austin, Texas, I ended up speaking more Cantonese than I did English. I was unconditionally accepted as one of the core members of a small group of students from Hong Kong, and through that association I became friends with most of the Hong Kong students attending UT. I ended up sharing an apartment with one of them, and soon after I moved in several others started invading our living room and kitchen on a regular basis. The apartment above blasted us with loud punk music, and we shot back with the machine-gun crackle of mahjong tiles.

Ironically, the experience was in some ways similar to being part of a Mormon community. I was invited to, and expected to attend, every single activity, whether I wanted to or not. There was a very strong sense of group identity, and I felt so much a part of it that I ran for president of the Hong Kong Students' Association. Apparently the students from Hong Kong thought I was a part of the group as well, because I won the election. The whole experience was an excellent trial run for my yet-to-come integration into a Chinese family.

Unfortunately I didn't couple my absence from church with research about the Church's history. This allowed the residual effects of my testimony to linger for years, preventing me from judging it in the light that it deserves.[17] One symptom of this lingering residue was the fear of harming the Church's reputation by allowing my "improper" behavior to be associated with it. I was no longer living a Mormon lifestyle, and I knew this would be the case even before I started attending UT, so I lied to all my Chinese friends about why I had lived in Hong Kong and learned to speak Cantonese. Instead of telling them I had been a missionary, I told them that my father's career took him there and that I had followed.

Having grown up inside The Mormon Show, I had been indoctrinated to believe that the sin of lying was less serious than the sin of harming the reputation of the Church. Members represent the Church, and they will be held accountable if they behave in a way that harms its image. It is a member's responsibility to demonstrate to nonmembers that being an obedient member of the LDS Church brings great happiness—even if this must be demonstrated through play acting.[18] Because I had been excommunicated, I was unable to boost the Church's reputation in this way. However, I felt that I was still capable of harming the Church's reputation. I believed that if I was going to laugh at my friends' dirty Cantonese jokes and drink beer with them, then I shouldn't let them know that I had been an Elder who was an

17. In his 1927 essay, "Why I Am Not a Christian," Bertrand Russell said, "There is a certain tendency in our practical age to consider that it does not much matter whether religious teaching is true or not, since the important question is whether it is useful. One question cannot, however, well be decided without the other. If we believe the Christian religion our notions of what is good will be different from what they will be if we do not believe it. Therefore, to Christians, the effects of Christianity may seem good, while to unbelievers they may seem bad."

18. There is nothing wrong with pretending to be happy when you're not. This is an admirable habit of many polite people who, even though they may feel tired or unhappy, want to make whomever they talk to feel good. When Mormons do it for the sake of the Church's reputation, the results are virtually identical. However, it can be very taxing on the members who don't actually feel that the lifestyle that they pretend is making them so happy is actually doing so. People frequently comment on how unusually nice, kind and pleasant Mormons are. Yet Utah is the state with the highest per-capita rate of anti-depressant use.

official representative of God. Doing so would damage both the Church and my soul. So I chose a lesser sin and lied.

Four years later, just before I graduated, I had grown out of this mindset and confessed my lie to a small group of friends from Hong Kong, while we were playing mahjong. In a very serious tone I said that I needed to tell them something. They stopped shuffling the mahjong tiles around and looked at me. There was a palpable silence that contrasted sharply with the loud crackling of the tiles a moment before.

"I didn't actually go with my parents to Hong Kong," I said. "In fact, my parents have never even been to Hong Kong." They remained still and attentive, assuming there must be more. "I went to Hong Kong as a missionary."

They pondered that for a second. "For which church?" one of them asked.

"The Mormon Church."

"You mean those guys that wear white shirts and have those black badges?" another one asked, gesturing with his hand over his shirt pocket to indicate where the black badges were positioned.

"Yes," I admitted.

"They used to come to our house. We never let 'em in."

"Is that all you wanted to tell us?" one of the others said.

"Yes. I'm really sorry."

I wondered what they thought of me, knowing that I had lied to them about who I was for so long.

The sound of the tiles resumed suddenly, and one of them laughed and said, "You sounded like you had something serious to say. I thought you were going to tell us you had a sex change and used to be a girl, or something like that." The others laughed. None of them thought that what I had just confessed was anything other than funny.

San Francisco

After graduating, I moved to San Francisco. I rented a car at the airport, drove to Chinatown, and bought a Chinese newspaper. I saw a room for rent and called the owner to ask about the price. I wanted to ask over the phone in Cantonese before they had a chance to see my face and raise the price. The room was on the second floor with a window overlooking Grant Street in North Beach, which is the district directly north of Chinatown. It was $230 a month and included free saxophone music from a man who played outside North Beach Pizza for spare change on weekend evenings. It would have been even better had the man learned a routine that lasted longer than fifteen minutes.

I quickly found a full-time job selling sofa beds and mattresses in a local store. The radio ads and window posters all said that we were having a half-price sale. People usually had to ask if things were half of the prices shown on the tags, because the implication was that the prices on the tags were either half of the normal price or twice the sale price, neither of which seemed realistic.

I had planned to work my way through graduate school, but ended up just working. I was a "sleep specialist," according to the the store's radio ads that played throughout the Bay Area. I sat at a desk against the back wall of the two thousand-square-foot display floor. I greeted, followed, and annoyed every third person who walked into the store, taking turns with the other two salesmen.

The job wore on me. But in spite of it, San Francisco provided a wonderful detour in my life. I was exposed to live music, art, and a free spirit that I found exhilarating. A brisk, constant wind from the west blew cool ocean air across the city, clearing away air pollution. Even—most San Franciscans would say "especially"—throughout the summer, an invigorating chill allowed me to remain stylish every evening in my leather jacket.

Ironically, I spoke much less Cantonese in San Francisco than I did in Austin, despite the fact that more people from Southern China live in San Francisco than in any other city in the United States.

For some reason that I don't quite understand, I maintained a strong desire to speak Cantonese. I wanted to find a career that would incorporate this rather unique ability of mine. There were a number of Cantonese speakers among the fascinating variety of customers to whom I sold furniture, and as a result I had the occasional opportunity to speak Cantonese on the job, but that wasn't the type of career I had in mind.

I frequently rented videos of television series made in Hong Kong and watched them for hours on end. One day while watching one of these videos, I saw a white man say his lines in Cantonese. [19] The real-

---

19. His name is Gregory Charles Rivers, and he's been acting in Hong Kong since 1987. He has a blog at: http://www.hokwokwing.hk/. (Hokwokwing is his Cantonese name.)

ization struck me instantly: I can do that. I immediately started making plans to go to Hong Kong and signed up for an acting class. Within months I was back in Hong Kong.

My Fifteen Minutes of Fame

The first thing I did when I arrived was to call both of the local TV stations and tell them that I wanted to act. "So do a lot of people," said a man at Asia Television, ready to hang up and get on with whatever he was doing.

"But I'm not Chinese," I told him, realizing that he apparently didn't think my Cantonese sounded like a foreigner's. It was that simple. I was soon acting full time in Hong Kong movies and television.

After two years I realized my acting was never going to go anywhere, and I didn't find it very rewarding. Most of my time was spent waiting my turn and trying to memorize lines in Cantonese that had just been written—scripts are usually an afterthought in the Hong Kong movie-making process. I never understood how my parts fit into the movies. I always asked, but nobody on the sets ever seemed to know. When it was finally my turn, I would get into position. Then, as often as not, someone would walk up to me with the script, scribble out a portion of my lines, write something else, and say, "Don't say that. Say this." Needless to say, it was virtually impossible to get into character when I didn't know what the character was, and it was all I could do just to remember the Cantonese words I was supposed to say. I'm not particularly proud of any of my acting, but I'm very glad I did it. It was a unique experience, and watching the old clips of me yelling at people, getting beaten up, or getting killed in creative ways is highly entertaining.

In one movie, I was a member of a group of European terrorists who had come to Hong Kong and taken an entire high school hostage. Of course the Hong Kong police force saved the day, and I ended up fighting to the finish alongside my terrorist friends. Poking my head up through a trap door I fired my automatic weapon until I was out of bullets. Tossing my gun aside, I pulled out a hand grenade and pulled the pin. Just before I could lob it over to where a few police officers were located, one of them shot me, making me fall where I stood with my hand still clenching the grenade. The trap door closed on top of me and was almost immediately thrown back open from the force of the grenade's explosion.

In another movie I was a corrupt police sergeant who double crossed a Triad (organized crime) boss that I had been cooperating with. Along with a few other corrupt police officers, I raided a house where this Triad boss had stashed away some heroin. We then sold the heroin in China, thinking the Triad boss would never be the wiser. We made some money from the deal and assumed that the Triad boss thought we were still on his side.

The Triad boss had arranged to meet me at a golf club a couple of days after we raided his stash and sold his heroin. I was hitting a bucket of golf balls off of a fifteen-foot-high platform when the Triad boss arrived. I (really, my character) was a little nervous, wondering whether he suspected something, but I acted calm and natural. He talked to me for a minute as I continued to hit balls onto the driving range. I felt relieved because I could tell from the way he was talking that he didn't suspect a thing.

After hitting a nice drive, I decided to stop and give him my full attention. When I turned to face him, I acted surprised to see him squatting in a batting stance with a putter over his right shoulder. He swung the putter like a bat as hard as he could, striking my left temple and spinning me around towards the edge of the driving platform.

CUT!

The camera was repositioned about fifteen yards up the driving range and aimed at the platform. While the next shot was being set up, my Chinese body double had his hair colored with a spray can until it looked like it belonged on a gold statue, and changed into the suit I was wearing, which was two sizes too large for him. Then he positioned himself where I had been on the platform.

ACTION!

He continued spinning around in the way I had begun to. Then he jumped from the platform to the ground fifteen feet below. After landing on his feet, he fell down and flopped about like a fish on land. After a bit of that he lay motionless on the grass.

CUT!

I was given one of those rubber bulbs that photographers use to blow dust off of their camera lenses. It was filled with red cough syrup from a factory in Guangzhou. A rubber tube was attached to the opening. The bulb was placed in my right hand and the tube was inserted into my shirt sleeve and ran up my arm and out the back side of my collar. I put the suit jacket on and lay on the grass in the position in which my double had died. The end of the tube was placed above my ear and my hair was carefully combed over the tube to hide it. The camera was positioned directly above me looking down.

ACTION!

My right hand went into action while the rest of me remained motionless. Pump, drip, pump, drip, pump . . . some of the sticky red cough syrup went in my ear.

CUT!

That's a wrap!

After finishing a television shoot one day very early on in my acting career, the director invited some of us out for a drink. We went to a pub called Rick's Café, whose name and décor were both inspired by the café in the movie *Casablanca*. The pub was underground, and as we came down the stairs I saw a very pretty girl drinking a coke at the bar. The director knew her and walked in her direction. Before he could introduce us, the pretty girl said, "He's quite good looking." I would have assumed she was talking about someone else if it wasn't for the fact that I was the only other person present. She didn't know that I could understand what she said since she was speaking Cantonese. If she had known she never would have said it, but I'm glad she did because it changed my life.

I still had makeup on from the filming. In addition to that, my hair had been styled and I was wearing a nice suit. I had originally planned to go to the bathroom to wash off my makeup, scruff up my hair a bit, take off my jacket, and roll up my sleeves. All of a sudden, however, I decided it would be best if I left everything just the way it was until I got home. And apparently I was right because it worked—I got that pretty girl's phone number.

Before long she and I started dating steadily, and after nearly two years we began talking about marriage. That meant I needed a real job. Since I saw the acting for what it was, it wasn't hard for me to walk away from it.

I saw a tiny ad in the *South China Morning Post* looking for a water pump salesman. I told the British owner of the company that I spoke Cantonese and that I had been a Mormon missionary in Hong Kong. "When can you start?" he asked. He knew water pumps were a tough sell, but that they had to be easier than religion.

I took the job and married that pretty girl. I spent the next nine years speaking Cantonese to her, to coworkers, to customers, and to my in-laws, who accepted me unconditionally as a member of their family. In the process I learned a few things about Hong Kong people.

Cultural Enlightenment

When shall we reach the time that we can dishonor our father and mother? Never! It is an eternal principal, and I am sorry to say—not sorry for the Japs and for the Chinese—these heathen nations, as we have been in the habit of calling them—I am not sorry for them, but for the comparison with them. Those heathen nations set the civilized Christian world an example in the honor they bestow upon their parents.

— Joseph F. Smith, the sixth prophet of the Church, from the October 1912 Conference Report, Gospel Doctrine, pp. 402–3

On the surface it may appear that the experiences of my post-mission life have little to do with the topic of this book. There is one major consequence of those experiences, however, that is entirely relevant to what this book is about. What I'm referring to is my personal cultural enlightenment. Because I continued to learn Cantonese and to experience Hong Kong life and culture, my mind gradually acquired the ability to understand a way of speaking, behaving, and thinking that is drastically different from the Mormon American culture I was raised in. The ethnocentric filter through which I had always judged human speech and behavior gradually disappeared.

As a consequence, I am better able, or perhaps just more willing, to see how similar we all are. At first I was surprised to notice the many similarities between Mormon and Chinese culture.

Each culture is founded on patriarchy, both within the family and within the society as a whole. Figures of authority are to be obeyed, not questioned. Democracy is an alien concept—especially where women and children are concerned. And the power automatically granted to male figures of authority has resulted in inevitable abuses of power.

The family is all important, and family relationships continue beyond the grave. Historically, men were allowed to have multiple wives, and the place for women has traditionally been in the home. Sex before marriage is wrong, especially for girls. When people marry, they are strongly encouraged to marry their own kind. Marrying and having children are essential—one doesn't fit comfortably into the community without them. Education, hard work, filial piety and self-sufficiency are all strongly emphasized and encouraged.

While growing up, I thought I had been born into the only group of people who actually knew what was going on: Mormons. I eventually discovered that that was total nonsense. Now I thought I had culturally assimilated into the only other culture in the world that, coincidentally, had so much in common with Mormonism. Thinking I was really onto something, I sent an e-mail to Dr. Jeanette Faurot, a former professor at UT who taught me Mandarin and Chinese culture. This was her reply:

> [B]eing brought up in any traditional society helps one understand any other traditional society, i.e., being brought up with clear and strict values (whether Mormon or any other) would help you understand Mexican, Iranian, Korean, or Ethiopian society as well as Chinese society. (I have always believed that the traditional and strictly enforced Christian/American values my parents taught me were virtually identical with Chinese Confucian values.)

Although we look at another culture and see behavior and speech that is drastically different from our own, we are all virtually the same underneath those thin surface layers. Being able to experience another culture so fully with this new perspective has been a wonderful and fulfilling experience.

The Tomb-Sweeping Festival

The Tomb-Sweeping Festival is an official holiday in Hong Kong. It is a ritual that I participate in annually. This festival reveals a lot about the customs and beliefs of popular Hong Kong religion, which, coincidentally, bears some interesting comparisons to Mormonism.

On that day, which comes each year in either late March or early April, I visit my father-in-law's tomb with my wife, daughter, and in-laws. At my mother-in-law's house, we load the car with everything that we need to carry out the ritual. We take a steamed chicken and a cooked baby pig with crispy skin. (Baby pig is almost always the first dish served at banquets on special occasions.) We bring along a bottle of rice wine to help wash it all down. We take two bouquets of flowers to place in the two small vases that are permanently attached to the tomb's floor. And, most importantly, we take several bags full of paper-simulacrum goods that we bought for my father-in-law to take care of his various wants and needs.

Every time we reach my father-in-law's tomb, the first thing we do is clean it up. My two brothers-in-law and I put on work gloves and clear away the leaves and vines that grow on the smooth cement base that extends about three feet out around the perimeter of the tomb. This cleaning part of the ritual is what gives the festival its name. My sisters-in-law scrub down the outside walls. My mother-in-law clears away the previous year's dried flowers and the remains of last year's incense sticks. Then she places the new flowers in the vases, lays the food out in front of the tomb's opening, and pours a glass of rice wine.

Chinese popular religion is a hybrid of Taoism, Buddhism, and Confucianism. In addition to burning incense and offering food and drink, people who believe in this religion burn paper models of earthly goods, believing that they will rematerialize in the place where their dead relatives and ancestors now "live." A paper mobile telephone, for example, becomes a real mobile telephone on the other side of the veil after it's been burned. We have burnt all sorts of things for my father-in-law over the years: suits, pajamas, shoes, watches, bars of gold, a car with a driver, umbrellas, a color TV, stacks and stacks of money, travel documents, plane and train tickets, a mobile phone, a maid, furniture, cigarettes, various types of *dimsum*, a radio, a bird cage with small birds covered in real feathers, a jar of instant coffee, a bottle of brandy, medicine, and much more. These things were all bought on the market, not made by the family, so it is no doubt a typical sampling of the sorts of things that are burnt by many families in Hong Kong for their deceased relatives.

My mother-in-law speaks to my father-in-law occasionally with the help of geomancers, who perform séances and serve as mediators between them. Three years ago we burnt mainly modern things like stylish Western clothes and a mobile phone. My dead father-in-law told my mother-in-law, through the geomancer, that he didn't have much use for that kind of stuff and that he prefers more traditional things. With that in mind, these past two years we burnt traditional Chinese clothes and more practical things, like lots of money and gold. My mother-in-law told us the geomancer had no way of knowing what we had burned the prior year, which, to her, proves that communication actually took place.

To start the ritual, my mother-in-law gives each of us three joss (incense) sticks. She hands them to us in the order of our status within the family, as clearly defined by this patriarchal society. My brother-in-law is first, even though he is not the oldest. I am second, because I am the oldest male in-law. Then it's my wife's turn since she is the oldest child, and on down the line. When we get our three lit joss sticks, we move them up and down vertically in front of ourselves at least three times. Then we each jab one into a small urn full of sand that lies front and center in the tomb. We then do the same thing with two other urns positioned to the right and left side of the tomb. These are for ghosts that guard the tomb.

When people move the incense up and down in front of themselves, they talk to the deceased and ask for blessings such as health, protection from bodily harm, help with careers and businesses, or anything else they might need help with. My sisters-in-law sometimes jokingly ask for the winning numbers to the lottery. Talking to deceased family members at their graves is not a strange thing to do. I imagine every culture does it, telling their lost family members about their current life situations, and even asking for help and advice. The only difference is the degree, if any, to which people actually believe that the deceased is able to hear and help.

There is a square fire pit made of brick in which all the paper items are burnt. My brother-in-law stirs the fire with a tree branch. After everything is thrown into the fire, item by item, my brother-in-law continues to stir the fire until everything is burnt completely. This is to make sure that my father-in-law doesn't end up with a piece of a shoe missing, a TV without a cord, or a birdcage with a hole in it from which the birds might escape. Once that is done, we light a few packs of firecrackers to scare away any bad ghosts who might steal what we had just burnt.

The parallels between Chinese popular religion and Mormonism are striking. They both create a fear of ghosts. They are both patriarchal, family-focused religions that are preoccupied with the dead, the afterlife, and cultural conformity. They even share the ritual of burnt offerings. These are not a physical part of Mormon culture, but burnt offerings are mentioned in the *Book of Mormon*. In First Nephi, Chapter 2, it says: "[T]hey did give thanks unto the Lord their God: and they did offer sacrifice and burnt offerings unto him." It seems that every time

Nephi and his brothers returned from one of their adventures, their father Lehi offered "sacrifice and burnt offerings."

There is a striking difference, however, in the way the two religions influence the way in which believers visualize their deceased relatives and the afterworld. My in-laws think of my father-in-law as being the same as he was when he was alive, and the place he lives as being very similar to our world. Burning paper bottles of brandy and cigarettes for him means he has retained his vices. Burning medicine for him means that those vices can still harm him. Burning a passport and train and plane tickets means he has to travel in the same way, and has the same kinds of border restrictions. So, to my in-laws, dad is still dad, and he always will be. He's frozen in time with the same habits, desires, personality, and knowledge he had when he left.

Mormons, on the other hand, think of their deceased relatives as being in their prime, dressed in white robes, and living in an environment that is a perfect and peaceful version of Earth.

In Conclusion

It's interesting to look at the beliefs and practices of my family and in-laws, observing the similarities and the differences much like an anthropologist would. Generalizing from what I've seen, it appears that religion addresses our natural fear of death. It provides an alternative to the idea that life won't continue, in one way or another, after we stop breathing. This is probably the main motivation for believing in religion. This fear of death is born from the fact that we don't ever want our short, interesting lives to end. That being the case, the last thing we should be doing is spending a large portion of our precious time following the orders of men who promise us breathtaking rewards after we are permanently breathless, if only we do what they say.

I don't want to die, but there's no rational reason for me to believe I won't. Believing that this life is all we have has changed my perspective. It makes life precious and beautiful. There is no rational reason to believe in a creator, especially one who plays favorites, elevating a "chosen people" above the rest. Believing that this life and this world are all we have makes environmental issues and social justice urgent matters. I can no longer assume that these are the latter days, that the world is about to end, and that there is therefore no need to make sustainability a high priority. And I can no longer assume that all the social injustices of the world will be rectified after everyone is dead.

Bertrand Russell explained that the moral objection to religion is that "religious precepts date from a time when men were more cruel than they are [now] and therefore tend to perpetuate inhumanities which the moral conscience of the age would otherwise outgrow."[20] The reason why this is true of religion, but not true of secular schools of thought, stems from the idea that God is eternal—the same yesterday, today, and forever. Taking the LDS Church as an example, if you believe that its prophets are spokesmen for God, then you will automatically accept their racist and sexist pronouncements. If you believe that the Bible and the *Book of Mormon* are the word of a moral God, then you will automatically accept the genocidal stories they contain as acceptable and righteous acts of mass murder.

As I have gone from being a believing Latter-day Saint to being entirely irreligious, I have changed in two major ways. First, my perspective and my priorities have changed because I now believe that all we have is this one life on this one planet. Second, I've changed morally; I no longer struggle with trying to understand why biblical genocide, *Book of Mormon* racism, and Mormon polygamy are examples of correct and righteous behavior. I have concluded that the Mormon Church is a fabrication, and that its historical record and teachings can therefore be judged in the same way, and by the same standards, that any other organization's historical record and teachings can be judged. For me it is now simple: genocide is bad; racism is bad; sexism is bad; etc. These things are unacceptable in any time and in any context. What I now struggle with is trying to understand why so many decent, caring people cling so dearly to ideas that, to me, are clearly immoral.

Many ex-Mormons come to similar conclusions. Bob McCue, a former bishop, said that his experience with Mormonism gave him a "healthy distrust for people who purport to speak with certainty for God." He now finds great joy in "learning to see the common threads of wisdom that unite humanity in a breathtaking tapestry." He has concluded that the "less someone knows about the spiritual experience of other people and how psychology and sociology work, the more likely they are to believe that a particular group of people—always their group—is favored by God." Bob also said:

---

20. *Why I Am Not a Christian*, by Bertand Russell, p. 30.

I have come to trust my own judgment more than that of any religious leader . . . People want certainty; religions that provide it are hence attractive. It is my view that this type of certainty is unhealthy. It discourages global thinking and the embracing of all humanity that will be required at some not-too-distant time to sustain life on Earth.[21]

After comparing English and Japanese attitudes about group loyalty and group concern, linguistic anthropologist Leger Brosnahan wrote the following:

Those in either group [English or Japanese] whose loyalties and concerns transcend their national or racial group, as the case may be, are very small minorities. Those concerned importantly with the East or the West or the northern or southern hemisphere or the Third, Second, or First World, not to mention those concerned with the whole world, the pollution of its oceans or atmosphere, or with outer space seem to be an honorable, growing, but very small minority of saints in either culture.[22]

If Brosnahan's observations are true, and I believe they are, then there is no reason not to assume that they generalize to all cultures. I like to think of myself as belonging to that small minority that is concerned with the whole world, rather than only being concerned primarily with those people who look, speak, and behave the way I do.

In 470 B.C., only nine years after Confucius died, a rival philosopher named Mozi was born. Mozi, a contemporary of Socrates, taught universal love. He believed that the same degree of good that one wishes for one's own parents or children should also be wished for the parents and children of others. He also taught that the identification one has with one's own community and nation should be extended to all communities and nations.

Mencius, Confucius's greatest and most influential apologist, argued against Mozi's ideas and "reaffirm[ed] the Confucian ideal of love measured within the context of different types of relationships. Confucianism, in rejecting [Mozi's philosophy], affirmed that seeking

---

21. These excerpts are from an interview of ex-Mormon and former bishop Bob McCue, by David Hedley, published in the *Calgary Herald*, May 30, 2004.

22. Brosnahan, Leger. *Japanese and English Gesture.* Taishukan Publishing, 1990. p. 53.

the good is expressed within a sphere of personal self-interests and systems of particular loyalties, especially those of family members. If [Mozi's] doctrine of nondifferentiated love were embraced, the whole of the Confucian system would be undermined."[23]

I hope that someday enough people will embrace Mozi's doctrine of nondifferentiated love to undermine Mormonism, Confucianism, and all other philosophies, religions, and world views that elevate one group of people, and one way of thinking, over all others.

---

23. McGreal, Ian P. *Great Thinkers of the Eastern World.* Harper Resource, 1995, pp. 18, 19.

Glossary

This glossary of Mormon terms has been adapted from a larger, more detailed glossary by Richard Packham. I am very grateful to Richard for permission to use his glossary, which can be seen at: http://home.teleport.com/~packham/glossary.htm.

Richard's website (http://home.teleport.com/~packham/) is an invaluable resource for information on Mormonism.

Aaronic priesthood—All worthy Mormon males are ordained to the Aaronic priesthood when they reach the age of twelve. The three offices of the Aaronic priesthood are, in order of ordination, deacon (age 12), teacher (age 14), and priest (age 16). They have specific duties. For example, priests bless the sacrament in sacrament meetings and deacons distribute the sacrament to the members attending the meeting.

Abraham, Book of—Joseph Smith's purported translation of some Egyptian papyrus rolls that came into his possession in 1835. He stated that one of the scrolls was written by the biblical Abraham "by his own hand." Smith's translation is now accepted as scripture by the LDS Church, as part of its *Pearl of Great Price*. Modern Egyptologists have also translated the scrolls, and they agree unanimously that the scrolls, which are now in the possession of the Mormon Church, are genuine, but they are common Egyptian funeral scrolls, entirely pagan in nature, having nothing to do with Abraham, and from a period two thousand years later than Abraham.

Adam-God doctrine—Brigham Young taught that God the Father was the same person as Adam. The present Church officially denies that he taught it, or, if he did, that it was only his opinion, and that it is "false doctrine."

Apostate—An apostate is a Mormon who no longer believes that Mormonism is true, especially one who expresses that conclusion. Many Mormons believe that members apostatize primarily because they are weak, they have sinned, they want to sin, or they never really had a testimony. Some Mormons believe that apostasy is an "unpardonable sin" and thus apostates are Sons of Perdition. That would mean that the author of this book is a Son of Perdition, but, as with most Mormon doctrine, it is hard to get a consistent view on this. See Hell and Blood Atonement.

Apostle—In Mormonism, there are three meanings of the term: 1) one of the original apostles named in the New Testament; 2) one of the twelve disciples appointed by Jesus in America while ministering there after his resurrection (see 3 Nephi in the *Book of Mormon*); 3) one of the members of the Quorum of the Twelve, the second highest governing body in the Mormon Church. They are addressed and referred to as "Elder [last name]."

Area representative—A Church official in charge of a relatively large geographical area including many stakes. Since 1997 they have been members of the Third, Fourth, and Fifth Quorums of Seventy.

Articles of Faith—The Articles of Faith are thirteen brief statements of Mormon beliefs, written by Joseph Smith. They are printed in copies of the *Doctrine and Covenants* and on cards and pamphlets distributed by missionaries. They are the closest thing in Mormonism to a creed. You can find them online at http://scriptures.lds.org/a_of_f/1.

Assistants to the president—Two Elder missionaries within each mission are called to serve as the mission president's assistants. They are usually referred to by other missionaries as APs or "apes."

Baby blessing—A ceremony in which a newborn baby is presented within a few weeks of birth at a sacrament meeting, where several Melchizedek priesthood holders form a circle holding the baby, pronounce a blessing on it, and give it the name chosen by the parents. If the father is worthy, he will participate and often pronounce the blessing. This is roughly the equivalent to the Christian "christening" ceremony.

Baptize, Baptism—The ritual (with confirmation) by which one becomes a member of the Mormon Church and becomes cleansed of sin. It is administered to Mormon children when they turn eight years old, and to all converts. It requires the complete immersion of the body in water, and the pronouncement of a short formula (*Book of Mormon*, 3 Nephi 11:25). Since a valid baptism can be performed only by a man holding the proper Mormon priesthood, Mormons consider baptisms performed in other churches to be invalid. Since baptism is required for salvation, Mormons provide for those who have died without the opportunity of being properly baptized by performing baptisms for the dead by proxy in Mormon temples.

Bible—Mormons believe the Bible to be "the word of God as far as it is translated correctly" (Eighth Article of Faith). They use the King James Version exclusively, supplemented by Joseph Smith's Inspired Version.

Bishop—A bishop is roughly equivalent to a pastor or minister in Protestant churches, that is, he is the head of a congregation (a ward), except that Mormon bishops are selected from the membership of the ward, they receive no formal training (they are lay clergy), and they receive no pay; they are expected to support themselves and their families without help from the Church. They generally serve five to ten years.

Bishopric—A bishop is assisted by two counselors, also selected from the ward membership. The three men comprise the bishopric.

Blessing—Mormons bless many things: a new baby, a sick person, a troubled person, the food at each meal. Any Mormon can bless the food (Mormons do not "say grace," but rather "ask the blessing"), but a Melchizedek priesthood holder is required to bless a baby or a sick or troubled person. Fathers occasionally give a "father's blessing" to a child on special occasions, such as before the child goes on a long trip or before he or she goes away to college. Such blessings by Melchizedek priesthood holders include anointing with consecrated oil.

Blood atonement—Mormons believe that some sins are so evil that Christ's atonement does not cover them, but that atonement can come only through the shedding of the sinner's blood (that is, through the violent death of the sinner). Murder is a "blood atonement" sin. In earlier days, the list of such sins included adultery and apostasy.

Book of Abraham—See Abraham, Book of.

Book of Commandments—See Commandments, Book of.

Book of Mormon—See *Mormon, Book of.*

Brethren (plural of brother)—"The Brethren" refers to the General Authorities.

Brigham Young—See Young, Brigham

Brother—Mormons address each other as "Brother" and "Sister," sometimes with the surname ("Brother Jones") but rarely with the given name. Mormons believe that Jesus and Lucifer are also our brothers. See Son of God.

Burning in the bosom—This refers to an intense feeling that Mormons claim is the Holy Ghost (Holy Spirit) confirming the truth of Mormonism. See *D&C* 9:7–9.

Cain, curse of—Mormons believe that the black race is descended from Cain, surviving the Great Flood through Ham's wife, who was black. They believe that black skin is a sign of this "curse." Since 1978 Mormons rarely discuss this doctrine, because until that time the curse of Cain was the basis for the Church excluding all blacks from holding the priesthood and from being admitted into the temple. In 1978, however, that ban was lifted, but without any change in the underlying doctrine.

Call, Calling—A Church job, usually unpaid. Many members have more than one calling. Callings may be teaching, heading a quorum, doing clerical or janitorial work, coaching an athletic team, missionary work, or practically anything. One does not apply or ask for a calling, but someone higher in authority "calls" a member to do a job, after receiving appropriate inspiration. The member is "set apart" in a brief ceremony, and sustained (accepted) by the other members in a public meeting by a show of hands.

Celestial kingdom (CK)—Mormon heaven consists of three levels or "degrees of glory," of which the highest is the Celestial Kingdom, where God actually dwells. Only good Mormons can attain the CK. The CK also is divided into three levels, and only Mormons who were married in the temple (in celestial marriage) will attain the top level. They can eventually become gods themselves. (*D&C* 76)

Celestial marriage—Marriage of a worthy Mormon man and woman performed in the temple in a ceremony which seals them together "for time and all eternity." Also called "temple marriage," "eternal marriage," and "the new and everlasting covenant [of marriage]." Until the Manifesto (1890), the term meant plural marriage (polygamy). (*D&C* 132)

Chapel—The building where a Mormon ward holds its meetings. Also called "ward house," "meeting house," or "church."

Chastity, law of—This law consists of all the commandments related to sexual behavior or thoughts. Members, especially sisters, must dress modestly. Sexual thoughts, masturbation, and premarital sex are sins. All forms of sexual perversion, including oral sex, are sinful, even if performed with a consenting spouse.

Church—When used by Mormons without any qualifier, the term refers to the Mormon Church. In this usage it is usually capitalized when written.

Church court—When a member is disciplined, the charges against the member are presented before a Church court, presided over by either the member's bishop or the stake president. These courts have recently been termed "courts of love," since the primary purpose is said to be to help the accused repent, rather than to punish. See high council.

Church Handbook of Instructions—The compilation of the rules and regulations for church operations. It is available only to church leaders. Members (or others) cannot obtain a copy. Abbreviated *CHI*.

Commandments—All the rules and regulations of the Church. Mormons are urged to "keep the commandments," meaning to be obedient to the Church's teachings and its leaders.

Commandments, Book of—The first collection of the revelations of Joseph Smith, published in Missouri in 1833. Enemies of the church destroyed the press and most copies. The revelations were revised and supplemented and later published in 1835 as the *Doctrine and Covenants*. Abbreviated as *D&C*. The complete text is online, showing the extensive revisions incorporated into it, at: http://www.2think.org/hundredsheep/boc/boc_main.shtml

Confirmation; confirm—The ritual performed immediately after baptism. It is performed by the laying on of hands by several priesthood holders, and confers the "Gift of the Holy Ghost." The recipient is thereafter an official member of the Church.

Consecrated oil—Olive oil used for anointing the sick when blessing them. The oil is blessed by several priesthood holders as they hold the open container and pronounce a short prayer. The oil is to be used for no other purpose. Some Mormons carry a tiny vial of such oil on their keychains, for use in emergencies.

Consecration, law of—A law which is presented in the temple during the endowment ritual, and which the participants must swear under oath to uphold. It requires that members give over on demand by the Church everything they may have or come to have, even their lives if necessary, for the "building up of the Kingdom of God [the Mormon Church]."

Counselor—All presiding officers in the Church, from the President of the Church down to the president of the local deacon's quorum of twelve-year-old boys, have two assistants, or vice-presidents, called counselors, ranked as "first counselor" and "second counselor."

Court of love—See Church court.

Covenant—Mormons are required to make numerous solemn promises to the Church, as God's representative on Earth. Many of these are made during the temple endowment ceremony. These are called "covenants." One of the covenants is the "New and Everlasting Covenant [of celestial marriage]." One of the questions in a worthiness interview is, "Have you kept all your covenants?" See also Born in the covenant.

Cumorah—(ka-MORE-a) A hill near Palmyra, New York, where Joseph Smith allegedly found the gold plates from which he translated the *Book of Mormon*. According to the *Book of Mormon*, it was also the site of the last great battle between the Nephites and the Lamanites, during which the Nephites were exterminated. It is now the site of an annual pageant presented by the Church, telling the Mormon story.

Deacon—The lowest office in the Aaronic priesthood. Worthy Mormon boys are ordained to this office at the age of twelve. The principle function of a deacon is to distribute the sacrament in meetings.

Discussions, missionary—A series of six lessons presented by missionaries to explain Mormonism to prospective converts, who are called "investigators." The goal is to baptize investigators as members of the Church. Discussions are usually presented in the investigator's home, and usually about a week apart.

Disfellowship—A lesser form of Church discipline than excommunication. It is imposed by a Church court ("court of love") for transgressions such as adultery. It is usually for a relatively short term, such as one year. Disfellowshipped Mormons still retain Church membership, but may not exercise their priesthood, enter the temple, partake of the sacrament, or speak in Church meetings. However, they can continue to wear their temple garments and pay tithing. If the member does not show repentance during his disfellowshipped period, he may be excommunicated.

District, District leader—Missions are divided into zones, and zones are divided into districts. Each district and zone has one Elder missionary that is called to serve as its leader. Districts often include Sister missionaries, but they are never called to serve as district leaders, or in any other position of authority over their male counterparts.

Doctrine and Covenants—One of the four standard works of Mormon scripture; a collection of the revelations of the prophets of the Church. All but a few are from the first prophet, Joseph Smith. Divided into numbered "sections." Cited as *D&C*. Available online at http://scriptures.lds.org/dc/contents.

Elder—1) The lowest office (rank) of the Melchizedek priesthood, to which all worthy Mormon men are ordained at about age 18 or soon thereafter; 2) a male Mormon missionary; 3) a title used with the surname to address a male missionary or a general authority.

Elders quorum—Every ward has an elders quorum to which all elders in the ward belong. One Elder is called to serve as Elders Quorum President.

Endowment(s), Endowed—The most important of the rituals performed in the temple, endowment is only for worthy adults. It involves ritual washings, anointings, observing a lengthy dramatic summary of the Mormon view of God's plan, learning secret passwords and handgrips, all while dressed in special ritual robes (called "temple clothing" or "temple robes"). Receiving the endowment (or "taking out your endowments") is a prerequisite to temple marriage. Mormons are forbidden to reveal or discuss the endowment outside the temple. After being endowed, Mormons are encouraged to repeat the ritual as often as possible, as proxy for dead persons, who thus become eligible for the celestial kingdom.

Ensign—The principal official Church magazine, published monthly.

Eternal marriage—See Celestial marriage.

Excommunication, Excommunicate—A form of Church discipline imposed by a Church court ("court of love") in which a Mormon is expelled from membership in the Church. Until 1985, excommunication was the only process recognized by the Church for ending Church membership. Excommunication is imposed for teaching false doctrine, for serious transgressions, especially violation of temple covenants, for murder or incest, or, in the case of prominent Church leaders, for embarrassing the Church. After someone has been excommunicated, they are subject to all the restrictions imposed on those who have been disfellowshipped. In addition, they are not allowed to pay tithing or wear their temple garments. See also Disfellowship.

Family home evening—On Monday evenings, family members are supposed to organize a meeting that includes an opening and closing prayer, a Church-related lesson, perhaps a game, and perhaps some refreshments. Members of the family take turns performing different part of family home evening. The Church website (www.lds.org) states that "Family home evening is a special time set aside each week that brings family members together and strengthens their love for each other, helps them draw closer to Heavenly Father, and encourages them to live righteously." The website also suggests lesson topics and activities.

Fast and testimony meeting—On "fast Sunday" (the first Sunday of each month) there is no regular sermon in sacrament meeting; instead, the members, as they are "moved by the Spirit," may speak, usually to "bear their testimony."

Fast offering—Mormons are requested to fast the first Sunday of each month by foregoing two meals (usually breakfast and lunch) and then donating the money saved to the Church for the benefit of the needy.

Fireside—A meeting in addition to regular Church meetings. These are usually held in the evening, are less formal than regular Church services, and are primarily for the youth of the Church. A relatively senior leader (i.e., higher ranking than bishop) is often, but not always, the key speaker at a fireside.

First Presidency—The First Presidency is the top ruling body of the Church, consisting of the president of the Church (the "prophet, seer and revelator") and his two counselors. They also almost always hold the office of apostle, in addition to the apostles in the Quorum of the Twelve.

Free agency—Mormons emphasize that human beings have free choice to obey or to disobey God.

Fundamentalist—Either as a noun or adjective, "fundamentalist" refers to Mormons who believe that the present Church has apostatized from the original teachings of Joseph Smith and Brigham Young, having abandoned plural marriage and other early doctrines (such as the Adam-God doctrine). Fundamentalists generally practice polygamy. They are considered apostates by the Church, and are excommunicated when discovered. Many live isolated from society.

GA—Abbreviation for General Authority.

Garments—The "garment of the holy priesthood" is a white undergarment which all endowed Mormons are required to wear at all times. Formerly it was a one-piece union suit-style garment ("longjohns"), extending to the wrists and ankles. It now extends only to below the knee, and just below the shoulder, and may be either a one-piece or two-piece garment. It has four special markings sewn into it, at the nipples, the navel, and the right knee. It must be purchased from the Church, which manufactures these garments, through special stores. Mormons believe that the garment protects them from physical and spiritual harm.

Genealogy—Because Mormons believe that it is their responsibility to perform the ordinances required for salvation for their own deceased ancestors (as well as for other dead persons), they must first identify those persons by name, so that they can act as their proxies in the temple. Thus the Mormons are very avid genealogists. The Church has one of the most valuable storehouses of genealogical data in the world, and makes it available free to everyone online: http://www.familysearch.org/.

General authorities—A collective term for the top leaders of the Church.

General conference—Twice a year, in early April and early October, the Church holds a general conference at its Conference Center in Salt Lake City, lasting two days. This consists mostly of addresses by the General Authorities. The conferences are broadcast on radio and television, and fed by satellite to stake centers all over the world so that Mormons everywhere can hear the proceedings.

Gentile—A non-Mormon. Mormons consider themselves to be the "true house of Israel," and therefore all non-Mormons are gentiles, including Jews.

Gold plates, Golden plates—According to Joseph Smith, an ancient set of records engraved by the ancient prophet Mormon on metal plates, and buried by his son Moroni about 421 A.D. in the Hill Cumorah in New York state, where Joseph Smith dug them up in 1827 and translated them as the *Book of Mormon.*

Glory, three degrees of—Heaven, which has three levels, or degrees: the celestial (highest), the terrestrial (middle), and the telestial (lowest). See *D&C* 76.

Gospel—When Mormons use this term, they normally mean Mormon scripture, even in the phrase "the gospel of Jesus Christ." In defense against criticisms aimed at the Church, members sometimes respond that "the gospel is true, the Church is not." They mean that the Church was set up and run by humans, who are imperfect, to help its members live the gospel. Mormons can, however, also use the term gospel to refer to the four canonical gospels (Matthew, Mark, Luke, and John).

Gospel doctrine—Adult members attend this class on Sundays while their children attend Sunday school. All the lessons are based on Gospel Doctrine lesson manuals that are written at Church headquarters in Salt Lake City.

Greenie—Refers to a missionary who has recently begun his mission (one who has just been "born" into the mission field).

Heaven—See Glory, three degrees of.

Heavenly Father—A common Mormon term for God the Father.

Hell—The Mormon doctrine of hell is contradictory. The *Book of Mormon* describes hell as a place of torment and burning to which all non-Christians will be condemned. But *D&C* 76 provides for relatively pleasant lower degrees of heaven for non-Christians (the Terrestrial Kingdom), and even for wicked people (the Telestial Kingdom). Only the Sons of Perdition (apostates from Mormonism) will be condemned to "outer darkness" to spend eternity in torment with Satan. (*D&C* 76:31-38)

High council—A body of twelve high priests in each stake, which functions as an advisory body to the stake president. It also serves as a Church court to try offenses by holders of the Melchizedek priesthood. (See Court of love). A member of the high council is called a "high councilor." High councilors often visit ward meetings as representatives of the stake president.

High priest—The highest office in the Melchizedek priesthood to which most Mormon males can be ordained (the office of apostle is higher). Most worthy Mormon males over the age of 35 are high priests.

Home teachers—Pairs of priesthood holders assigned by the bishop to visit all families in the ward every month. Each family is assigned a pair of home teachers, who call on all of their assigned families once a month to present a short lesson, to inquire about the families' welfare, and to report any problems to the bishop.

Intelligence—1) In Mormonism, the basic material of the universe, which has existed eternally and from which all gods and spirits are produced; the first stage in the development of a human being or god: intelligence > spirit > human being with a body > existence after death as spirit > resurrected body > god. 2) An oft-cited Mormon scripture says: "The Glory of God is intelligence, or, in other words, light and truth." (*D&C* 93:36)

Interpreters—See Urim and Thummim.

Interview—Interviews with Church leaders are an important part of Mormon culture. Before people are baptized, they must successfully pass an interview to ensure they are worthy. Ward members must pass interviews with their bishops before they can obtain a temple recommend. Children, beginning at age twelve, are interviewed before progressing onto the next level of the Mormon hierarchal structure. For example, a 16-year-old boy who holds the Aaronic Priesthood rank of teacher must pass a bishop's interview before he can be ordained to the rank of priest. Successfully passing an interview means that the person answered "yes" to questions regarding belief (e.g., "Do you believe that Joseph Smith was a prophet of God?", and "no" to questions regarding forbidden behavior (e.g., "Do you masturbate?").

Investigator—See Discussions, missionary

Jack Mormon—A Mormon who is not active, who does not keep the commandments; a Mormon who is Mormon in name only.

Joseph Smith, Jr.—See Smith, Joseph, Jr.

Journal—Similar to a personal diary. Members are strongly encouraged to keep a journal.

Journal of Discourses—A printed collection of 26 volumes of the sermons of early church leaders, principally from the days of Brigham Young. Online at: http://journalofdiscourses.org/.

Junior companion—One companion of a missionary companionship is assigned to be the senior companion. The other is the junior companion. Juniors are supposed to obey their seniors.

Kolob—(KOH-lobb) A distant star (not otherwise identified) near which, according to the Book of Abraham, Chapter 3:2–9, is the planet on which God dwells and from which He governs the universe.

LDS—An abbreviation for Latter-day Saint (Mormon), from the official name of the church: The Church of Jesus Christ of Latter-day Saints; used as an adjective or a noun.

Lamanite—(LAY-mu-nite) Noun or adjective. Originally referred to the descendants and followers of Laman, a brother of Nephi (in the *Book of Mormon*), who generally were unrighteous and warred against the more righteous Nephites, eventually completely exterminating them. Mormon doctrine asserts that the Lamanites are the ancestors of the Native American (Indian) tribes. Thus, Mormons frequently use the term to refer to present-day Native Americans.

Lucifer—A Son of God, our brother, and a brother of Jesus. In the pre-existence, when Lucifer's proposed plan for man's salvation was rejected by the Council in Heaven, he rebelled and one-third of the spirits followed him. He is the devil, Satan.

Meetings—Mormons have many meetings, and Mormons are asked in every worthiness interview, "Do you attend your meetings?" In addition to the meetings during the Sunday block, there may be other auxiliary or quorum meetings and committee meetings. If a member has many callings (most of which include attending committee meetings), there may not be much free time in the week for family or leisure.

Melchizedek priesthood—The higher of the two Mormon priesthoods. (The other is the Aaronic priesthood). The Melchizedek ranks (offices) are apostle (highest), high priest, elder. Until recently, there was also the office of seventy between high priest and elder, but that office is no longer granted. All worthy adult Mormon males are ordained to some office in the Melchizedek priesthood.

Member—Used without any qualifier, a member of the Church, especially in heavily Mormon areas in the West, or when speaking with other Mormons. Strangers in Utah might be asked, "Are you a member?"

Mission, Missionaries—The Mormons are avid missionaries. All 19-year-old boys are commanded to serve a two-year, full-time mission. Missionaries, or their families, are supposed to pay all the expenses of a mission, except travel. to and from the mission locale. Missionaries' only training is several weeks at a Missionary Training Center (MTC), which may include some foreign language training. Missionaries are assigned to an area (also called a "mission") presided over by a mission president, with headquarters at a "mission home." According to the Church's official website, there are more than 50,000 full-time missionaries serving in nearly 350 missions all over the world. Unlike missionaries of some other denominations, who are medical or teaching personnel and whose primary purpose is to ease human suffering in underdeveloped areas, Mormon missionaries (at least until relatively recently) were sent mostly to the industrialized, Christian nations, with the sole purpose of proselytizing. In addition to the full-time missionaries, many Mormons are called to serve part-time missions in their own communities ("ward missionaries," formerly called "stake missionaries"). See also Discussions, missionary.

Mission call—The calling to serve a mission. Coming in the form of an official letter from Church headquarters in Salt Lake City, a mission call announces which mission the missionary has been assigned to serve in, which language if any he or she will learn, and on which date he or she is to begin.

Missionary companion—Mormon missionaries always work in pairs. Thus, every missionary has a companion of the same sex. No missionary is supposed to be away from the presence of his or her companion at any time.

Morally clean—Equivalent of sexually "pure." Mormonism severely condemns all types of premarital or extramarital sexual activity, including masturbation, "French" kissing, petting, watching R-rated movies, and looking at pornography. (Rodin's statue "The Kiss" was banned from an art display at BYU.)

Mormon—As a noun: 1) The name of the ancient Nephite who supposedly compiled and edited the *Book of Mormon* and inscribed it on the gold plates; 2) A member of the Mormon Church. As an adjective: 1) Referring to the Church of Jesus Christ of Latter-day Saints or its members; 2) Referring to anything derived from the *Book of Mormon* or the teachings of Joseph Smith. Officially the Church dislikes the use of the term.

Mormon, Book of—Published in 1830 in Palmyra, New York, by Joseph Smith, it purports to be a translation of the gold plates delivered to Joseph Smith by the angel Moroni in 1827. It claims to be a record of the ancient inhabitants of America, from about 2200 BC to 421 AD. Allegedly written in "Reformed Egyptian," the present English edition is 521 pages long. After the Bible, it is the second of the four standard works of scripture for Mormons. A free copy of the *Book of Mormon* can be obtained from any Mormon bishop or missionary, or almost any thrift store. The text of the Book of Mormon is online at http://scriptures.lds.org/. The original 1830 version, with the thousands of changes made in subsequent versions, is online at http://ww2.think.org/hundredsheep/bom1830/bom_main.shtml.

Moroni—(mu-ROH-nigh) In the *Book of Mormon*, the son of Mormon, and the last surviving Nephite, who buried the sacred records of his people, written on the gold plates, in the Hill Cumorah, and, as an angel, guarded them until 1827, when he loaned them to Joseph Smith for translation. Moroni is believed to be the angel referred to in Revelation 14:6–7 (*D&C* 133:36). His statue, depicting him blowing a trumpet, tops the steeple of most Mormon temples.

MTC—Missionary Training Center. The principal center is in Provo, Utah. Others are located in South America and England. After being called to a mission, new missionaries spend several weeks at the MTC for training. Because of the need for language instruction, this training is somewhat longer for missionaries who will be sent to a country in which a different language is spoken.

Nephi—(NEE-figh) An important *Book of Mormon* prophet. See Nephite.

Nephite—(NEE-fight) Noun and adjective. In the B*ook of Mormon*, a descendant or follower of Nephi, one of the sons of Lehi, who (according to the Book of Mormon) brought his family from Jerusalem to America about 590 BC. The Nephites were generally more righteous than their cousins the Lamanites, but were completely exterminated by them at the Hill Cumorah about 421 A.D.

Obedience, law of—This law requires Mormons to obey all commandments of God as given through the leaders of the Mormon Church and the Mormon scriptures. As part of the endowment, temple Mormons take an oath to obey this law.

Ordinance—Any ritual in Mormonism, including baptism, confirmation, endowment (which consists of numerous ordinances, such as washing and anointing), and temple marriage. Often used in the phrase "laws and ordinances of the Gospel."

Outer darkness—See Hell.

Patriarch—1) One of the ancestors of the House of Israel, as portrayed especially in Genesis; 2) An office of the Melchizedek priesthood, the primary function of which is to give patriarchal blessings to members. Usually each stake has a patriarch, most often an older man.

Patriarchal blessing—A blessing pronounced upon a Mormon by a patriarch, usually only once in a lifetime, and usually when the member is a teenager or young adult. The purpose is to outline for the member what blessings and dangers can be expected in life. Guided by the Holy Spirit, the patriarch also identifies the tribe of Israel to which the member belongs (usually Ephraim or Manasseh). The blessing is transcribed into writing, and one copy is given to the member and another retained in Church records.

Pearl of Great Price—The fourth of the standard Mormon scriptures. (The others are the Bible, *Book of Mormon*, and *D&C*.) *Pearl of Great Price* contains the Book of Moses, the Book of Abraham, and some writings of Joseph Smith.

Perdition, Sons of—See Hell.

Pioneers—The early Mormon settlers of Utah, also called the Mormon Pioneers. "Pioneer Day" commemorates the entrance into the Salt Lake Valley of the first wagon train of Mormons on July 24, 1847, and is celebrated as an official state holiday in Utah, with parades and pageants.

Plural marriage—The common Mormon term for polygamy, the practice of one husband having more than one wife at the same time. It was practiced secretly by Joseph Smith beginning in the 1830s. He introduced the practice secretly to his closest confederates in the 1840s, and produced a revelation in 1843 in which God commanded its practice as the "new and everlasting covenant of marriage" (*D&C* 132). The doctrine was kept secret from the general membership of the Church until 1852, after which all faithful Mormons were urged to practice it. The practice outraged the American public, with the U.S. government passing ever more stringent laws to try to stop its practice. Finally the Church reluctantly abandoned the practice in 1890, although the doctrine itself has never been repudiated by the Church. Plural marriage is still practiced by many fundamentalists. See also Celestial marriage.

Polygamy—See Plural marriage.

Pre-existence—Also called "pre-mortal existence." Mormons believe that humans existed individually before birth into this life, first as "intelligences," and then as "spirit children" of God and one of his wives. Our status in this life—whether born into miserable poverty in a backward country in primitive times, or born to good and prosperous Mormon parents in modern times—depends on how righteous we were during the pre-existence. See also Cain, curse of, and Lucifer.

Preparation day—Also P-day. This is the only day of the week that missionaries are allowed to do things other than proselytize. They can do things such as write letters, wash clothes, shop, visit tourist attractions, etc.

President of the Church—The top Church leadership position. The president and his two counselors make up the First Presidency. The president is considered to be a "prophet, seer and revelator." He holds office for life. In modern times, upon the death of the president, the First Presidency is dissolved and the senior member of the Quorum of the Twelve succeeds to the office.

Priest—The highest of the offices of the Aaronic (lower) priesthood, usually conferred upon young men when they reach the age of sixteen. A priest has authority to baptize and to bless the sacrament.

Priesthood—The authority to act in God's name in performing rituals (ordinances) and other religious offices. It can only be obtained via ordination by laying on of hands by one already holding the priesthood being conferred. Mormons believe that only they hold authentic priesthood. All worthy Mormon males over the age of 12 are ordained to some office (rank) in the priesthood. The first (lower) is the Aaronic priesthood, the higher is the Melchizedek priesthood. Each includes all the authority of the lower offices. Women are not allowed to hold the priesthood. Black people, whether male or female, were barred from the priesthood until 1978. See Cain, curse of.

Priesthood meeting—This is the Sunday meeting attended by all males who are old enough to hold the priesthood. Girls and women attend separate meetings at the same time.

Primary—A church auxiliary organization for children from pre-school to age 12. The Primary meets every Sunday during the Sunday block.

Prophet—A person through whom God supposedly speaks to the world. Mormons believe that God has inspired prophets with his messages at all times, in all dispensations. Mormons believe that the founder of the Mormon Church, Joseph Smith, Jr., was a prophet on an equal footing with the Biblical prophets, and that each of his successors as president of the Mormon Church was likewise a prophet, as is the current president, who is referred to as "the living prophet." Although the Biblical prophets and Joseph Smith made many prophecies, few Mormon prophets in the last hundred years have done so.

Rather, they restrict themselves to giving advice and speaking on doctrinal matters. The modern apostles are also considered to be prophets. Until the 1960s, when Mormons used the term "the prophet" they were generally referring to Joseph Smith. Nowadays the term is used to mean also "the living prophet," i.e., the current president of the Church. Primary children are taught a song, "Follow the Prophet—he knows the way!," meaning do what the president of the Church tells you to do.

Quorum—All priesthood holders are organized into small local groups called quorums. Each quorum has a president and two counselors at the head. Also the general authorities are organized into quorums, such as the Quorum of the Twelve [Apostles], the First Quorum of Seventy, etc.

Quorum of the Twelve—The second-highest governing body in the Church after the First Presidency. Also called the Council of the Twelve. It consists of twelve apostles, who serve for life. The senior member is the president of the Twelve, and is next in line to succeed the president of the Church.

Recommend—See Temple recommend.

Relief Society—The women's auxiliary organization of the Church. It is also the name of the meeting that women attend when men attend priesthood meeting.

Returned missionary—A person who has served a full-time mission for the church.

Revelation—Mormons believe in "continuing revelation," i.e., that God is continually revealing important truths to the living prophet, in contrast to most Christians, who contend that God's revelations were complete when the Bible canon was closed.

RM—Abbreviation for returned missionary.

Sabbath—Like most Christian sects, Mormons designate Sunday as the Sabbath. Members are commanded to "keep the Sabbath" by attending Sunday meetings and refraining from working or patronizing any type of business.

Sacrament, Sacrament service—The Mormon name for the "Lord's Supper," "communion," or "eucharist," the ritual part of the weekly sacrament meeting, consisting of a ceremonial eating of a small piece of bread and drinking a small cup of water, each having been consecrated by a priest with a set prayer (*Book of Mormon*, Moroni 4:3 and 5:2) and distributed to the congregation in the pews by the deacons. Only members in good standing are to "take the sacrament."

Sacrament meeting—The principal weekly Mormon worship service in each ward, part of the Sunday block, usually presided over by the bishop. It is opened and closed with a prayer offered by a priesthood holder, and it includes the singing of hymns, the sacrament service, one or two sermons by members called by the bishop, and possibly other music, perhaps by the ward choir. It is the most important meeting all Mormons are required to attend.

Seal, Sealing—Mormons believe that families who are ceremonially joined to each other ("sealed"—husband to wife, parents to children) will enjoy that same relationship in the next life. This belief is the basis for the Mormon slogan "Families Are Forever!" See also Celestial marriage.

Seer—One to whom God has given the ability to know hidden truths, especially one who is authorized to receive knowledge through the use of the Urim and Thummim or a seer stone. It is a higher calling than prophet. (*Book of Mormon*, Mosiah 8:15-18) The president of the Church, as well as being a prophet, is also a seer. (*D&C* 107:92, 124:94).

Seer stone—See Urim and Thummim, and Seer.

Senior companion—One companion of a missionary companionship is assigned to be the senior companion. The other is the junior companion. Seniors technically have authority over their junior companions.

Seventy—Formerly an office in the Melchizedek priesthood, above elder and below high priest. Now no longer used, except as a designation for the General Authorities of the third tier, the First Quorum of Seventy, etc., including area representatives, who are organized into quorums of seventy. Based on the seventy men sent out by Jesus (Luke 10:1).

Sister—The female equivalent of brother. Female missionaries are addressed as "Sister" (surname), as with "Elder" (surname) for male missionaries.

Smith, Joseph, Jr. (1805–1844)—The founder of Mormonism, "translator" of the *Book of Mormon*, revered by Mormons as a prophet.

Son of God—Brigham Young taught that Jesus is literally the son of God the Father, both spiritually and physically, his spirit first having been sired by God in the pre-existence, and his body of flesh later also sired by God the Father through normal sexual relations with Mary. (Today Mormons believe in the miraculous virgin birth of Jesus, and most are unaware that Brigham ever taught otherwise.) All humans also have spirits created the same way as Jesus' spirit was created, thus we are all spiritual children of God, and Jesus is our spiritual brother.

Sons of Perdition—See Hell.

Split—When two pairs of missionary companionships trade companions temporarily, it is called a split or a switch.

Spirit, the—The Holy Ghost. Worthy members receive inspiration and guidance in their lives when they are "in tune" with the Spirit.

Spirit world—The place where we resided in the pre-existence.

Square, the—The act of holding one's right arm up as one does when being sworn into public office or in a court of law. The upper arm is held parallel to the ground and the forearm is pointed straight up with the hand held open, flat, and facing forward. Priesthood holders raise their right arm to the square when performing baptisms or when casting away evil spirits. Both men and women hold their right arm to the square when making their covenants during the temple ceremony. All members hold their right arm to the square when asked during sacrament meeting or general conference if they "sustain" newly appointed Church leaders, providing a requisite visual show of support.

Stake—A stake consists of several neighboring wards, usually five to ten. Roughly equivalent to, but much smaller than, a Catholic diocese.

Stake presidency, Stake president—Each stake is presided over by a stake president, assisted by two counselors. These three men are the stake presidency.

Street display—Missionaries throughout the world occasionally set up a portable signboard of some kind in public. They stand around the signboard and attempt to talk to members of the public who may be sitting close by or walking past. The aim of the missionaries is to arrange future meetings with people in their homes so that they can teach those people the missionary discussions.

Switch—See Split.

Teacher—An office in the Aaronic priesthood, given to worthy Mormon boys when they turn 14. See also Home teacher.

Telestial kingdom—The lowest of the Three Degrees of Glory (heaven), described at *D&C* 76:81–90, also called hell (v. 84).

Temple—The most sacred Mormon buildings are temples. Only special ordinances are performed there, including endowments, sealings (including temple marriages), and baptisms for the dead. Only worthy Mormons are admitted, by presenting a temple recommend. There are now over a hundred Mormon temples; they are in most major U.S. and world cities and in many smaller U.S. cities. The only thing that Mormon temples have in common with the temples described in the Bible is the name.

Temple marriage—See Celestial marriage.

Temple recommend—A written pass which must be presented by a Mormon before being admitted to the temple. It is obtained from a bishop, who conducts a private interview to determine the applicant's worthiness, since only worthy Mormons are allowed to participate in the temple ordinances. The interview questions inquire about the member's testimony, faithfulness to covenants, obedience to the commandments, especially keeping the Word of Wisdom, whether the member is morally clean, whether the member has paid a full tithing, whether the member attends meetings regularly, and whether the member sustains the Church leaders. A recommend is valid for two years. It must be surrendered if the member is disfellowshipped.

Terrestrial kingdom—The second of the Three Degrees of Glory in Mormon heaven, above the Telestial Kingdom and below the Celestial Kingdom. See *D&C* 76:71–80

Testimony—Every Mormon is expected to have a testimony of the truthfulness of the gospel, that is, to "know" that Mormonism is true. This knowledge is usually obtained through prayer (see the *Book of Mormon*, Moroni 10:4), fasting, study, reading the standard works, or through personal revelation. It is the equivalent of what Christians call "faith." Mormons are expected to be always ready to "bear" their testimony, especially in fast and testimony meeting. Testimony is often formulaic: "I know with every fiber of my being that the Gospel is true; I know that Joseph Smith was a prophet of God; and I know that the present president of the Church is a living prophet. I know that the *Book of Mormon* is true, and I have received a firm witness thereto from the Holy Ghost. I bear this testimony to you in the name of Jesus Christ. Amen." Bearing testimony is the Mormon equivalent of Christian "witnessing." To have a "weak" testimony is to have doubts about Mormonism, and to "lose" one's testimony is to become an apostate.

Tithing, Tithe—The practice of giving one-tenth of one's income to one's bishop. It is a major source of income for the Church, estimated at five billion dollars per year. The payment of a full tithe is a requirement for a temple recommend and for advancement in the priesthood.

Tract (verb)—The most common form of proselytizing by Mormon missionaries. The door-to-door approach with which nearly everyone is familiar. Most missionaries "go tracting" nearly every day.

Transfers—The monthly reassignment of missionaries to various districts within their mission.

Trunky—An adjective describing a missionary who has psychologically packed his or her trunks and is anxious to return home.

United Order—Also called the Order of Enoch. This refers to several attempts in the early Church to require all members to transfer their private property to the Church, which would then distribute it more equally, as needed. It is the logical conclusion of the Law of Consecration. See *D&C* 42:32, 51:3, 82:17.

Urim and Thummim—Also called "interpreters" in the *Book of Mormon*, and sometimes used to refer to a seer stone, especially the stone owned by Joseph Smith. In Mormon lore, they are described as two transparent stones set in a bowed frame attached to a breast plate, which, when worn by the seer, allows him to see through the stones and interpret writings in foreign languages. Joseph Smith claimed that he obtained the ancient interpreters when he was given the gold plates by Moroni. Although the official Mormon history says that Smith used the Urim and Thummim on the breastplate to translate the *Book of Mormon*, most witnesses said that he used the same seer stone which he had used as a young man in seeking buried treasure. Smith's seer stone is still in the possession of the church.

Visitors' center—Almost all Mormon historical sites and temples have a visitors' center, where guides (who are often missionaries) explain the significance of the place and at the same time tell the visitors about Mormonism. These centers are sometimes very elaborate, with museum-like displays, motion picture theaters, dioramas, etc.

Ward—A Mormon congregation, equivalent to a Catholic parish, usually with 300 to 500 members, presided over by a lay bishop. Every ward covers an exclusive geographical area, and Mormons are required to be members of the ward in which their home is located.

Ward house—See Chapel.

Word of Wisdom—Section 89 of the *D&C*. It advises Mormons to avoid strong drink, hot beverages, tobacco, and, except in winter, meat. It has been interpreted to forbid all use of alcohol, tobacco, tea, and coffee. Especially strict members interpret it to forbid all caffeine, as well as decaffeinated drinks, either hot or cold. Although it was worded as merely advisory, it is now strictly enforced, and to "keep" the Word of Wisdom is a primary requirement for obtaining a temple recommend or for completing a satisfactory worthiness interview.

Worthy, Worthiness—Only those who are considered worthy will advance in the Church, receive higher callings, or receive a temple recommend. At each such step, the member is interviewed by the bishop, who asks probing questions (see temple recommend). The first such interview occurs when a Mormon child is eight years old and is to be baptized.

Young, Brigham (1801–1877)—The successor to Joseph Smith as president of the Church. Upon Smith's death in 1844, Young led the majority of the Church members to Utah.

Zone, Zone leader—Missions are divided into zones, and zones are divided into districts. Each district and zone has one Elder missionary that is called to serve as its leader. Zones often include Sister missionaries, but they are never called to serve as district leaders, or to serve in any other position of authority over their male counterparts.

Recommended Reading
and Viewing

CD-ROM

Smith Research Associates, *New Mormon Studies CDROM: A Comprehensive Resource Library*. Salt Lake City: Signature Books, 1997.

> This user-friendly, searchable CD-ROM is by far the best single-source resource for researching Mormonism. It includes the complete texts of numerous books and magazines about Mormonism, transcripts of early general conference talks, copies of all the Mormon scriptures, and the 26-volume set of the *Journal of Discourses*.

DVD

Grooters, John (director). *The Lost Book of Abraham: Investigating a Remarkable Mormon Claim*. The Institute for Religious Studies, 2002.

Messer, Bobby Lee (producer/director). *Line Upon Line: Mormonism Transcended*. Salt Lake City: The Exmormon Foundation, 2007.
(Available at www.exmormonfoundation.org)

Public Broadcasting System. *The Mormons*. "Frontline" and "American Experience," 2006.
(Available at www.pbs.org/mormons/)

Web Sites

http://contentdm.lib.byu.edu/cgi-bin/browseresults.exe
> Brigham Young University's online collection of scanned and searchable early Mormon documents; it includes Mormon pioneer diaries and the entire 26-volume set of the *Journal of Discourses*.

www.2think.org/hundredsheep/boc/boc_main.shtml
> The first collection of the revelations of Joseph Smith, published in Missouri in 1833, were called the *Book of Commandments*. Enemies of the Church destroyed the press and most copies. The revelations were revised and supplemented and later published in 1835 as the *Doctrine and Covenants*. The complete text of the *Book of Commandments* is online, showing the extensive revisions made to the *Doctrine and Covenants*.

www.exmormon.org
> A very popular web site titled "Recovery from Mormonism" that was started in 1995 to help former Mormons make the transition out of Mormonism. It includes hundreds of stories from ex-Mormons.

www.exmormonfoundation.org/
> The web site of the Exmormon Foundation, a nonprofit organization set up to "support those who are questioning their Mormon faith."

www.lds.org
> The official web site of The Church of Jesus Christ of Latter-day Saints.

www.pbs.org/mormons/view/
> The PBS documentary about Mormons and their history can be viewed here in its entirety.

http://home.teleport.com/~packham/index.htm
> Richard Packham's very informative, interesting, and often entertaining web site about Mormonism and other topics. Richard also keeps a mirror site because his main site occasionally gets too much traffic: www.geocities.com/packham33

www.utlm.org/
> The web site of Utah Lighthouse Ministry, which includes an impressive amount of information about the LDS Church by Sandra Tanner and her late husband Jerald Tanner, who were both born and raised as Mormons.

Books

Brodie, Fawn M. *No Man Knows My History: The Life of Joseph Smith (2nd Revised Enlarged Edition)*. New York: Vintage, 1995.

Buerger, David John. *The Mysteries of Godliness: A History of Mormon Temple Worship*. Salt Lake City: Signature Books, 2002.

Compton, Todd. *In Sacred Loneliness: The Plural Wives of Joseph Smith*. Salt Lake City. Signature Books, 1997.

Cornwall, Marie; Heaton, Tim B.; Young, Lawrence A (Editors). *Contemporary Mormonism: Social Science Perspectives*. Champaign, IL: University of Illinois Press, 2001.

Krakauer, Jon. *Under the Banner of Heaven: A Story of Violent Faith*. New York: Anchor, 2004.

Larsen, Charles M. *By His Own Hand on Papyrus: A New Look at the Joseph Smith Papyri*. Institute for Religious Research, 1992.

Metcalfe, Brent Lee (Editor). *New Approaches to the Book of Mormon: Explorations in Critical Methodology*. Salt Lake City: Signature Books, 1993.

Naifeh, Steven and Smith, Gregory White. *The Mormon Murders: A True Story of Greed, Forgery, Deceit, and Death*. New York: St. Martins Paperbacks, 2005.

Ostling, Richard and Joan. *Mormon America*. San Francisco: HarperSanFrancisco, 1999.

Palmer, Grant H. *An Insiders View of Mormon Origins*. Salt Lake City: Signature Books, 2002.

Quinn, D. Michael. *The Mormon Hierarchy: Origins of Power*. Salt Lake City: Signature Books, 1994.

Quinn, D. Michael. *The Mormon Hierarchy: Extensions of Power*. Salt Lake City: Signature Books, 1997.

Souterton, Simon. *Losing a Lost Tribe: Native Americans, DNA, and the Mormon Church*. Salt Lake City: Signature Books, 2004.

Smith, Joseph. *The Book of Mormon: The Original 1830 Edition*. Berkeley, CA: Apocryphile Press, 2005.

Tanner, Jerald and Sandra. *Mormonism—Shadow or Reality*. Salt Lake City: Utah Lighthouse Ministry, 1987.

Index

Aaronic priesthood . . . 11, 57, 59
Aaronic Priesthood: Manual 2 . . . 154f
Andrews, Wes . . . 35
Arizona Republic . . . 158, 173, 174
Beck, Julie B. . . . 40
Benson, Ezra Taft . . . 34–36, 46
Bible . . . 12, 16, 33, 37
Black Hammer . . . 35
Blackman, Robert L. . . . 46
Blood atonement . . . 39, 40
Book of Mormon . . . 9–13, 23, 24, 26f, 33,
        37, 38, 57, 60, 66, 128, 188
    Gold plates . . . 10, 11
Borden, Bradley . . . 5, 6, 158, 159
Borden, Christopher . . . 157
Bradford, William R. . . . 47
Brigham Young University . . . 32, 36, 61,
        62, 76, 162, 175
Brosnahan, Leger . . . 189
Buddhism . . . 185
BYU . . . See Brigham Young University
Cantonese . . . 67, 72, 73, 81, 83–85, 93,
        94, 100–102, 137, 178, 179, 182, 183
Chapman, Stephen . . . 37
Chomsky, Noam . . . 34
Church Handbook of Instructions . . . 112,
        154, 156 , 164–169, 171, 172
Church of Jesus Christ of Latter-day
        Saints . . . 1–3, 5–7, 9–13, 16–51,
            53–159, 161–177, 183, 184,
            186–190
    Baby blessing . . . 51, 52
    Church court . . . 152, 154–156,
        165–167
    Disfellowshipment . . . 153, 154, 160,
        161
    Endowments . . . 68–71
    Excommunication . . . 155, 156,
        165–167, 173
    Family home evening . . . 19, 23, 54
    General conference . . . 40
    Indoctrination . . . 15–51, 55, 58–63
    Law of chastity . . . 44, 167
    Polygamy . . . 13, 38, 41–43
    Racism . . . 12, 31–36, 80

Relief society . . . 165
Sexual repression in . . . 44, 45
        60–62, 65, 79, 123, 134, 142,
        143, 147–159, 163–167
    Tithing . . . 40, 41, 156
    Word of Wisdom . . . 44, 54
Confucianism . . . 189, 190
Connolly, Billy . . . 65
Contemporary Mormonism . . . 75, 76
Cook, Carl B. . . . 22, 23
Cowdery, Oliver . . . 10, 11
Cowley, Matthias F. . . . 17
Cumorah . . . 10
D&C . . . See *Doctrine & Covenants*
Dalton, Clyde . . . 35
Darwin, Charles . . . 48
Dawkins, Richard . . . 21f
Demon-Haunted World . . . 166f
Doctrine & Covenants . . . 12, 16
Doman, Glenn . . . 20
Dunn, Loren C. . . . 22
Dunn, Paul H. . . . 173, 174
Ensign . . . 18, 24, 41
Eyring, Henry B. . . . 22
Faurot, Jeannette . . . 184
Faust, James E. . . . 16
Featherstone, Vaughn J. . . . 61
Fundamentalist Church of Jesus Christ
        of Latter Day Saints . . . 58
Garden of Eden . . . 30
Goaslind, Jack H. . . . 57, 58
Gorton, H. Clay . . . 79f, 80f
Grant, Heber J. . . . 158
Hales, Robert D. . . . 34
Hall, Edward T. . . . 26, 27
Hans, Christian . . . 46
Harris, Martin . . . 10f
Hasler, John . . . 19, 126
Hasler, Marjorie . . . 19, 126
Heaven . . . 41, 43, 47, 48
        Celestial kingdom . . . 43, 47, 67, 68,
            97
        Telestial kingdom . . . 48
        Terrestrial kingdom . . . 47, 48
Hinckley, Gordon B. . . . 18, 35, 41, 43

Hitler, Adolf . . . 99f
Hong Kong . . . 2, 3, 66, 67, 81–149, 174, 179–187
    Cinema . . . 179–182
Internal Revenue Service . . . 36
Jack Mormons . . . 56
Jackson County, Missouri . . . 30
Jeffs, Rulon . . . 58
Jesus Christ . . . 9, 29, 30, 37
Jesus the Christ . . . 66
Johnson, Maurey . . . 167
Kimball, Spencer . . . 18, 45, 157
Kissinger, Henry . . . 35
Kolob . . . 27
Krasny, Michael . . . 21f
Laman . . . 12
Lamanites . . . 12, 33, 36
LDS Church . . . See "Church of Jesus Christ of Latter-day Saints"
Lucifer . . . See Satan
Mackintosh, José Manuel . . . 6, 159
Masonic rituals . . . 69
McConkie, Bruce R. . . . 45, 158
McCue, Bob . . . 188, 189
McKay, David O. . . . 157
Melchizedek priesthood . . . 11, 51, 165
Miracle of Forgiveness . . . 157
Missionaries . . . 1–3, 45, 46, 65–67, 71–159, 162, 168
    Assistants to the president (APEs) . . . 81, 82, 119, 156
    Proselytizing . . . 89–99, 102–104, 107–113, 116–118, 120, 122–129, 132–137, 140, 141, 144–146
Missionary Training Center . . . 1, 68, 71–75, 77, 78, 82, 83, 115
Monson, Thomas F. . . . 19, 46
Mormon Church . . . See "Church of Jesus Christ of Latter-day Saints"
Mormon Doctrine . . . 158
Mormonism . . . See "Church of Jesus Christ of Latter-day Saints"
Moroni . . . 9–11, 83
Mozi . . . 189
National Geographic . . . 173
Native Americans . . . See "Lamanites"
Nephi . . . 12, 186
Nephites . . . 12
New Era . . . 46, 173
Nixon, Richard . . . 35
Oaks, Dallin H. . . . 45
Order of Enoch . . . 40
Orwell, George . . . 171

Packer, Boyd K. . . . 24
Packham, Richard . . . 12f, 68, 191, 194
Palmyra, New York . . . 9
Petersen, Mark E. . . . 32
Ponder, Kent . . . 45f
Provo, Utah . . . 1, 68
Quorum of the Seventy . . . 22, 46, 47
Parry, Keith . . . 93
Pearl of Great Price . . . 12
Returned missionaries . . . 2, 76, 78, 94, 162, 168–172, 174
Richards, George F. . . . 31, 32
Richards, H. Bryan . . . 46
Rivers, Gregory Charles . . . 179f
RMs . . . See "Returned Missionaries"
Roughing It . . . 11
Russell, Bertrand . . . 34, 76f, 77f, 176f
Sagan, Carl . . . 166
San Francisco . . . 178, 179
Satan . . . 25, 29, 30, 139
Seer stone(s) . . . 10
Smith, Emma . . . 10f
Smith, Joseph Jr. . . . 10–13, 16, 38, 40, 69, 167
Smithsonian Institution . . . 26
South China Morning Post . . . 182
Southerton, Simon . . . 26
Talmage, James E. . . . 66
Tanner, Eldon, N. . . . 45
Taoism . . . 185
Taylor, John . . . 24
Testimony . . . 22, 23, 58, 122, 126, 168–174
Thatcher, Margaret . . . 93
Truman Show . . . 15, 16
Twain, Mark . . . 11
Urim and Thummim . . . 10
University of Texas . . . 175–177
War in Heaven . . . 31–36, 151
West, Emerson R. . . . 24
Whitmer family . . . 11
Wilson, William A. . . . 75–77
Wirthlin, Anne G. . . . 20, 21
Worthy, Jack B. . . . 1, 2, 53–61, 65–159, 161–190
Young, Brigham . . . 13, 28–32, 38–40, 42, 48, 50
Young, Dwan B. . . . 18